Upper Saddle River, New Jersey • Boston, Massachusetts
Chandler, Arizona • Glenview, Illinois • Shoreview, Minnesota

Cover image credit: Cover (Bkgd L) Getty Images, (Bkgd R) Dennis MacDonald/Alamy; (L) Paul Burns/Getty Images, (C) Dennis MacDonald/Alamy, (CL) Dex Image/Jupiter Images; (CR) Dynamic Graphics/Jupiter Image, (R) Dennis MacDonald/Alamy

ISBN-13: 978-0-13-367516-0

ISBN-10:   0-13-367516-5

10 11 12 V011 17 16 15 14

TABLE OF CONTENTS

ABOUT YOUR BOOK

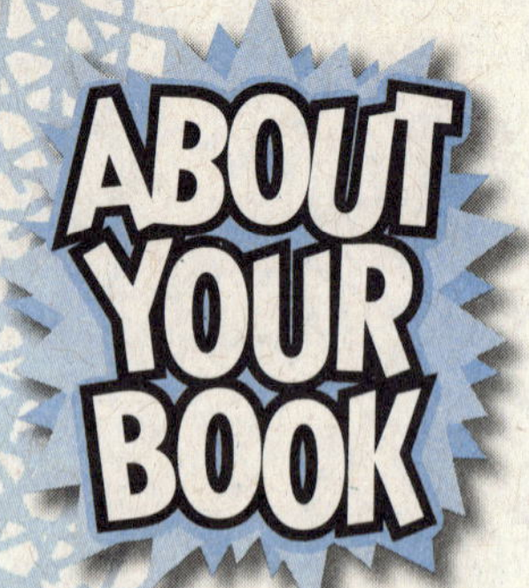

The What and Why of This Book

This book is designed to help you develop strategies you can use in writing, grammar, usage, mechanics, and vocabulary. While you write and work with vocabulary, you will return to the articles in your student book. You will think more about the Big Questions.

Write About It!

Each article in your student book has an opportunity for you to Write About It! A writing assignment helps you think more deeply about the Big Question.

Draft It
A writing frame helps you organize your writing.

Writing Prompt
A prompt explains the assignment.

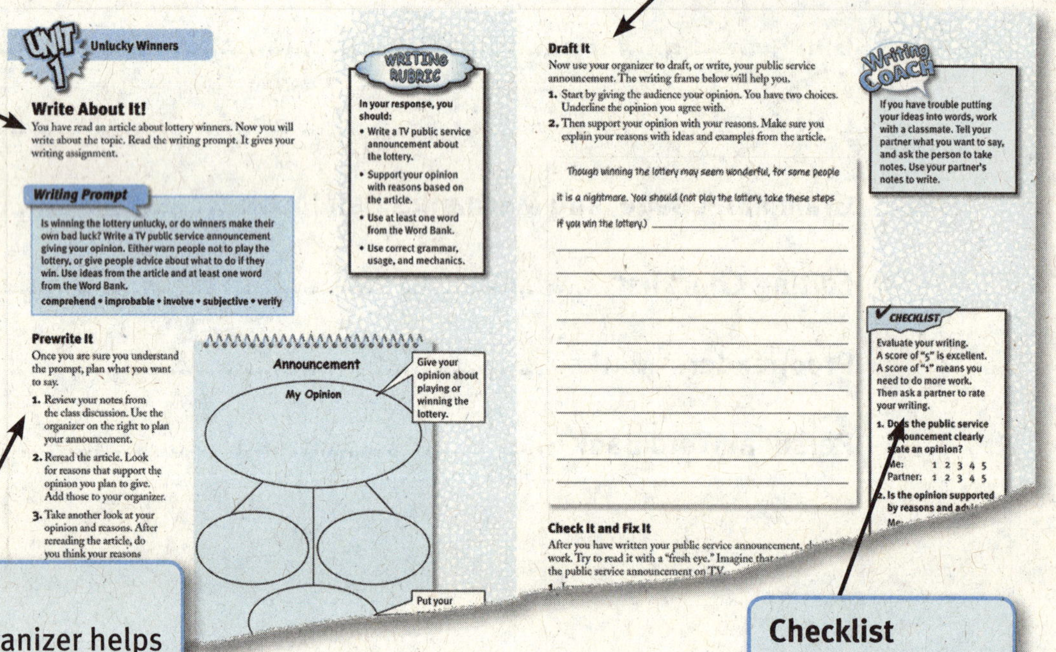

Prewrite It
A graphic organizer helps you collect your thoughts before you write.

Checklist
A checklist helps you evaluate and revise your writing.

Vocabulary Workshop

Each article in your student book has a Vocabulary Workshop. In the workshop, you deepen your understanding of words from the Word Bank as you use them in different ways. Expanding your vocabulary will help you become a better reader and writer.

Your Choice
Record other words you want to remember.

Show You Know
Check your understanding about words by writing stories, crafting clues, or answering questions.

Partner Up
Use these suggestions for working with partners.

Define It
Graphic organizers expand your thinking about words.

Word Parts
Studying and using word parts will help you figure out words you may not know.

All in the Family
Explore variations of words that are all in the same word family.

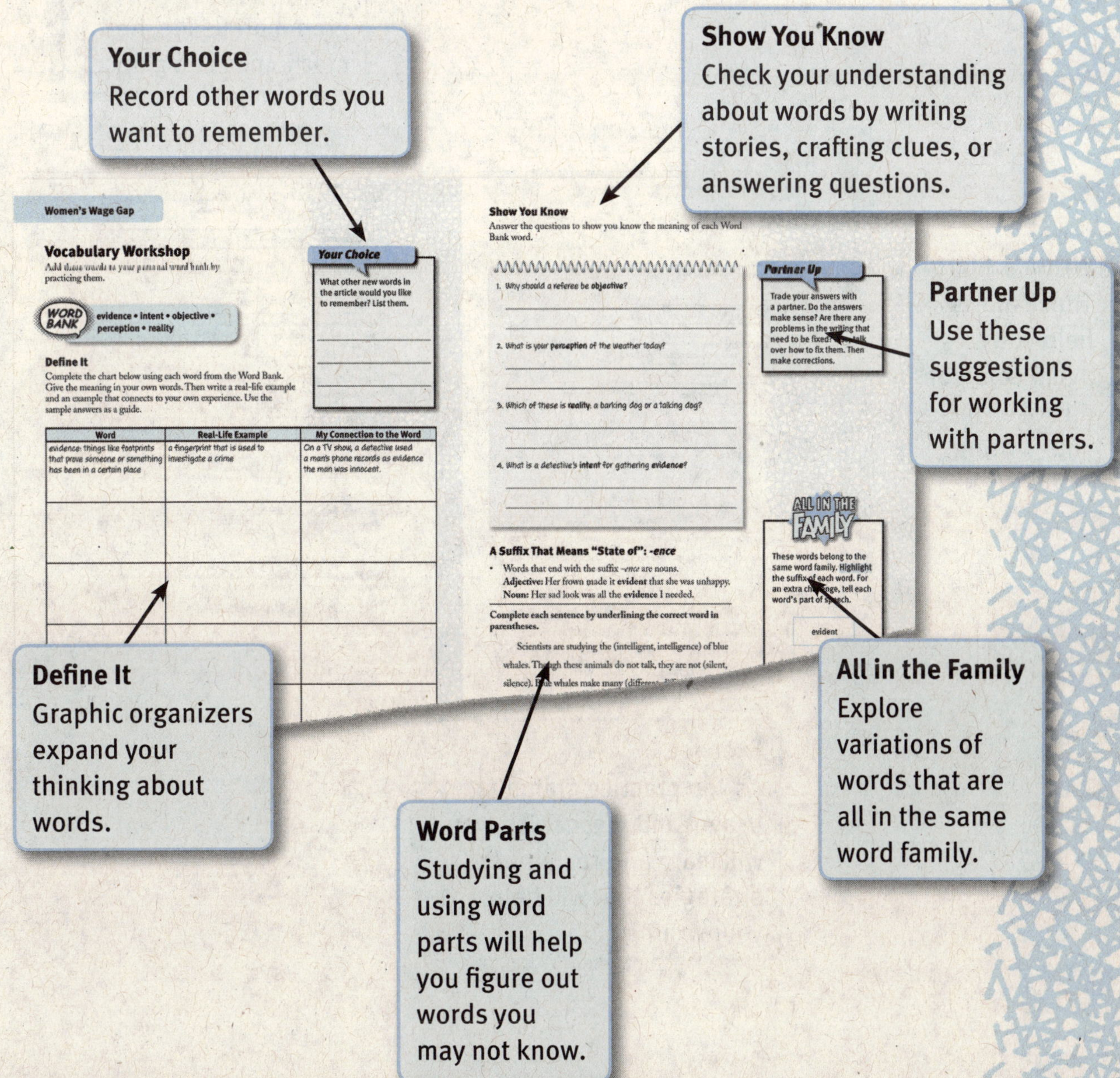

Grammar, Usage, and Mechanics Handbook

The Grammar, Usage, and Mechanics Handbook answers questions you may have during and after writing. It will help you correctly write and punctuate sentences. It will help you spell words that are commonly misspelled or confused.

Charts
Charts like this one help you find useful information about grammar, usage, and mechanics at a glance.

Writer's Alert
These alerts help you avoid common mistakes in your writing.

Exercise
As you practice grammar, usage, and mechanics, you will learn and remember strategies that will help your writing.

Is there a difference between reality and truth?

Write About It!

You have read an article about lottery winners. Now you will write about the topic. Read the writing prompt. It gives your writing assignment.

In your response, you should:

- Write a TV public service announcement about the lottery.

- Support your opinion with reasons based on the article.

- Use at least one word from the Word Bank.

- Use correct grammar, usage, and mechanics.

Writing Prompt

Is winning the lottery unlucky, or do winners make their own bad luck? Write a TV public service announcement giving your opinion. Either warn people not to play the lottery, or give people advice about what to do if they win. Use ideas from the article and at least one word from the Word Bank.

comprehend • improbable • involve • subjective • verify

Prewrite It

Once you are sure you understand the prompt, plan what you want to say.

1. Review your notes from the class discussion. Use the organizer on the right to plan your announcement.

2. Reread the article. Look for reasons that support the opinion you plan to give. Add those to your organizer.

3. Take another look at your opinion and reasons. After rereading the article, do you think your reasons are convincing? If not, change them.

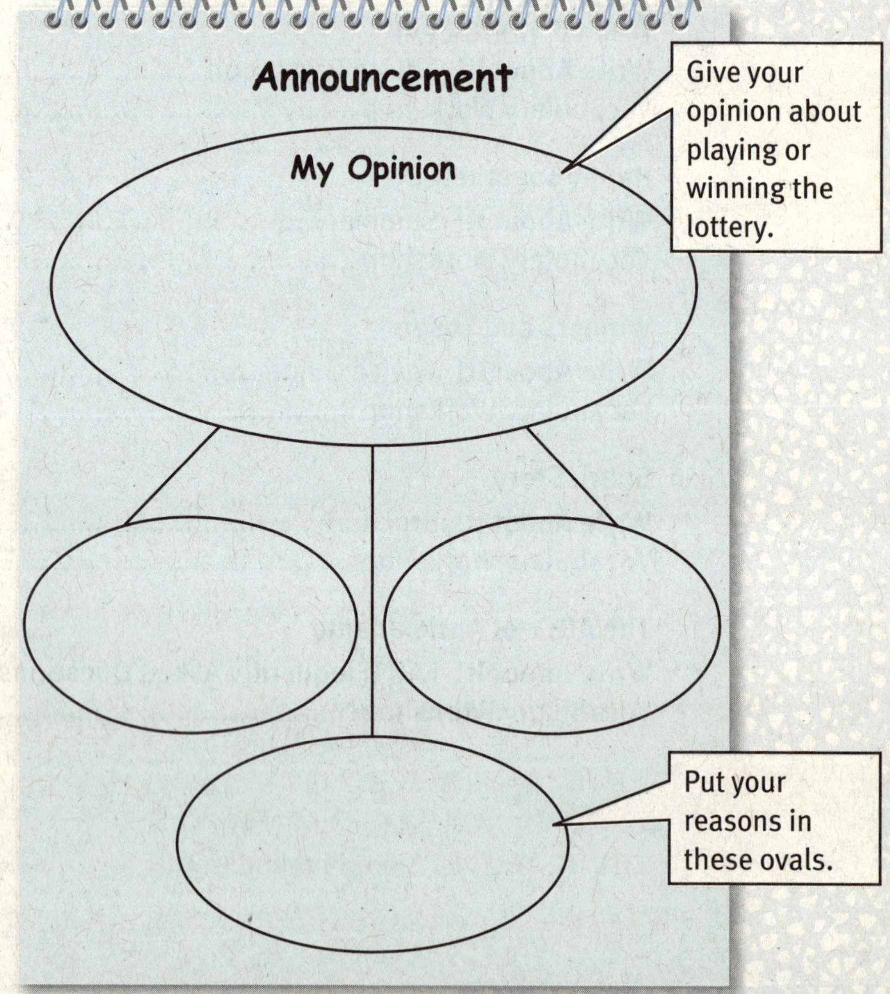

Draft It

Now use your organizer to draft, or write, your public service announcement. The writing frame below will help you.

1. Start by giving the audience your opinion. You have two choices. Underline the opinion you agree with.
2. Then support your opinion with your reasons. Make sure you explain your reasons with ideas and examples from the article.

Though winning the lottery may seem wonderful, for some people

it is a nightmare. You should (not play the lottery, take these steps

if you win the lottery.) ___________________________________

____

____

____

____

____

____

____

____

____

Check It and Fix It

After you have written your public service announcement, check your work. Try to read it with a "fresh eye." Imagine that you are watching the public service announcement on TV.

1. Is your message written clearly and correctly? Use the checklist on the right to decide.
2. Then work with a classmate. Read your announcements to each other. Talk over ways you might improve them. Use the ideas to revise your work.
3. For help with grammar, usage, and mechanics, go to the Handbook on pages 189–231.

If you have trouble putting your ideas into words, work with a classmate. Tell your partner what you want to say, and ask the person to take notes. Use your partner's notes to write.

✔ CHECKLIST

Evaluate your writing. A score of "5" is excellent. A score of "1" means you need to do more work. Then ask a partner to rate your writing.

1. **Does the public service announcement clearly state an opinion?**

   Me: 1 2 3 4 5
   Partner: 1 2 3 4 5

2. **Is the opinion supported by reasons and advice?**

   Me: 1 2 3 4 5
   Partner: 1 2 3 4 5

3. **Is there at least one word from the Word Bank?**

   Me: 1 2 3 4 5
   Partner: 1 2 3 4 5

4. **Are grammar, usage, and mechanics correct?**

   Me: 1 2 3 4 5
   Partner: 1 2 3 4 5

Vocabulary Workshop

Add these words to your personal word bank by practicing them.

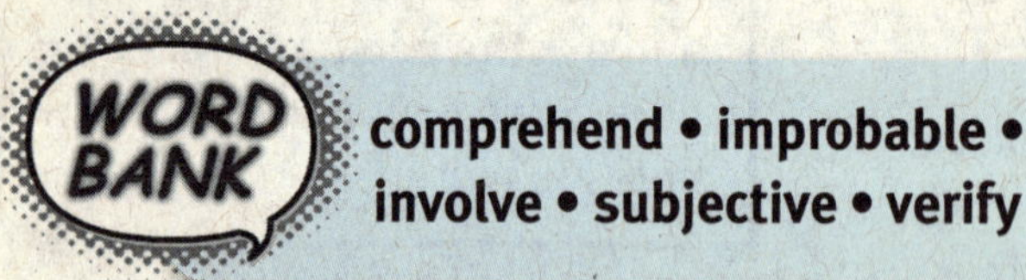

comprehend • improbable • involve • subjective • verify

Your Choice

What other new words in the article would you like to remember? List them.

____

____

____

Define It

Fill in the chart with the Word Bank words. In your own words, tell what each word means. Then circle the number that tells how well you understand each word. Circle "4" if you understand it completely. Circle "1" if you are not sure you understand the word at all. Use the example as a model.

What It Means	comprehend
To comprehend something is to understand it or "get" it.	**How Well I Understand It** 1 2 3 ④
What It Means	
	How Well I Understand It 1 2 3 4
What It Means	
	How Well I Understand It 1 2 3 4
What It Means	
	How Well I Understand It 1 2 3 4
What It Means	
	How Well I Understand It 1 2 3 4

Word COACH

To remember new words, practice using them. Use a new word at least three times on the day you first study it. Try to use the word when you are talking as well as writing.

Show You Know

To show that you understand the Word Bank words, write a clue for each word. Exchange clues with a partner. See whether your partner can identify the correct word for each clue. Use the clue for the word *improbable*, below, as a model.

- If something is unlikely to happen, it is this.

1. ____

2. ____

3. ____

4. ____

5. ____

Prefixes That Mean "Not": *il-, im-, in-, un-*

- You can improve your word skills by memorizing the prefixes that usually mean "not" or "the opposite of." Knowing these by heart can help you figure out the meanings of unfamiliar words. For example, what does the word *impersonal* mean in the following sentence? Find and think about the parts of the word.

The e-mail invitation seemed very **impersonal** to me.

(*im* = "not"; *personal* = "friendly"; *impersonal* = not friendly)

Complete each sentence by underlining the correct word in parentheses.

I was (happy, unhappy) when I got home and did not have my keys. I had an (important, unimportant) report due. It would be (possible, impossible) to do it without my computer. I was (afraid, unafraid) I would get a grade of (complete, incomplete). My kind neighbor (politely, impolitely) told me to check my pockets. It sounds (logical, illogical), but the keys were there the whole time!

These words are part of the same word family. What are some other words that have the word *probable* in them? Add one to the list.

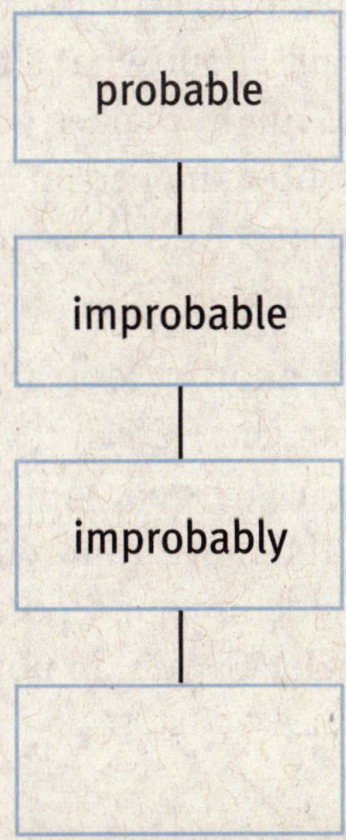

High Flyers

Write About It!

You have read an article about trapeze artists. Now you will write about the topic. Read the writing prompt. It gives your writing assignment.

Writing Prompt

Imagine that you are a writer for "Crazy Careers," a teen radio show about unusual jobs. Write a report on what a trapeze artist is, who might enjoy being a "flyer," and how people can get safe and proper training. Use ideas from the article and at least one word from the Word Bank.

associate • context • differentiate • perception • uncertainty

WRITING RUBRIC

In your response, you should:

- Write a radio report for teens about "flying" as a career.

- Use facts and details from the article.

- Use at least one word from the Word Bank.

- Use correct grammar, usage, and mechanics.

Prewrite It

Once you are sure you understand the prompt, plan what you want to say.

1. Review your notes from the class discussion. Use the organizer on the right to jot down ideas.

2. Reread the article. Look for details about what a flyer is, who might make a good flyer, and how the person can get training. Add those to your organizer.

3. Take another look at your organizer. Reread the details you have listed. Which details are the most important to include in your report? Cross out details you do not want to use.

Report on Flyers

What a Flyer Does

Who Might Make a Good Flyer

How to Get Training

Draft It

Now use your organizer to draft, or write, your radio news report.
The writing frame below will help you.

1. Start by explaining what trapeze artists do. Read the first sentence below and complete it.

2. Then write your report about the flying trapeze. Complete the second sentence below. End your report by informing teens about trapeze schools.

If you have trouble getting your ideas down on paper, work with a classmate. Ask your partner to look at your organizer. Together, choose ideas for your report, and talk about how to word them.

You might say "flyers," or trapeze artists, have one of the most exciting jobs around because they ________________________

____ .

To be a good trapeze artist, you need these qualities: ________

____

____

____

____ .

If these qualities describe you, you can get training by ________

____

____

____ .

✔ CHECKLIST

Evaluate your writing.
A score of "5" is excellent.
A score of "1" means you need to do more work.
Then ask a partner to rate your writing.

1. **Does the report describe what flyers do?**

   Me: 1 2 3 4 5
   Partner: 1 2 3 4 5

2. **Does it describe qualities of good flyers?**

   Me: 1 2 3 4 5
   Partner: 1 2 3 4 5

3. **Does it inform teens about flying schools?**

   Me: 1 2 3 4 5
   Partner: 1 2 3 4 5

4. **Is there at least one word from the Word Bank?**

   Me: 1 2 3 4 5
   Partner: 1 2 3 4 5

5. **Are grammar, usage, and mechanics correct?**

   Me: 1 2 3 4 5
   Partner: 1 2 3 4 5

Check It and Fix It

After you have written your report, check your work. Try to read it as if you have never before seen it. Imagine what it would be like to hear the report on the radio.

1. Is your writing clear and correct? Use the checklist on the right to decide.

2. Then trade reports with a classmate. Talk over ways you might improve your reports. Use the ideas to revise your work.

3. For help with grammar, usage, and mechanics, go to the Handbook on pages 189–231.

Vocabulary Workshop

Add these words to your personal word bank by practicing them.

associate • context • differentiate • perception • uncertainty

Define It

Complete the chart below using the Word Bank words. First, tell what the word means. Then tell what the word does not mean. Use the example as a guide.

Your Choice

What other new words in the article would you like to remember? List them.

____

____

____

Word	What It Is	What It Is Not
associate	to make connections or link things together in your mind	to separate things

Show You Know

To show that you understand the Word Bank words, write three
sentences. In each sentence, use and highlight two of the words.
(You will use one word twice.) Use the example as a model.

- Many people associate being high in the air with feelings of fear

  and uncertainty.

1. ____

   ____

2. ____

   ____

3. ____

   ____

Suffixes That Mean "State of": *-tion, -ty*

- When you add the suffix *-tion* to a verb, you change the verb
  into a noun. Sometimes, adding a suffix changes the spelling
  of the base word as well.
  Verb: I **perceive** that there is a net below the trapeze artists.
  Noun: My **perception** is that the trapeze artist fell into the net.

- When you add the suffix *-ty* to an adjective, you turn the word
  into a noun.
  Adjective: He was **uncertain** about how high the trapeze was.
  Noun: When it was time to fly, he was filled with **uncertainty.**

**Complete each sentence by underlining the correct word in
parentheses.**

I am afraid of heights, so I was (uncertain, uncertainty)

about taking a trapeze class. The coach was (certain, certainty)

that the class could help me get over my fear. Once I was on the

platform, my (perceive, perception) of being in the air changed.

I (perceived, perception) that this could be a lot of fun!

Going to Extremes

Write About It!

You have read an article about extreme sports. Now you will write about the topic. Read the writing prompt. It gives your writing assignment.

In your response, you should:

- Write a paragraph explaining your opinion.

- Give reasons and examples from the article.

- Use at least one word from the Word Bank.

- Use correct grammar, usage, and mechanics.

Writing Prompt

When people who take risks for the sake of adventure need to be rescued, should they have to help pay for the cost of the rescue? Write a paragraph giving your opinion. Use ideas from the article and at least one word from the Word Bank.

comprehend • confirm • evaluate • focus • improbable

Prewrite It

Once you are sure you understand the prompt, plan what you want to say.

1. Review your notes from the class discussion. Use the organizer on the right to jot down ideas about what you might say in your paragraph.

2. Reread the article. Look for reasons that support or explain your opinion. Add those to your organizer.

3. Reread all the reasons you have listed on your organizer. Cross out reasons that you do not plan to use in your paragraph.

Paragraph Plan

My Opinion

Your opinion answers the question in the prompt.

My Reasons and Examples

Your reasons and examples support your opinion.

Draft It

Now use your organizer to draft, or write, an opinion paragraph. The writing frame below will help you.

1. Start by giving your opinion. You have two choices. Underline your choice.

2. Then give your reasons and examples. Read the second sentence below. Finish the thought by giving a reason. Follow up the reason with an example from the article.

Paying for Rescues

In my opinion, risk-takers who need rescuing (should, should not)

have to help pay for their rescues. The reason I think this is that

____

____

____

____ .

For example, ___________________________________

____

____

____

____ .

Check It and Fix It

After you have written your paragraph, check your work. Imagine that you are reading it for the first time.

1. Is your paragraph written clearly and correctly? Use the checklist on the right to decide.

2. Then trade paragraphs with a classmate. Talk over ways you might improve your paragraphs. Use the ideas to revise your work.

3. For help with grammar, usage, and mechanics, go to the Handbook on pages 189–231.

If you have trouble supporting your opinion, work with a partner. Tell your partner which reasons you plan to use. Ask your partner which reasons are the most convincing. Use your partner's suggestions when you write.

✔ CHECKLIST

Evaluate your writing. A score of "5" is excellent. A score of "1" means you need to do more work. Then ask a partner to rate your writing.

1. Does the paragraph clearly state an opinion?

Me:　　　1　2　3　4　5
Partner:　1　2　3　4　5

2. Are there reasons and examples that support the opinion?

Me:　　　1　2　3　4　5
Partner:　1　2　3　4　5

3. Is there at least one word from the Word Bank?

Me:　　　1　2　3　4　5
Partner:　1　2　3　4　5

4. Are grammar, usage, and mechanics correct?

Me:　　　1　2　3　4　5
Partner:　1　2　3　4　5

　　　　Going to Extremes　　**11**

Vocabulary Workshop

Add these words to your personal word bank by practicing them.

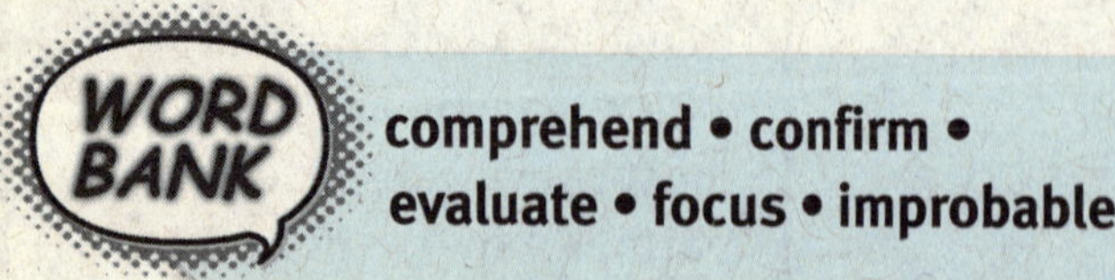

Define It

Fill in the chart. In the center oval, write two or three subjects you could write about using the Word Bank words. Use the examples as a model.

confirm		
What It Means	**What It Means**	**What It Means**
to make sure something is right and true		
	Subjects — schoolwork: confirm due date	
What It Means		**What It Means**

Your Choice

What other new words in the article would you like to remember? List them.

____

____

____

Word COACH

Use note cards to study new words. Write a word on one side of the card. On the other side, write examples and things related to the word. Review your examples later. Use them to guess what the word is.

Show You Know

In the space below, write a short, short story (just a paragraph!) using the Word Bank words. Be sure your sentences show that you understand the meanings of the words.

Once upon a time, ___________________________

____

____

____

____

____

Trade short, short stories with a partner. Circle the Word Bank words. If your partner used any word incorrectly, suggest a way to fix the mistake. Then, if necessary, make corrections to your story based on your partner's suggestions.

Word Play

Using words with exact meanings can make your writing more lively and specific. In the chart below, list words that mean the same or about the same as the Word Bank words. Think of words that have a precise meaning. Check a dictionary or thesaurus if you need to, and use the examples as models.

Word Bank Word	Words with Similar Meanings
comprehend	understand, grasp
confirm	prove, guarantee

Now try some of the words to see how they can make your writing more precise. Rewrite each of the sentences below, substituting one of your words for the boldface word.

1. Is it hard to **comprehend** why adventurers like to take risks?

____

2. Adventurers should **evaluate** risks before taking them.

____

Women's Wage Gap

Write About It!

You have read an article about the women's wage gap. Now you will write about the topic. Read the writing prompt. It gives your writing assignment.

Writing Prompt

Imagine that you work at a small neighborhood fast-food restaurant. You find out that male workers are paid more than female workers who do the same job. What advice would you give to the female workers and why? Write a few paragraphs giving your advice. Use ideas from the article and at least one word from the Word Bank.

evidence • intent • objective • perception • reality

Prewrite It

Once you are sure you understand the prompt, plan what you want to say.

1. Review your notes from the class discussion. Use the organizer on the right to plan your response.

2. Reread the article. Look for information that supports the advice you would give. Add that to your organizer.

3. Reread what you said you would advise. Do you want to change your mind after rereading the article? If so, make the change. Then reread your reasons. Which reasons are the best? Cross out ideas that you do not want to use.

WRITING RUBRIC

In your response, you should:

- Write a few paragraphs giving advice.

- Give reasons for the advice you give.

- Use at least one word from the Word Bank.

- Use correct grammar, usage, and mechanics.

Wage Gap at Work

What I Would Advise	Why I Would Advise This

Draft It

Now use your organizer to draft, or write, your paragraphs of advice.
The writing frame below will help you.

1. Start by saying what you think the female workers should do.
   Read and complete the first sentence below.

2. Then give your reason. Read the second sentence below. Finish the
   thought by giving a reason for your actions. Make sure you explain
   your reason with ideas from the article.

If you have trouble organizing your thoughts, work with a partner. Tell your partner what advice you would give and why. Have your partner write the ideas down in outline form. Use your partner's outline to write.

Take My Advice

My advice to female workers who are paid less than male

workers is to ____

____

____

____ .

I think the female workers should do this because ____________

____

____

____

____ .

✔ **CHECKLIST**

Evaluate your writing. A score of "5" is excellent. A score of "1" means you need to do more work. Then ask a partner to rate your writing.

1. **Do the paragraphs clearly state advice?**
   Me: 1 2 3 4 5
   Partner: 1 2 3 4 5

2. **Are there ideas from the article to explain the advice?**
   Me: 1 2 3 4 5
   Partner: 1 2 3 4 5

3. **Is there at least one word from the Word Bank?**
   Me: 1 2 3 4 5
   Partner: 1 2 3 4 5

4. **Are grammar, usage, and mechanics correct?**
   Me: 1 2 3 4 5
   Partner: 1 2 3 4 5

Check It and Fix It

After you have written your paragraphs, check your work. Try to read them with a "fresh eye."

1. Are your ideas written clearly and correctly? Use the checklist on the right to decide.

2. Exchange paragraphs with a classmate. Talk over ways you both might improve your paragraphs. Use the ideas to revise your work.

3. For help with grammar, usage, and mechanics, go to the Handbook on pages 189–231.

Vocabulary Workshop

Add these words to your personal word bank by
practicing them.

**evidence • intent • objective •
perception • reality**

Your Choice

What other new words in
the article would you like
to remember? List them.

____

____

____

Define It

Complete the chart below using each word from the Word Bank.
Give the meaning in your own words. Then write a real-life example
and an example that connects to your own experience. Use the
sample answers as a guide.

Word	Real-Life Example	My Connection to the Word
evidence: things like footprints that prove someone or something has been in a certain place	a fingerprint that is used to investigate a crime	On a TV show, a detective used a man's phone records as evidence the man was innocent.

Show You Know

Answer the questions to show you know the meaning of each Word Bank word.

1. Why should a referee be **objective**?

   ____

   ____

2. What is your **perception** of the weather today?

   ____

   ____

3. Which of these is **reality**: a barking dog or a talking dog?

   ____

   ____

4. What is a detective's **intent** for gathering **evidence**?

   ____

   ____

Partner Up

Trade your answers with a partner. Do the answers make sense? Are there any problems in the writing that need to be fixed? If so, talk over how to fix them. Then make corrections.

A Suffix That Means "State of": *-ence*

- Words that end with the suffix *-ence* are nouns.
  Adjective: Her frown made it **evident** that she was unhappy.
  Noun: Her sad look was all the **evidence** I needed.

Complete each sentence by underlining the correct word in parentheses.

Scientists are studying the (intelligent, intelligence) of blue whales. Though these animals do not talk, they are not (silent, silence). Blue whales make many (different, difference) sounds. The sounds are (dependent, dependence) on the situation.

These words belong to the same word family. Highlight the suffix of each word. For an extra challenge, tell each word's part of speech.

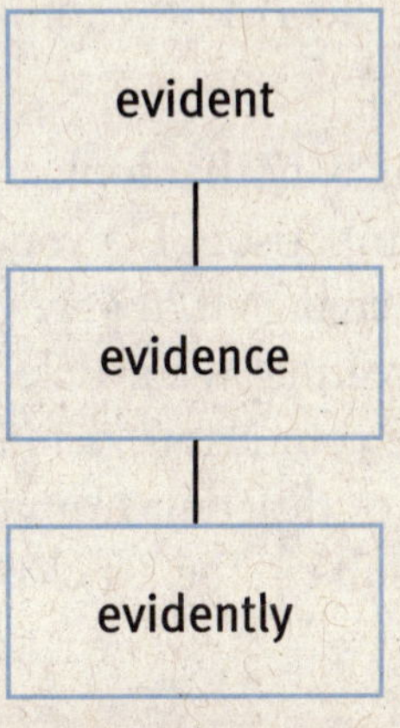

Write About It!

You have read an article about what makes people happy. Now you will write about the topic. Read the writing prompt. It gives your writing assignment.

Writing Prompt

After reading "Happy Together," ask your classmates the question "What makes you happy?" Have each student write an answer on a folded slip of paper. Count the answers to see which were the most popular. Then write a summary of your class's top answers, and compare them with the top answers in the poll. Use ideas from the article and at least one word from the Word Bank.

concrete • discern • evaluate • results • uncertainty

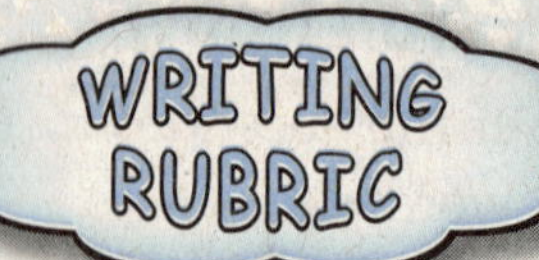

In your response, you should:

- Write a summary describing your class's top answers about happiness.

- Compare your class's top answers to those in the poll.

- Use at least one word from the Word Bank.

- Use correct grammar, usage, and mechanics.

Prewrite It

Once you are sure you understand the prompt, plan what you want to say.

1. Review your notes from the class discussion. Use the organizer on the right to record and summarize how your class voted.

2. Reread the article. Compare your class results to the results of the poll described in the article. Add the information to your organizer.

3. Take another look at your comparison. Do you need to change it in any way after rereading the article? How are your class's results similar to or different from the survey results in the article?

Happiness Survey

Class Survey: What Makes You Happy?	Number of Votes
1.	
2.	
3.	
4.	

Record what classmates voted for here.

Summary of Class Results:

The summary describes how your class voted.

Comparison of Class and Article Results:

The comparison compares your class to the article.

Draft It

Now use your organizer to draft, or write, a summary of your class's answers. The writing frame below will help you.

1. Start by stating which answers received the most votes. Use the results from your graphic organizer to complete the second sentence.

2. Then compare your class's results to the poll's results. You have three choices. Underline how your class compares. Then explain your comparison. Make sure you include the results of the survey described in the article.

For help making comparisons, work with a partner. Tell your partner the class's voting results and the poll's results. Have your partner make two lists. Use your partner's lists for comparing.

> ### Happiness Summary
>
> The students in our class voted on what makes us happy. The most
>
> votes were for ____
>
> ____ .
>
> Compared to the results in the poll, our class's results were (the same
>
> as, similar to, different from) those in the article. This is because
>
> ____
>
> ____
>
> ____
>
> ____
>
> ____ .

✔ CHECKLIST

Evaluate your writing. A score of "5" is excellent. A score of "1" means you need to do more work. Then ask a partner to rate your writing.

1. **Does the report correctly sum up how your class voted?**

   Me: 1 2 3 4 5
   Partner: 1 2 3 4 5

2. **Does the report compare your class results to the poll's results?**

   Me: 1 2 3 4 5
   Partner: 1 2 3 4 5

3. **Is there at least one word from the Word Bank?**

   Me: 1 2 3 4 5
   Partner: 1 2 3 4 5

4. **Are grammar, usage, and mechanics correct?**

   Me: 1 2 3 4 5
   Partner: 1 2 3 4 5

Check It and Fix It

After you have written your summary and comparison, check your work. Try to read it with a "fresh eye."

1. Is everything written clearly and correctly? Use the checklist on the right to decide.

2. Then trade reports with a classmate. Talk over ways to improve your reports. Use the ideas to revise your work.

3. For help with grammar, usage, and mechanics, go to the Handbook on pages 189–231.

Vocabulary Workshop

Add these words to your personal word bank by practicing them.

concrete • discern • evaluate • results • uncertainty

Define It

For each organizer below, do as follows. Choose two words from the Word Bank and write them on either side of the triangle. (One word will appear twice.) On the blank "because" lines, tell why the two words are connected. Use the examples as a guide.

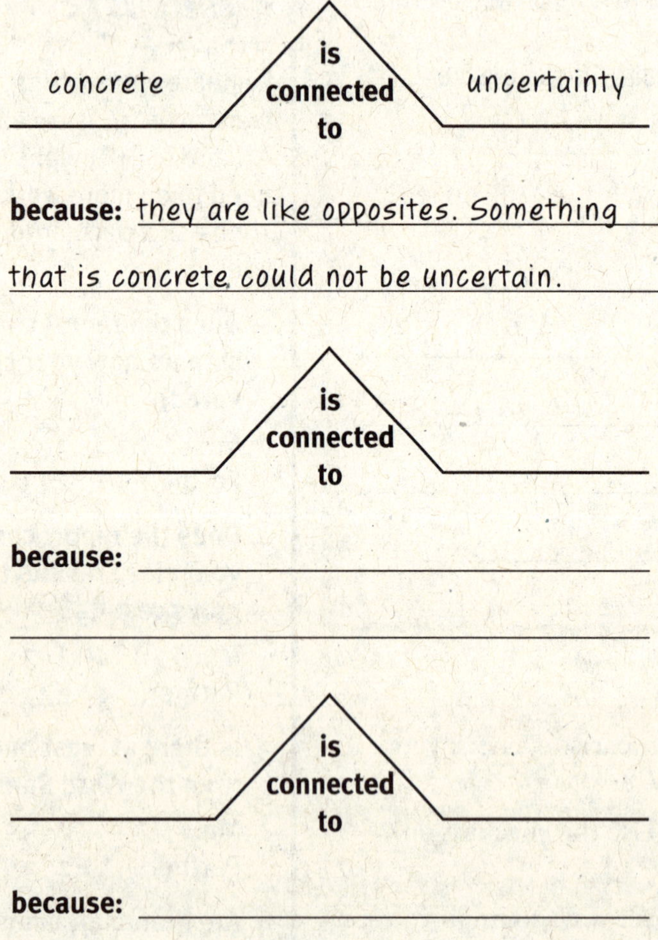

Show You Know

Write a dialogue, or a conversation between people, in the space below. In your dialogue, use all the Word Bank words in a way that shows you understand their meanings.

_______________ : _______________________________

____

_______________ : _______________________________

____

_______________ : _______________________________

____

_______________ : _______________________________

____

Choose a part, and act out your dialogue with a partner. Listen for how the Word Bank words are used. If something sounds wrong, discuss what might need to be fixed. Then make corrections.

Multiple-Meaning Words

When you use a dictionary to find the meaning of a word, you often find more than one definition for the word. How can you tell which definition is the right one? Look at how the word is used in the context of a sentence. For example, which definition for _concrete_ makes sense below?

- My teacher asked us for a **concrete** example of a mammal.
  concrete: (a) strong building material; (b) real and specific
  If you chose definition (b), you are right! That definition makes sense in the sentence.

Underline the correct meaning for each boldface word below.

Word in Sentence	Meaning 1	Meaning 2
Joining school **clubs** can help you stay happy.	sticks used for hitting golf balls	groups that meet to do an activity
Kids learn to **form** good relationships.	to create or put together	printed paper with blanks to fill in
What makes people **depressed**?	sad or deeply unhappy	pushed in or down

Write About It!

You have read an article about competition. Now you will write about the topic. Read the writing prompt. It gives your writing assignment.

Writing Prompt

After reading "Winners and Losers," what advice would you give parents about competition for their young children? Write a short guide. Tell parents your opinion of competition. Depending on your opinion, explain positive or negative aspects of competition. Use ideas from the article and at least one word from the Word Bank.

context • crucial • differentiate • evidence • subjective

WRITING RUBRIC

In your response, you should:

- Write a guide for parents stating your opinion about competition.

- Describe positive or negative points about competition.

- Use at least one word from the Word Bank.

- Use correct grammar, usage, and mechanics.

Prewrite It

Once you are sure you understand the prompt, plan what you want to say.

1. Review your notes from the class discussion. Use the organizer on the right to jot down your thoughts.

2. Reread the article. Look for positive or negative points about competition—whichever support your opinion. Add those to your organizer.

3. Take another look at your opinion. Do you need to change it in any way after rereading the article? If so, make the change. Reread all the points you have listed. Which are the most important? Use those points in your guide.

Competition for Kids

My Opinion:

Positives	Negatives

Draft It

Now use your organizer to draft, or write, a guide for parents. The writing frame below will help you.

1. Start by giving your opinion. You have three choices of opinion. Underline your choice.

2. Then, depending on your opinion, use ideas from the article to give positive, negative, or both positive and negative points about competition.

Competition: A Guide for Parents

Competition is (good, bad, both good and bad) for children. I say

this because ____

____

____

____

____

____

____

____

____

____ .

If you want, ask a partner to help you identify positive or negative points about competition. Tell your partner something about competition, and have your partner write it on the organizer under "Positives" or "Negatives."

Check It and Fix It

After you have written your guide, check your work. Imagine that you are a parent reading the guide for the first time.

1. Is everything written clearly and correctly? Use the checklist on the right to decide.

2. Then trade guides with a classmate. Talk over ways you both might improve your guides. Use the ideas to revise your work.

3. For help with grammar, usage, and mechanics, go to the Handbook on pages 189–231.

✔ **CHECKLIST**

Evaluate your writing. A score of "5" is excellent. A score of "1" means you need to do more work. Then ask a partner to rate your writing.

1. **Does the guide state a clear opinion about competition?**

   Me: 1 2 3 4 5
   Partner: 1 2 3 4 5

2. **Does the guide give positive points, negative points, or both, based on the opinion that is given?**

   Me: 1 2 3 4 5
   Partner: 1 2 3 4 5

3. **Is there at least one word from the Word Bank?**

   Me: 1 2 3 4 5
   Partner: 1 2 3 4 5

4. **Are grammar, usage, and mechanics correct?**

   Me: 1 2 3 4 5
   Partner: 1 2 3 4 5

Vocabulary Workshop

Add these words to your personal word bank by practicing them.

context • crucial • differentiate • evidence • subjective

Define It

Fill in the chart with the Word Bank words. In your own words, tell what each word means. Then circle the number that tells how well you understand each word. Circle "4" if you understand it completely. Circle "1" if you are not sure you understand the word at all.

Your Choice

What other new words in the article would you like to remember? List them.

____

____

____

What It Means		How Well I Understand It
		1 2 3 4
What It Means		**How Well I Understand It**
		1 2 3 4
What It Means		**How Well I Understand It**
		1 2 3 4
What It Means		**How Well I Understand It**
		1 2 3 4
What It Means		**How Well I Understand It**
		1 2 3 4

Show You Know

To show that you understand the Word Bank words, write a clue for
each word. Exchange clues with a partner. See whether your partner
can identify the correct word for each clue.

1. ____

2. ____

3. ____

4. ____

5. ____

A Suffix That Means "To Make" or "To Do": -ate

- The suffix -*ate* is found at the end of verbs. When you see
  this suffix on a word, use it for help in figuring out the word's
  meaning. For example, what does the word *differentiate* mean
  in the following sentence? Use the word parts to help you.

You can **differentiate** between the twins by their clothes.

(-*ate* = "to make"; *different* = "not the same"; *differentiate* =
"to make not the same.")

**Complete each sentence by underlining the correct word in
parentheses.**

There is no one (medicine, medicate) that cures the measles.

That is why doctors (vaccine, vaccinate) children against

measles. The (vaccine, vaccinate) prevents kids from getting the

measles. Unlike the measles, the kinds of flu that are (active,

activate) each year change. Therefore, you need to (participant,

participate) in getting a flu shot each year.

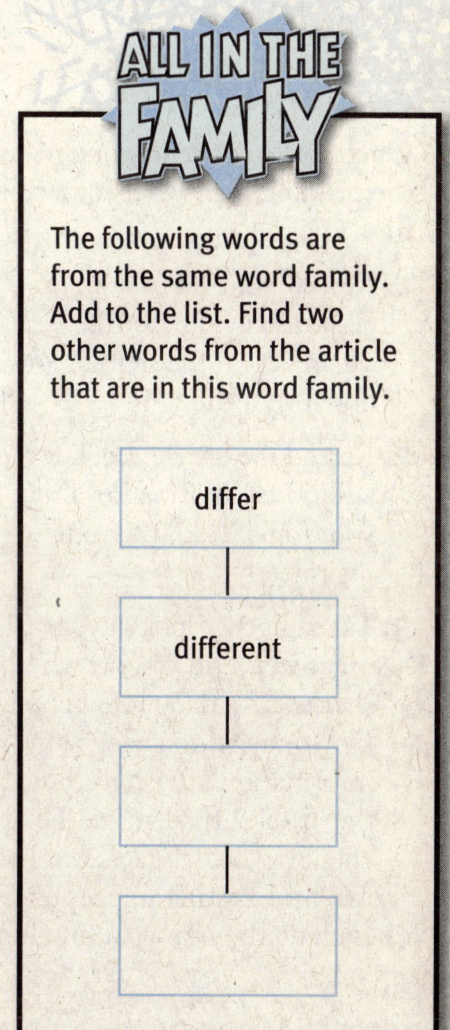

The following words are
from the same word family.
Add to the list. Find two
other words from the article
that are in this word family.

Shark Story

Write About It!

You have read an article about sharks. Now you will write about the topic. Read the writing prompt. It gives your writing assignment.

Writing Prompt

Imagine that you live near a sea park where people come to view sharks. Write a short brochure for park visitors, giving information about sharks. Tell whether sharks are a danger to people. Use ideas from the article and at least one word from the Word Bank.

approach • confirm • objective • observe • reality

In your response, you should:

- Write an informational brochure about sharks.

- Tell people whether sharks are a danger to them.

- Use at least one word from the Word Bank.

- Use correct grammar, usage, and mechanics.

Prewrite It

Once you are sure you understand the prompt, plan what you want to say.

1. Review your notes from the class discussion. Use the organizer on the right to jot down your thoughts.

2. Reread the article. Look for additional information about your topic. Add it to your organizer.

3. Take another look at your organizer. Did you say whether sharks are a danger to people? Do you need to change any information after rereading the article? If so, make the changes. Which facts will be most interesting to people? Include them in your brochure.

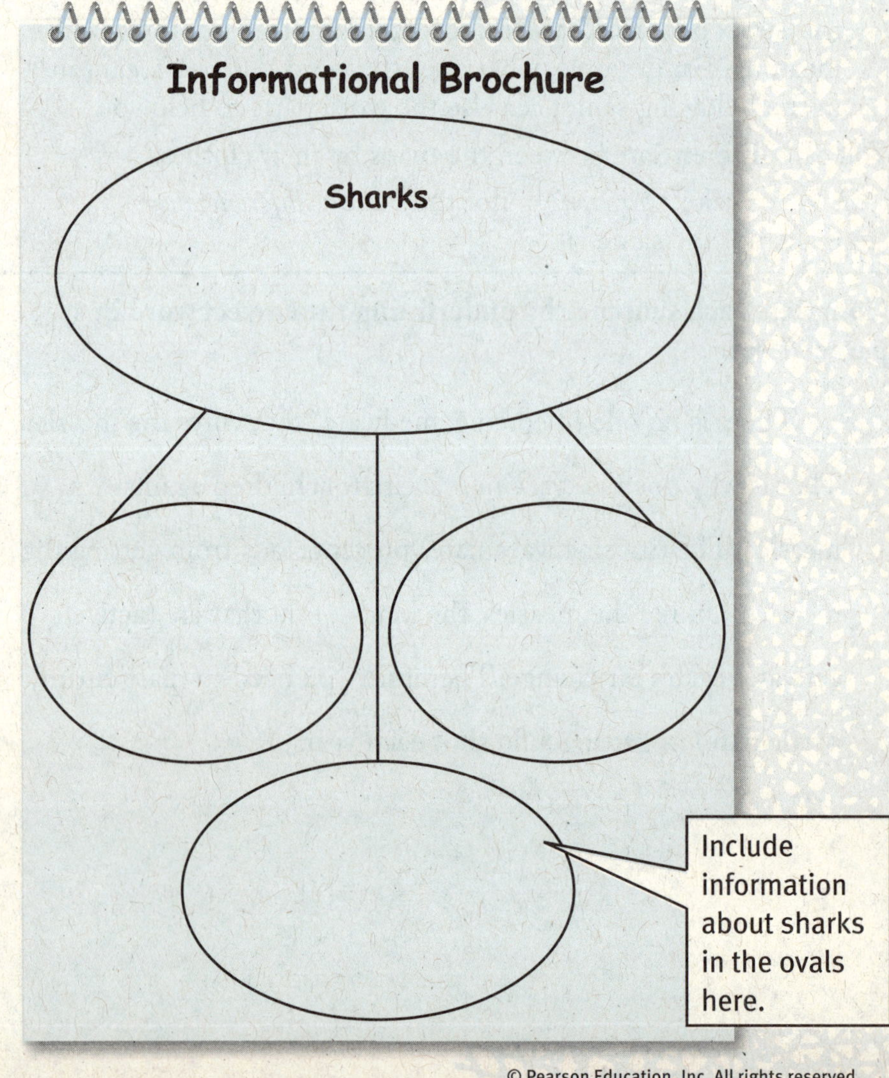

Draft It

Now use your organizer to draft, or write, an informational brochure. The writing frame below will help you.

1. Start by describing whether sharks are harmful to people. You have three choices. Underline your choice, and explain your thinking.
2. Then give information about sharks in the section "Shark Facts." Make sure you include facts and details from the article.

All About Sharks

Though many people think sharks are especially dangerous

animals, sharks (never, often, rarely) harm swimmers. Sharks

and people ____

____

Shark Facts: ____

____

____

____

____

____

Check It and Fix It

After you have written your brochure, check your work. Try to read it with a "fresh eye." Imagine that you are a visitor to the park reading the brochure.

1. Is everything written clearly and correctly? Use the checklist on the right to decide.
2. Then trade brochures with a classmate. Talk over ways you both might improve your brochures. Use the ideas to revise your work.
3. For help with grammar, usage, and mechanics, go to the Handbook on pages 189–231.

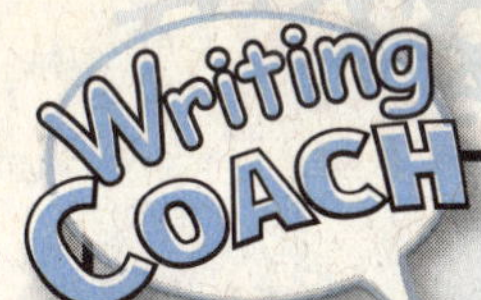

If you have trouble finding information, work with a partner. Ask your partner to scan the article and write down some facts. Use your partner's notes as you write.

✔ **CHECKLIST**

Evaluate your writing. A score of "5" is excellent. A score of "1" means you need to do more work. Then ask a partner to rate your writing.

1. **Does the brochure clearly tell whether sharks are a danger?**

   Me: 1 2 3 4 5
   Partner: 1 2 3 4 5

2. **Are there facts and information from the article in the brochure?**

   Me: 1 2 3 4 5
   Partner: 1 2 3 4 5

3. **Is there at least one word from the Word Bank?**

   Me: 1 2 3 4 5
   Partner: 1 2 3 4 5

4. **Are grammar, usage, and mechanics correct?**

   Me: 1 2 3 4 5
   Partner: 1 2 3 4 5

Vocabulary Workshop

Add these words to your personal word bank by practicing them.

approach • confirm • objective • observe • reality

What other new words in the article would you like to remember? List them.

____

____

____

Define It

Complete the chart below. Write each Word Bank word, its meaning, and a word it reminds you of. Use the example as a guide.

What It Means	approach	
a method or a way of doing something		**A Word It Reminds Me Of** strategy
What It Means		
		A Word It Reminds Me Of
What It Means		
		A Word It Reminds Me Of
What It Means		
		A Word It Reminds Me Of
What It Means		
		A Word It Reminds Me Of

Show You Know

In the space below, write a short, short story (just a paragraph!) using the Word Bank words. Be sure your sentences show that you understand the meanings of the words.

Once upon a time, ______________________________

____

____

____

____

Trade short stories with a partner. Read each other's stories. Are the Word Bank words used correctly? If something needs to be fixed, talk over how to fix it. Then make corrections.

Word Sort

Sort the Word Bank words into the correct columns in the chart below. Read the article and add your own words to each category. Use the examples as a guide.

Nouns	Verbs	Adjectives
approach	confirm	

Now that you have sorted your words, pick two from different categories and combine them into a sentence. For a challenge, pick more than two.

____

____

The following words are in the same word family. What are some other words that have *confirm* in them? Add two to the list.

confirm

confirmation

Shark Story　29

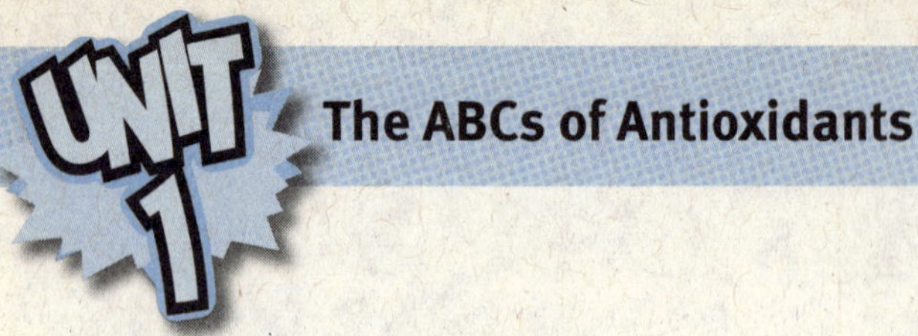

In your response, you should:

- Write an FAQ feature for a Web page on healthful eating.

- Use facts and information from the article.

- Use at least one word from the Word Bank.

- Use correct grammar, usage, and mechanics.

Write About It!

You have read an article about antioxidants in food. Now you will write about the topic. Read the writing prompt. It gives your writing assignment.

Writing Prompt

After reading "The ABCs of Antioxidants," what common questions do you think teens have about antioxidants? Imagine that you are a writer for a school Web site. Write a Frequently Asked Questions (FAQ) feature that gives questions and answers about antioxidants. Use ideas from the article and at least one word from the Word Bank.

concrete • consequence • discern • refer • verify

Prewrite It

Once you are sure you understand the prompt, plan what you want to say.

1. Review your notes from the class discussion. Use the organizer on the right to write questions that teens might have.

2. Reread the article. Look for facts and details that answer the questions. Add those to your organizer.

3. Reread all the questions and answers you have listed. Which questions are most important? Use those in your FAQs.

FAQs About Antioxidants

Question 1: _______________________

Answer: _______________________

____

Question 2: _______________________

Answer: _______________________

____

Question 3: _______________________

Answer: _______________________

____

Question 4: _______________________

Answer: _______________________

____

Draft It

Now use your organizer to draft, or write, your FAQs. The writing frame below will help you.

1. Start by writing your first question. Then write an answer for the question.

2. Then write two more questions and answers. Make sure your answers use facts and details from the article.

If you have trouble coming up with questions for your FAQs, work with a partner. Ask your partner what he or she would want to know about the topic. Use your partner's questions to write your FAQs.

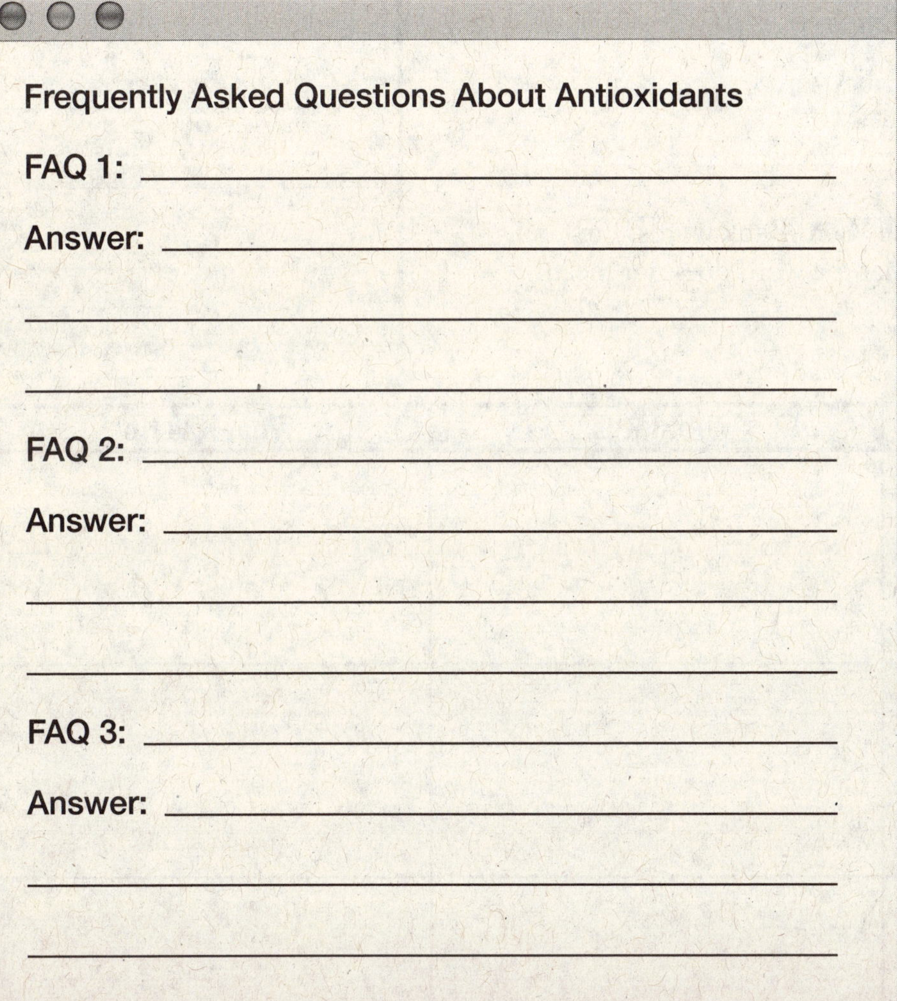

Frequently Asked Questions About Antioxidants

FAQ 1: _______________________________________

Answer: _______________________________________

____

____

FAQ 2: _______________________________________

Answer: _______________________________________

____

____

FAQ 3: _______________________________________

Answer: _______________________________________

____

____

✔ CHECKLIST

Evaluate your writing. A score of "5" is excellent. A score of "1" means you need to do more work. Then ask a partner to rate your writing.

1. **Does the FAQ feature ask questions that teens would ask?**

   Me: 1 2 3 4 5
   Partner: 1 2 3 4 5

2. **Are questions answered with facts and details from the article?**

   Me: 1 2 3 4 5
   Partner: 1 2 3 4 5

3. **Is there at least one word from the Word Bank?**

   Me: 1 2 3 4 5
   Partner: 1 2 3 4 5

4. **Are grammar, usage, and mechanics correct?**

   Me: 1 2 3 4 5
   Partner: 1 2 3 4 5

Check It and Fix It

After you have written your FAQs, check your work. Try to read it with a "fresh eye."

1. Is everything written clearly and correctly? Use the checklist on the right to decide.

2. Then trade FAQs with a classmate. Talk over ways you both might improve your questions and answers. Use the ideas to revise your work.

3. For help with grammar, usage, and mechanics, go to the Handbook on pages 189–231.

Vocabulary Workshop

Add these words to your personal word bank by
practicing them.

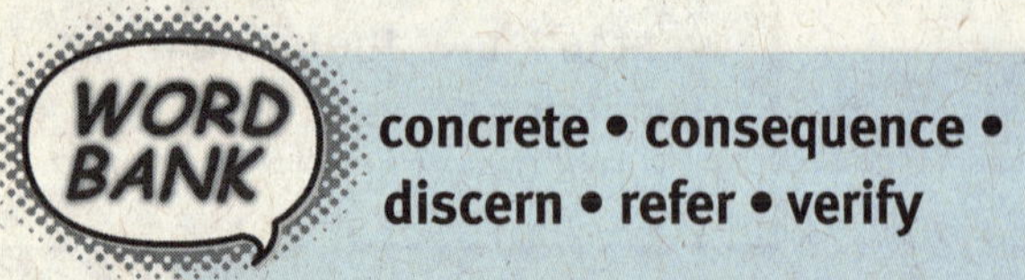

concrete • consequence •
discern • refer • verify

Your Choice

What other new words in
the article would you like
to remember? List them.

____

____

____

Define It

Complete the chart below using the Word Bank words. First, tell
what the word means. Then tell what the word does not mean.

Word	What It Is	What It Is Not

Show You Know

To show that you understand the Word Bank words, write three
sentences. In each sentence, use and highlight two of the words.
(You will use one word twice.)

1. ____

   ____

2. ____

   ____

3. ____

   ____

A Root That Means "To Bring" or "To Carry": *fer*

- The root of a word contains the word's main meaning. Roots
  are combined with prefixes and suffixes to form new words.
  You can use the meaning of the root *fer* and common prefixes
  and suffixes to figure out the meaning of a word.

The scientists **refer** to other studies on organic food.

(*re–* = "again"; *fer* = "to bring." *Refer* = "bring again," as in bringing
attention to something again.)

**Complete each sentence by underlining the correct word in
parentheses.**

I (refer, prefer, confer) to ride my bike to work, but I took

the bus today because it was raining. I was not sure which bus to

take, so I (conferred, transferred, referred) with people at the bus

stop. They (preferred, referred, inferred) me to the map of bus

routes. I had to (prefer, infer, transfer) from one bus to another.

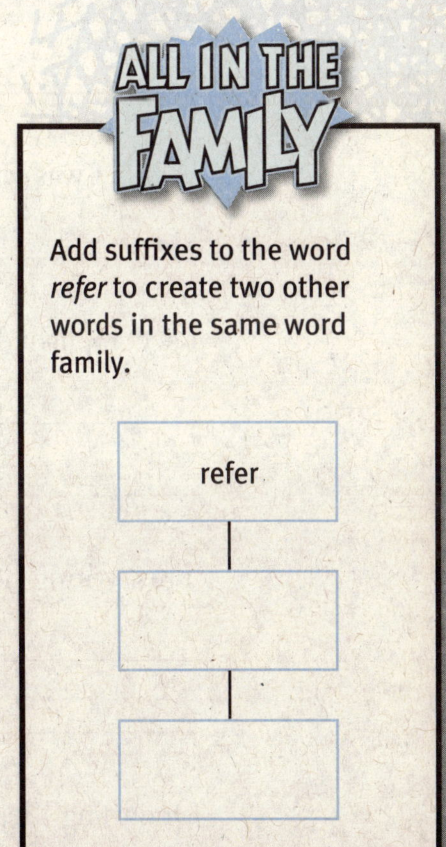

Writing Reflection

Is there a difference between reality and truth?

Look through your writing from this unit and choose the best piece. Reflect on this piece of writing by completing each sentence below.

My best piece of writing from this unit is _________________________

____

I chose this piece because _______________________________________

____

____

While I was writing, one goal I had was ___________________________

____

I accomplished this goal by ______________________________________

____

____

This writing helped me think more about the Big Question because

____

____

One thing I learned while writing that can help me in the future is

____

____

Can progress be made without conflict?

Write About It!

You have read an article about rivalry between brothers and sisters. Now you will write about the topic. Read the writing prompt. It gives your writing assignment.

In your response, you should:

- Explain sibling rivalry and its possible benefits.

- Use ideas from the article.

- Use at least one word from the Word Bank.

- Use correct grammar, usage, and mechanics.

Writing Prompt

Imagine that you are a writer for a teen magazine on the Internet. Write an article about sibling rivalry. Explain what it is, what causes it, and how siblings may benefit from it. Use ideas from the article and at least one word from the Word Bank.

compromise • concession • confrontation • discuss • reconciliation

Prewrite It

Once you are sure you understand the prompt, plan what you want to say.

1. Review your notes from the class discussion. Are there ideas that you can use in your article? Jot them down on the organizer on the right.

2. Reread the article. Look for other facts and ideas you might include in your article. Add those to your organizer.

3. Take a final look at your organizer. Decide which facts and ideas to include in your article.

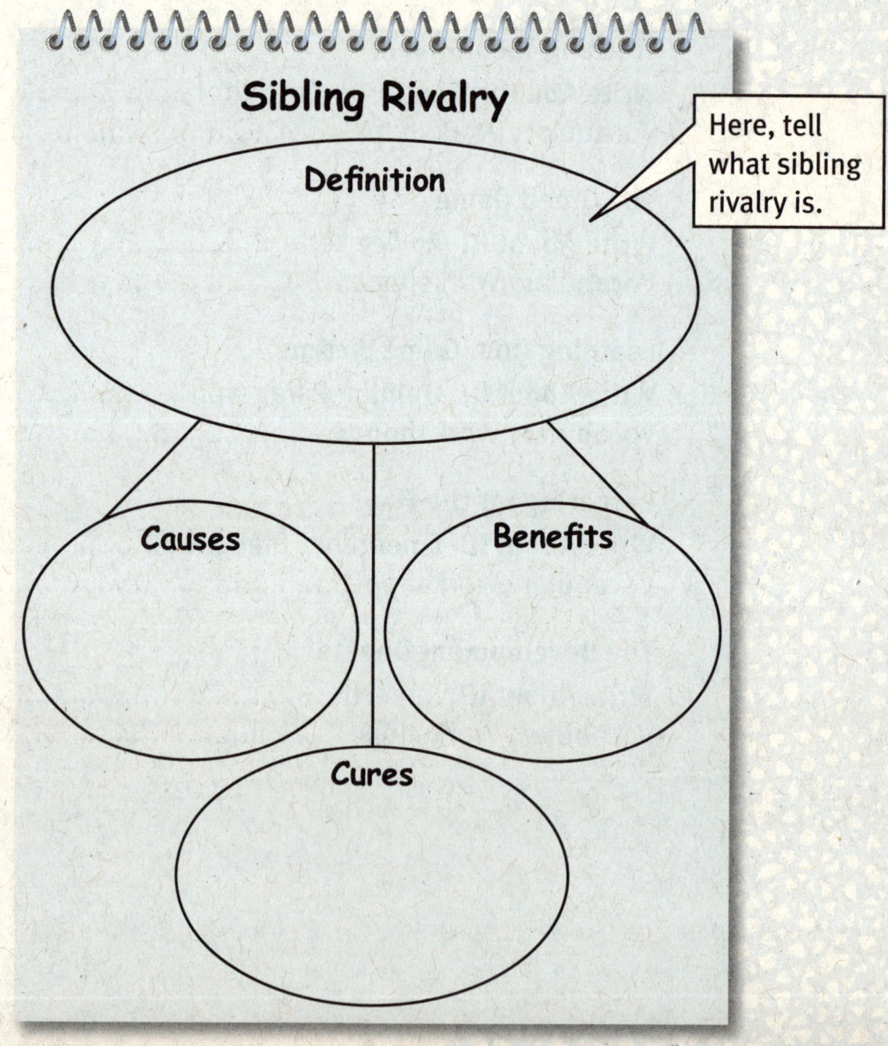

Draft It

Now use your organizer to draft, or write, your online magazine article. The writing frame below will help you.

1. Read the first sentence. Then complete the second sentence by defining sibling rivalry.

2. In a second paragraph, explain a main cause of sibling rivalry. In a third, explain a possible benefit. Make sure you include ideas from the article.

If you have trouble writing, work with a partner. Ask the person to take notes as you explain what you want to say. Use the notes to write.

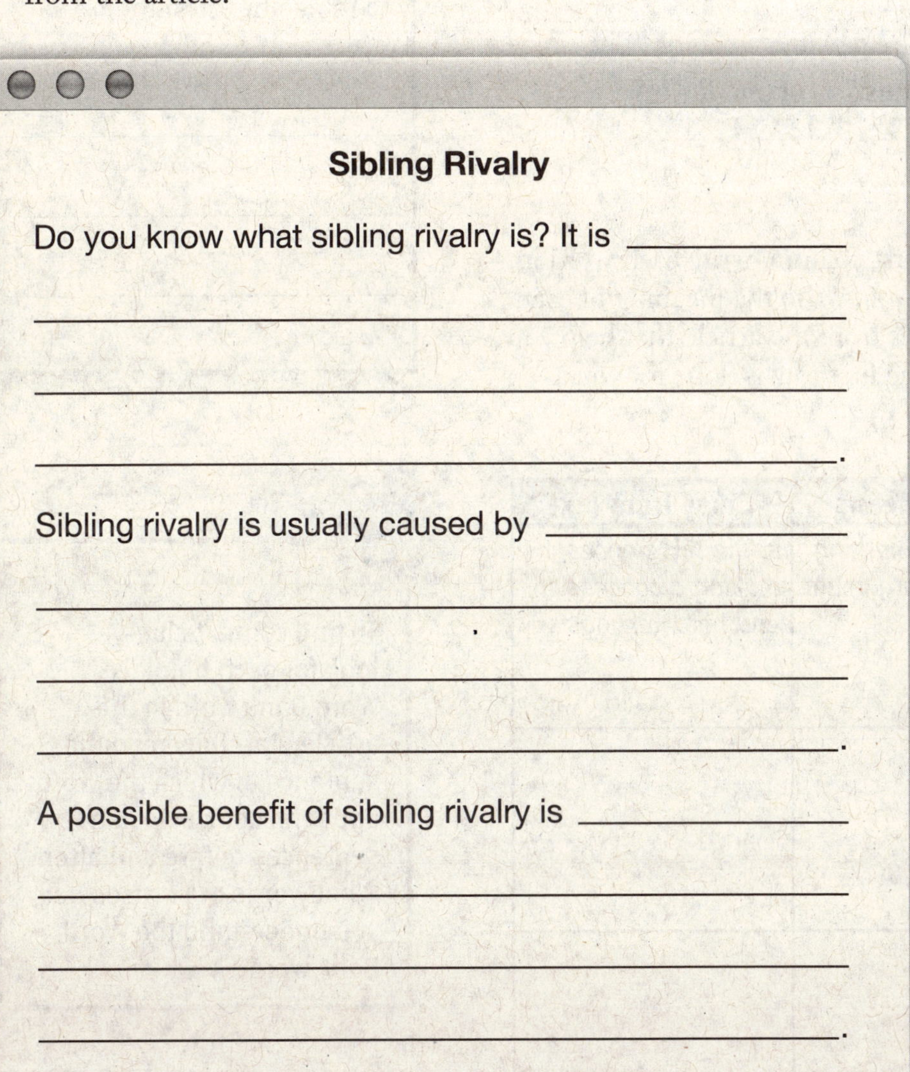

Sibling Rivalry

Do you know what sibling rivalry is? It is _______________

____

____

____ .

Sibling rivalry is usually caused by _______________

____

____

____ .

A possible benefit of sibling rivalry is _______________

____

____

____ .

✔ **CHECKLIST**

Evaluate your writing. A score of "5" is excellent. A score of "1" means you need to do more work. Then ask a partner to rate your writing.

1. **Does the article clearly define sibling rivalry?**

   Me: 1 2 3 4 5
   Partner: 1 2 3 4 5

2. **Does the article give a cause and a benefit?**

   Me: 1 2 3 4 5
   Partner: 1 2 3 4 5

3. **Is there at least one word from the Word Bank?**

   Me: 1 2 3 4 5
   Partner: 1 2 3 4 5

4. **Are grammar, usage, and mechanics correct?**

   Me: 1 2 3 4 5
   Partner: 1 2 3 4 5

Check It and Fix It

After you write your article, check your work. Try to read it with a "fresh eye," as if you have never before seen it.

1. Is everything written clearly and correctly? Use the checklist on the right to decide.

2. Trade articles with a classmate. Discuss ways you might improve your articles. Use the ideas to revise your work.

3. For help with grammar, usage, and mechanics, go to the Handbook on pages 189–231.

Vocabulary Workshop

Add these words to your personal word bank by
practicing them.

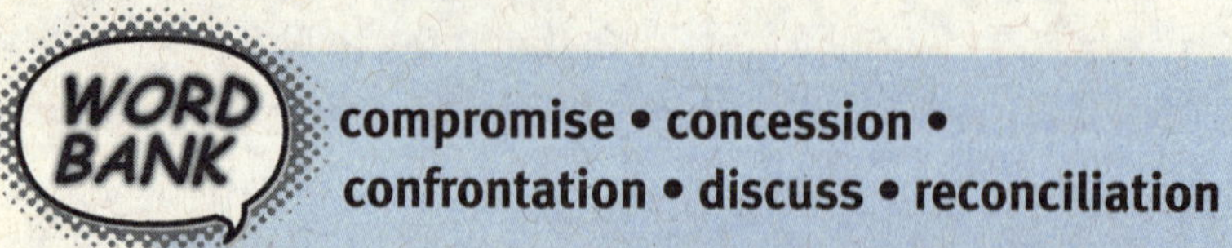

Define It

Complete the chart below. In the first column, write each word in
the Word Bank. In the second column, write the meaning of each
word. In the last column, write clues from the article that help you
understand the word's meaning. The first row is done for you as
a guide.

Word	What It Means	Clues from Text
compromise	to give up something to settle an argument	settle differences, making a concession, end hard feelings

What other new words in
the article would you like
to remember? List them.

____

____

____

To find context clues,
look for each boldface
Word Bank word in the
article. Carefully read the
sentence in which the word
appears. Look also at a few
sentences before and after.
What words or phrases help
you understand the Word
Bank word?

Show You Know

Answer the questions below to show you know the meaning of each
Word Bank word. Explain each answer.

1. Union members and management may **compromise** to end a strike. What do they do?

   ____

2. A candidate for office makes a **concession** speech when losing an election. What does the candidate do

   in the speech? ____

3. Malory is so shy that she will do almost anything to avoid a **confrontation**. What does she try to avoid?

   ____

4. When you disagree with someone, **discuss** why you disagree. How might you do this?

   ____

5. My sister and parents said they were sorry in order to find **reconciliation**. What did they find?

   ____

Prefixes That Mean "With": *co-*, *com-*, *con-*

- The prefixes *co-*, *com-*, and *con-* all mean "with" or "together."
  The Latin root of the word *confrontation—frontis—*means
  "forehead." Over time, "two foreheads together" has come to
  mean "a face-to-face meeting."

- The prefixes *co-*, *com-*, and *con-* can be added to roots, as in
  confrontation, or to whole words, as in *compromise*, or "promise
  together."

**Complete each sentence by underlining the correct word
in parentheses.**

Few people want to have a (compromise, concession,
confrontation). However, if you and a neighbor disagree and
cannot reach a (compromise, concession, confrontation), you may
decide to go to court. Most courts want you to work out your
differences before the judge is called, so your lawyer may ask you
to make a (compromise, concession, confrontation) or two.

Write About It!

You have read an article about holding parents responsible when their teenagers break laws. Now you will write about the topic. Read the writing prompt. It gives your writing assignment.

Writing Prompt

Imagine that your state government is thinking about strengthening its parental responsibility laws. Write a letter to your senator giving your views. Should strong laws be passed? Why or why not? Use ideas from the article and at least one word from the Word Bank.

change • defend • inclined • oppose • struggle

WRITING RUBRIC

In your response, you should:

- Give your opinion of parental responsibility laws.

- Support your opinion with reasons and examples from the article.

- Use at least one word from the Word Bank.

- Use correct grammar, usage, and mechanics.

Prewrite It

Once you are sure you understand the prompt, plan what you want to say.

1. Review your notes from the class discussion. Use the organizer on the right to jot down your thoughts.

2. Reread the article. On your organizer, note reasons and examples you might include in your letter.

3. Review your organizer. Decide which reasons and examples to include in your letter.

Parental Responsibility Laws

My View

> Your view is your opinion of the laws.

My Arguments

> Your arguments are your reasons and supporting examples.

Draft It

Now use your organizer to draft, or write, the letter to your senator.
The writing frame below will help you.

1. Start by stating your opinion in the first sentence. You have two
   choices. Underline your choice.
2. Then give the main reason for your opinion. Follow up by giving
   a second reason. Then underline what you want the senator to
   do—support or oppose the law change.

Dear Senator:

   I am (for, against) stronger parental responsibility laws. The main

reason is that ____

____

____

____.

   Another reason is that ______________________________________

____

____

____.

For these reasons, I hope you will (support, oppose) stronger parental

responsibility laws.

Yours truly,

____

The purpose of your letter
is to convince your senator
to agree with you and take
action. Make sure your
reasons are convincing.
Discuss them with
classmates. Ask how you
could make your letter more
persuasive.

✔ CHECKLIST

Evaluate your writing.
A score of "5" is excellent.
A score of "1" means you
need to do more work.
Then ask a partner to rate
your writing.

1. **Does the letter state an
   opinion about the issue?**

   Me: 1 2 3 4 5
   Partner: 1 2 3 4 5

2. **Are there reasons and
   examples from the article?**

   Me: 1 2 3 4 5
   Partner: 1 2 3 4 5

3. **Is there at least one word
   from the Word Bank?**

   Me: 1 2 3 4 5
   Partner: 1 2 3 4 5

4. **Are grammar, usage, and
   mechanics correct?**

   Me: 1 2 3 4 5
   Partner: 1 2 3 4 5

Check It and Fix It

After you have written your letter, check your work. Read it as if you
were the senator receiving it.

1. Is everything written clearly and correctly? Use the checklist on the
   right to see.
2. Trade letters with a classmate. Talk over ways you might make your
   letters more convincing. Then revise your work if necessary.
3. For help with grammar, usage, and mechanics, go to the Handbook
   on pages 189–231.

Vocabulary Workshop

Add these words to your personal word bank by
practicing them.

change • defend • inclined • oppose • struggle

What other new words in
the article would you like
to remember? List them.

____

____

____

Define It

For each organizer below, do the following. Choose two words from
the Word Bank and write them on either side of the triangle. (One
word will appear twice.) On the blank "because" lines, tell why the
two words are connected. Use the examples as a guide.

oppose   **is connected to**   struggle

because: you often have to struggle when you oppose something.

____

      is connected to

because: _____________________________________

____

      is connected to

because: _____________________________________

____

Show You Know

Write a comic strip in the space below. Use all the Word Bank words in a way that shows you understand their meanings.

Roots That Mean "Put": *pos, posit*

- You might be able to guess the meaning of the Word Bank word *oppose* by looking at its parts. *Oppose* is made up of the prefix *op-*, meaning "against," and the root *pos*, meaning "to put or place." The literal meaning of *oppose* is "to put or place against." That is very similar to the Word Bank definition "to be against."

For each sentence below, underline the root in the boldface word. Then think about the meaning of the root as well as the sentence, and write what you think each word means.

1. The artist wants me to **pose** for a portrait.

Meaning: ___________________________________

2. What soccer **position** is behind center forward?

Meaning: ___________________________________

3. Will you take the seat **opposite** me on the aisle?

Meaning: ___________________________________

4. You can get a sunburn if you **expose** too much skin.

Meaning: ___________________________________

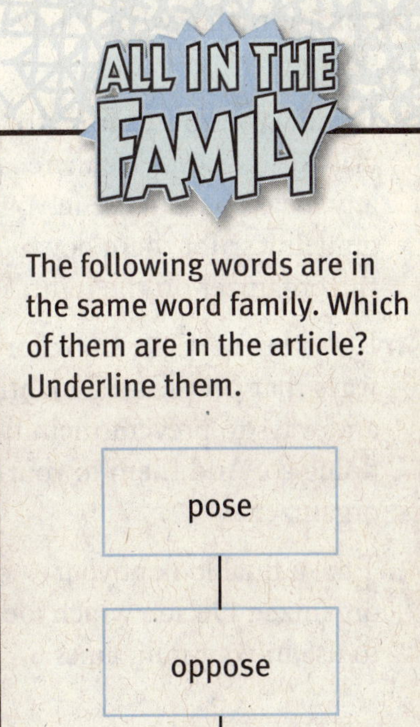

Identity Theft

Write About It!

You have read an article about identity theft. Now you will write about the topic. Read the writing prompt. It gives your writing assignment.

In your response, you should:

- Write guidelines for preventing identity theft.

- Include information from the article.

- Use at least one word from the Word Bank.

- Use correct grammar, usage, and mechanics.

Writing Prompt

Help keep kids safe from identity theft. Write a list of guidelines called "Safe Internet Use." Imagine that your guidelines will hang in your school library or computer lab. Use information from the article and at least one word from the Word Bank.

concession • motive • produce • progress • radical

Prewrite It

Once you are sure you understand the prompt, plan what you want to say.

1. Review your notes from the class discussion. Are there any ideas you can use in your guidelines? Jot them down on the organizer on the right.

2. Reread the article. Look for ways that people steal identities and ways to prevent them from doing so. Add them to your organizer.

3. Take a final look at your organizer. Decide which ideas to use in your guidelines.

Safe Internet Use

Scams	Protections

List ways that thieves steal identities.

List ways to protect yourself.

Draft It

Now use your organizer to draft, or write, your guidelines.
The writing frame below will help you.

1. Read the first sentence. It states the main idea. Then finish the sentence starter by describing a few common Internet scams.

2. Next, describe ways that teens can protect their identities. Be sure to use ideas from the article.

To make your guidelines easy to read, put them in a numbered list, or put a bullet point (•) in front of each guideline. If you are not sure which form to use, talk it over with a classmate.

Safe Internet Use

Protect yourself from identity theft! Beware of these Internet

scams: __________________________________

____

____

____

__________________________________.

Here are some ways to protect your identity: __________

____

____

____

____

__________________________________.

✔ **CHECKLIST**

Evaluate your writing.
A score of "5" is excellent.
A score of "1" means you need to do more work.
Then ask a partner to rate your writing.

1. **Do the guidelines clearly explain what to do and not do?**

   Me: 1 2 3 4 5
   Partner: 1 2 3 4 5

2. **Do the guidelines include ideas from the article?**

   Me: 1 2 3 4 5
   Partner: 1 2 3 4 5

3. **Is there at least one word from the Word Bank?**

   Me: 1 2 3 4 5
   Partner: 1 2 3 4 5

4. **Are grammar, usage, and mechanics correct?**

   Me: 1 2 3 4 5
   Partner: 1 2 3 4 5

Check It and Fix It

After you have written your guidelines, check your work. Try to read them as if you have never before seen them.

1. Is everything written clearly and correctly? Use the checklist on the right to see.

2. Trade guidelines with a classmate. Discuss ways you might improve them. Use your ideas to revise your work.

3. For help with grammar, usage, and mechanics, go to the Handbook on pages 189–231.

Vocabulary Workshop

Add these words to your personal word bank by practicing them.

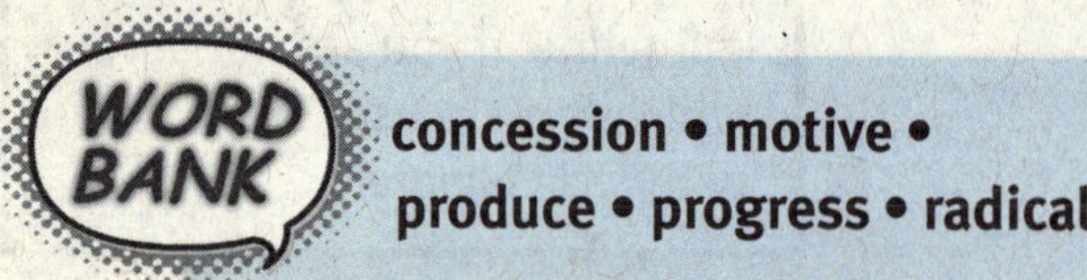

Your Choice

What other new words in the article would you like to remember? List them.

____

____

____

Define It

In your own words, write what each word in the Word Bank means. Then think of a word that has the same or a very similar meaning. Write that word as shown in the example below.

What It Means	concession
a thing you give up without really wanting to	**A Word It Reminds Me Of** sacrifice
What It Means	
	A Word It Reminds Me Of ____________
What It Means	
	A Word It Reminds Me Of ____________
What It Means	
	A Word It Reminds Me Of ____________
What It Means	
	A Word It Reminds Me Of ____________

Show You Know

To show that you understand the Word Bank words, write a clue
for each word. Exchange clues with a partner. See whether your
partner can identify the correct word for each clue. Use the clue for
concession, below, as a model.

- This is something you give up, often without wanting to.

1. ____

2. ____

3. ____

4. ____

5. ____

A Root That Means "Move": *gress*

- If you know the meaning of the root of a word, you may be able
  to figure out the meaning of other words that contain the same
  root. The root *gress* comes from a Latin word meaning "to move,
  step, or walk." Add the prefix *pro-*, meaning "forward," to the root,
  to get *progress,* which means "to move forward" or "an advance."

**Write the meanings of the following *gress* words in your own words.
The prefixes are defined for you.**

1. **transgress** (*trans-* = "across")

   ____

2. **regress** (*re-* = "back" or "again")

   ____

3. **digress** (*di-* = "two")

   ____

4. **egress** (*e-* = "out" or "away")

   ____

5. **congress** (*con-* = "with" or "together")

   ____

The following words are
in the same word family.
Underline the word or words
that are used in the article.

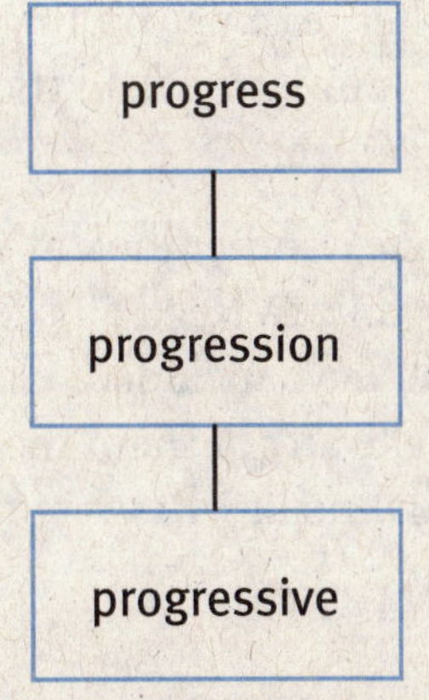

Write About It!

You have read an article about devices used to track teen drivers. Now you will write about the topic. Read the writing prompt. It gives your writing assignment.

Writing Prompt

After reading "Tracking Teen Drivers," do you think the benefits of tracking devices outweigh the drawbacks? Do the devices help save lives or only invade privacy? State your opinion and support it in a letter to a newspaper editor. Use ideas from the article and at least one word from the Word Bank.

adversity • compromise • oppose • reveal • unify

WRITING RUBRIC

In your response, you should:

- State your opinion of tracking devices.

- Support your opinion with reasons from the article.

- Use at least one word from the Word Bank.

- Use correct grammar, usage, and mechanics.

Prewrite It

Once you are sure you understand the prompt, plan what you want to say.

1. Review your notes from the class discussion. Use the organizer to jot down ideas you might use in your letter.

2. Reread the article. Look for other reasons you might include in your letter. Add those to your organizer.

3. Take another look at your organizer. Read all the reasons you have included. Can you make any of them more convincing? Rewrite them.

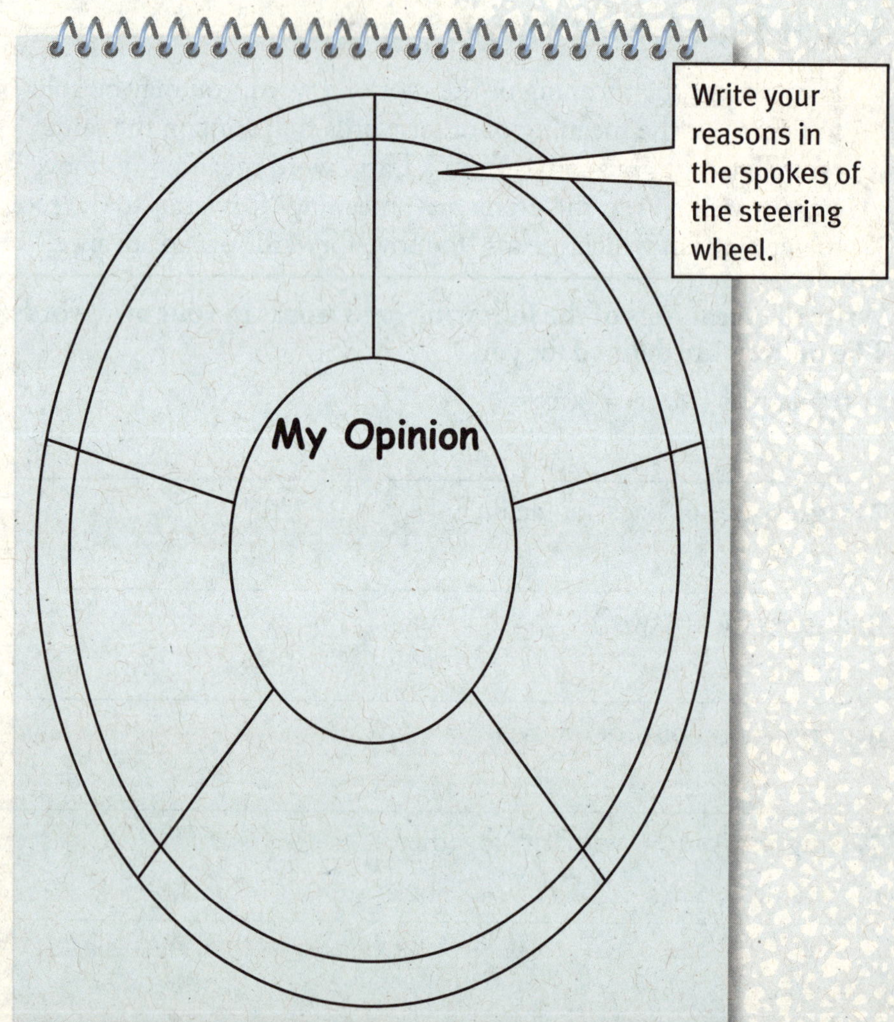

Draft It

Now use your organizer to draft, or write, your letter to the editor. The writing frame below will help you.

1. Read the first sentence. You have two choices of opinion. Underline your choice. Then give the main reason for your opinion.

2. Next, state another reason for your opinion. Be sure to include reasons from the article. Finally, sign your letter.

To strengthen your letter, talk over the issue with a partner whose opinion is different from yours. See if your reasons stand up to his or hers. If not, discuss how to make your letter more convincing.

Dear Editor:

Tracking devices that monitor teen drivers are a (good, bad) idea.

The main reason is that _______________________________

____

____

____

____

____.

Another reason is that _______________________________

____

____

____

____

____.

✔ CHECKLIST

Evaluate your writing. A score of "5" is excellent. A score of "1" means you need to do more work. Then ask a partner to rate your writing.

1. **Does the letter clearly state an opinion?**

   Me: 1 2 3 4 5
   Partner: 1 2 3 4 5

2. **Is the opinion supported by reasons from the article?**

   Me: 1 2 3 4 5
   Partner: 1 2 3 4 5

3. **Is there at least one word from the Word Bank?**

   Me: 1 2 3 4 5
   Partner: 1 2 3 4 5

4. **Are grammar, usage, and mechanics correct?**

   Me: 1 2 3 4 5
   Partner: 1 2 3 4 5

Check It and Fix It

After you have written your letter, check your work. Read it as though you have just opened the newspaper and know little about the issue.

1. Is everything written clearly and correctly? Use the checklist on the right to see.

2. Trade letters with a classmate. Discuss ways you might make your letters more persuasive. Use your ideas to revise your work.

3. For help with grammar, usage, and mechanics, go to the Handbook on pages 189–231.

Vocabulary Workshop

Add these words to your personal word bank by
practicing them.

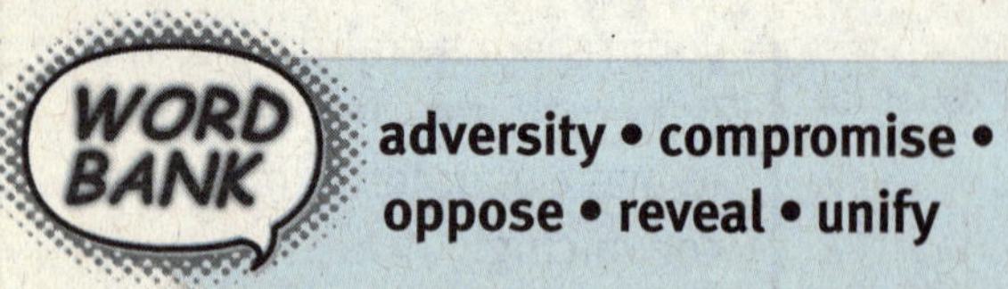

**adversity • compromise •
oppose • reveal • unify**

Your Choice

What other new words in
the article would you like
to remember? List them.

____

____

____

Define It

Complete the chart below using the Word Bank words. First, tell
what each word means. Then tell what the word does not mean.
Use the example as a guide.

Word	What It Is	What It Is Not
adversity	trouble; hard times	good luck

Show You Know

In the space below, write a short, short story (just a paragraph!) using the Word Bank words. Be sure your sentences show that you understand the meanings of the words.

Once upon a time, ____

____

____

____

____

Suffixes That Mean "Condition": *-ity, -ty*

- When you add the suffix *-ity* or *-ty* to an adjective, you change the word into a noun. For example, if something is *adverse,* it is opposed to, acts against, or is harmful. The Word Bank word *adversity,* then, means "a condition of harm or bad luck, or opposed to well-being."

Form a noun by adding the suffix *-ity* or *-ty* to each adjective below. Then write a sentence for each noun you form.

1. loyal ____

Sentence: ____

____

2. equal ____

Sentence: ____

____

3. safe ____

Sentence: ____

____

4. creative ____

Sentence: ____

____

The Greed Game

Write About It!

You have read an article about teenagers and consumerism. Now you will write about the topic. Read the writing prompt. It gives your writing assignment.

In your response, you should:

- Give advice to a teen who cannot afford to buy trendy items.
- Include ideas from the article.
- Use at least one word from the Word Bank.
- Use correct grammar, usage, and mechanics.

Writing Prompt

Imagine that you are a writer for an advice blog for teenagers. You get a posting from a young person who says she feels pressure to buy an Mp3 player and more to keep up with friends. Her parents say they cannot afford to buy her what she wants. What advice would you give her? Use ideas from the article and at least one word from the Word Bank.

conclude • debate • former • negotiate

Prewrite It

Once you are sure you understand the prompt, plan what you want to say.

1. Review your notes from the class discussion. On the organizer on the right, jot down ideas you might use in your blog posting.

2. Reread the article. Look for advice in the article that you might include in your posting. Add it to your organizer.

3. Take another look at your organizer. Read over all the advice you have given. Will it be helpful? If not, brainstorm, and then revise your ideas.

Blog Posting

My Advice

Your advice is your suggestions and reasons.

Draft It

Now use your organizer to draft, or write, your blog response.
The writing frame below will help you.

1. Start by reading the first sentence. It introduces your topic.

2. Then finish the sentence starter by stating your advice. Be sure
to use ideas from the article.

Dear Teenager:

You say you feel pressure from friends to buy things
you cannot afford. Here is my advice to you:

____

____

____

____

____

____

____

____

____

____

Your posting should sound
kind and helpful. Ask a
partner to read your posting
and describe the tone, or
the way the posting sounds.
If the tone is not friendly
and helpful, discuss how to
improve it.

✔ **CHECKLIST**

Evaluate your writing.
A score of "5" is excellent.
A score of "1" means you
need to do more work.
Then ask a partner to rate
your writing.

**1. Does the posting give
clear, helpful advice?**

Me: 1   2   3   4   5
Partner: 1   2   3   4   5

**2. Does the posting include
ideas from the article?**

Me: 1   2   3   4   5
Partner: 1   2   3   4   5

**3. Is there at least one word
from the Word Bank?**

Me: 1   2   3   4   5
Partner: 1   2   3   4   5

**4. Are grammar, usage, and
mechanics correct?**

Me: 1   2   3   4   5
Partner: 1   2   3   4   5

Check It and Fix It

After you have written your blog advice posting, check your work.
Try to read it as if you are the teen who needs the advice.

1. Is everything written clearly and correctly? Use the checklist on the
right to see.

2. Trade advice postings with a classmate. Discuss ways you might
make your advice more helpful or practical. Use your ideas to revise
your work.

3. For help with grammar, usage, and mechanics, go to the Handbook
on pages 189–231.

Vocabulary Workshop

Add these words to your personal word bank by practicing them.

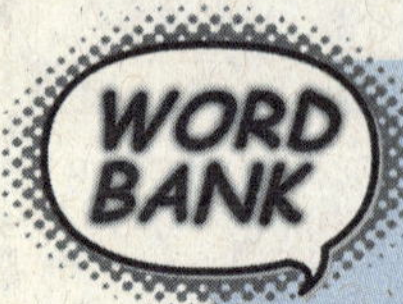

WORD BANK conclude • debate • former • negotiate

Define It

Complete Venn diagrams to show how words are different and alike. Choose a pair of words from the Word Bank. Write the words on the lines inside the diagram. On the sides of the circles, tell how the two words are different. In between, write how they are similar. The first pair is done for you as a model. Do this for two more pairs of words. You will use one word twice.

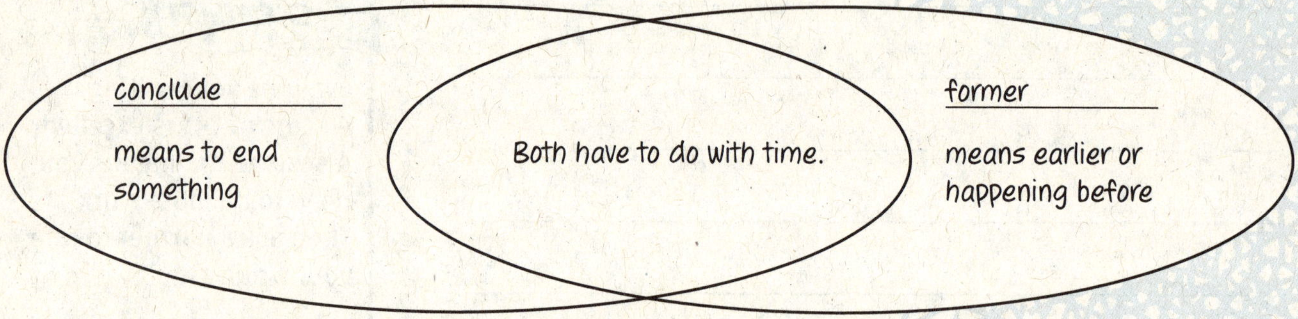
conclude
means to end something
Both have to do with time.
former
means earlier or happening before

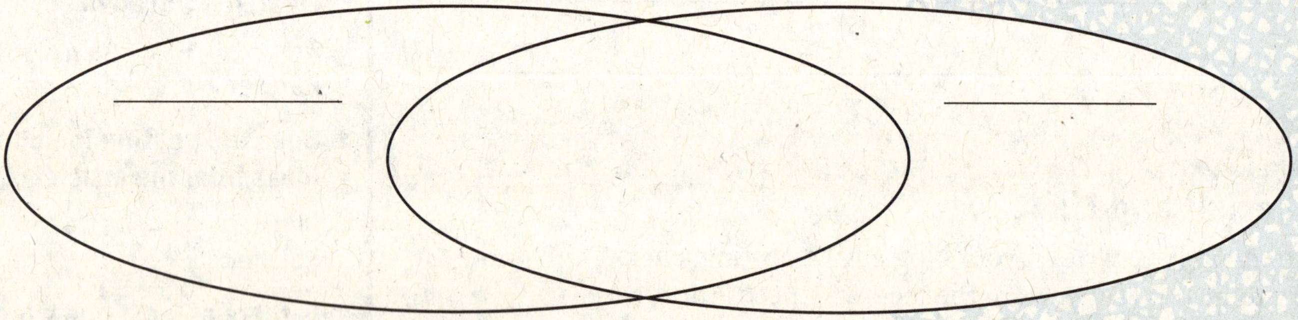

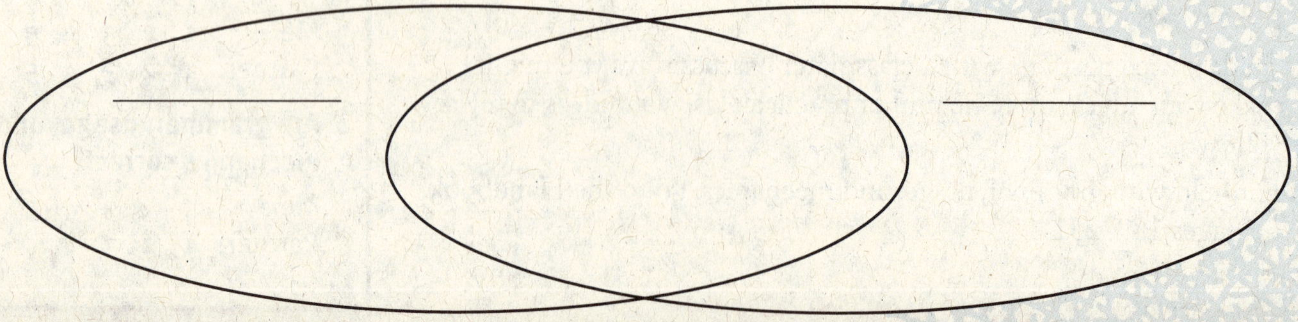

Your Choice

What other new words in the article would you like to remember? List them.

____

____

____

Show You Know

To show that you understand the Word Bank words, write two
sentences. In each sentence, use and highlight two of the words.
Use the example as a model.

- When you negotiate, you may engage in a debate.

1. ____

   ____

2. ____

   ____

Trade sentences with a
partner and read them. Are
the words used correctly?
If not, discuss how to revise
the sentences. Then revise.

Word Play

In the chart below, list words that mean the same or about the same
as the Word Bank words. Use the examples as models.

Word Bank Word	Words with Similar Meanings
conclude	infer, understand, judge

Rewrite each sentence, substituting one of your words for the
underlined word.

1. Dad and Juan had a <u>debate</u> about driving at age sixteen.

____

2. I consider Jean my <u>former</u> girlfriend because she refuses to call me.

____

3. How can we end our differences if we do not <u>negotiate</u>?

____

4. From the evidence, the officer will <u>conclude</u> the suspect is guilty.

____

Write About It!

You have read an article about meetings between offenders and their victims. Now you will write about the topic. Read the writing prompt. It gives your writing assignment.

Writing Prompt

Should teenage offenders be required to meet and talk over their differences with their victims? Write a paragraph in which you state your opinion. Use ideas from the article and at least one word from the Word Bank.

adversity • change • confrontation • inestimable • reconciliation

WRITING RUBRIC

In your response, you should:

- State whether you think offenders should be required to meet with their victims.

- Support your opinion with ideas from the article.

- Use at least one word from the Word Bank.

- Use correct grammar, usage, and mechanics.

Prewrite It

Once you are sure you understand the prompt, plan what you want to say.

1. Review your notes from the class discussion. Which ideas could you use in your paragraph? Jot them down on the organizer on the right.

2. Reread the article. Look for descriptions of victim-offender meetings as well as benefits and drawbacks of the meetings. Add them to your organizer.

3. Take another look at your organizer. Read all the ideas you have included. Which ones are you sure you want to use? Underline them.

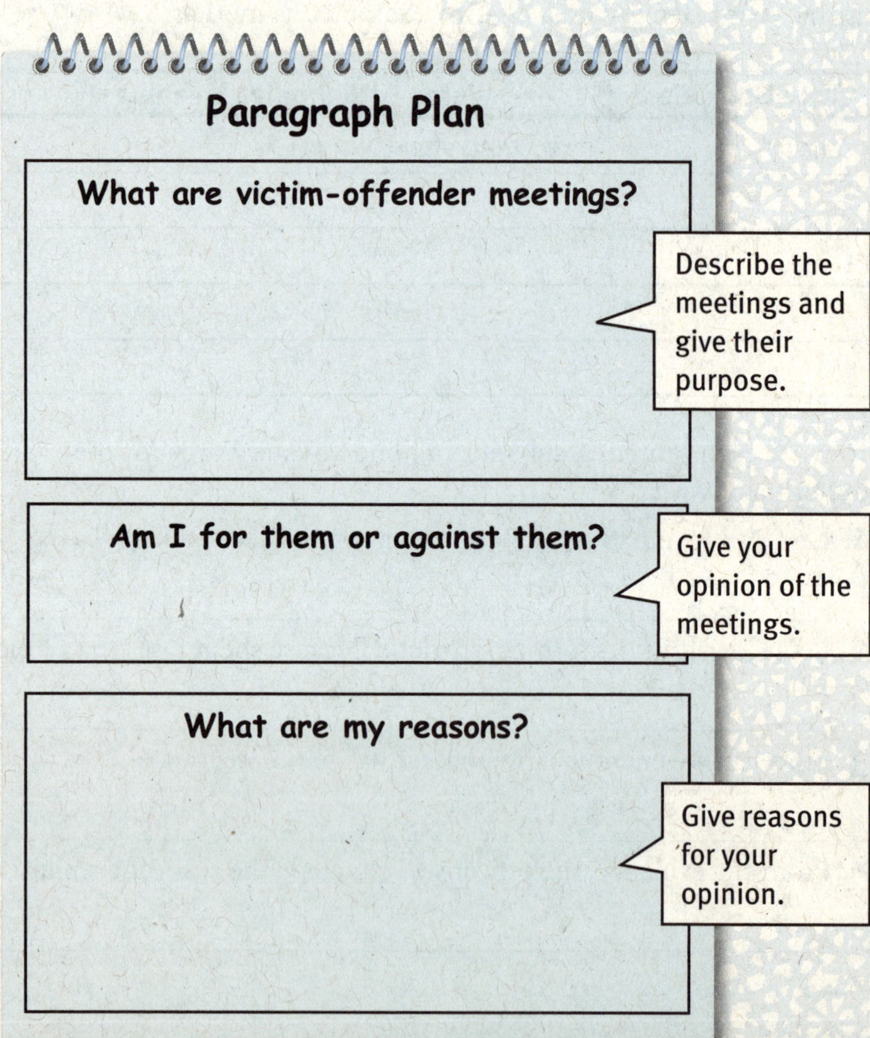

Draft It

Now use your organizer to draft, or write, your opinion paragraph.
The writing frame below will help you.

1. Start by reading the first sentence. It states the general topic of
   your paragraph. Then finish the sentence starter by describing the
   meetings and giving their purpose.

2. Next, underline your opinion of the meetings. Then give a reason
   or two for your opinion. Include ideas from the article.

Ask a partner to read your
paragraph aloud. When you
listen, does any part seem
confusing? Discuss ways
to revise that part of your
paragraph.

Victim-Offender Meetings

Some high schools set up victim-offender meetings. These are

____

____

____

____

____.

I am (for, against) victim-offender meetings because ___________

____

____

____

____

____

____.

✔ **CHECKLIST**

Evaluate your writing.
A score of "5" is excellent.
A score of "1" means you
need to do more work.
Then ask a partner to rate
your writing.

1. **Does the paragraph
   clearly describe the
   meetings?**

   Me: 1 2 3 4 5
   Partner: 1 2 3 4 5

2. **Does it state an opinion
   and support it with ideas
   from the article?**

   Me: 1 2 3 4 5
   Partner: 1 2 3 4 5

3. **Is there at least one word
   from the Word Bank?**

   Me: 1 2 3 4 5
   Partner: 1 2 3 4 5

4. **Are grammar, usage, and
   mechanics correct?**

   Me: 1 2 3 4 5
   Partner: 1 2 3 4 5

Check It and Fix It

After you have written your opinion paragraph, check your work.
Try to read it as if you have never before seen it.

1. Is everything written clearly and correctly? The checklist on the
   right will help you see.

2. Trade paragraphs with a classmate. Discuss ways you might improve
   your paragraphs. Use your suggestions to revise your work.

3. For help with grammar, usage, and mechanics, go to the Handbook
   on pages 189–231.

Vocabulary Workshop

Add these words to your personal word bank by
practicing them.

**adversity • change • confrontation •
inestimable • reconciliation**

Your Choice

What other new words in
the article would you like
to remember? List them.

____

____

____

Define It

In your own words, write what each word in the Word Bank means.
Then think of a word that has the same or a very similar meaning.
Write that word as shown in the example below.

What It Means	adversity
bad luck or obstacles in your path	**A Word It Reminds Me Of** misfortune
What It Means	
	A Word It Reminds Me Of _____________
What It Means	
	A Word It Reminds Me Of _____________
What It Means	
	A Word It Reminds Me Of _____________
What It Means	
	A Word It Reminds Me Of _____________

Show You Know

Answer the questions below to show you know the meaning of each
Word Bank word.

1. What are some ways that victims of Hurricane Katrina met with **adversity**?

   ____

2. What is a **change** you would like to make in yourself?

   ____

3. Everyone in the hallway heard the **confrontation** between Alex and Zack. What did they hear?

   ____

4. My history teacher has **inestimable** knowledge about the Civil War. How much knowledge does he have?

   ____

5. The referee called for **reconciliation** between the opposing teams. What did he want?

   ____

A Suffix That Means "Can": *-able*

- When you add the suffix *-able* to a verb, you change the word
  into an adjective.

  Verb: I cannot **estimate** how much I appreciate my mom.

  Adjective: My appreciation for my mom is **inestimable**.

  This suffix is usually added to complete words, as in *breakable*
  and *enjoyable*. When the word ends in the letter *e*, drop the letter
  when you add the suffix, as in *livable* and *adorable*.

Form an adjective by adding the suffix *-able* to each verb below.
Then write a sentence for each adjective you form.

1. wash ____

   Sentence: _____________________________________

2. use ____

   Sentence: _____________________________________

3. conceive ____

   Sentence: _____________________________________

4. microwave ____

   Sentence: _____________________________________

The following words are in
the same word family. What
are some other words that
have a form of *estimate* in
them? Add one to the list.

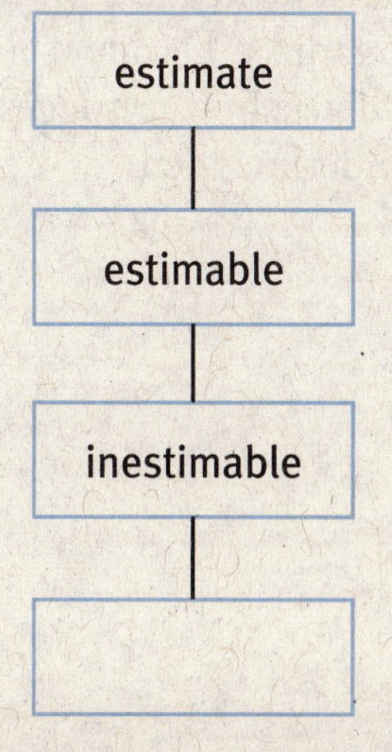

Learning from Crime Victims

Write About It!

You have read an article about coping with a possible worldwide outbreak of flu. Now you will write about the topic. Read the writing prompt. It gives your writing assignment.

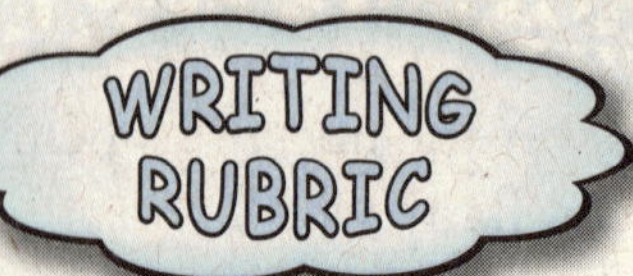

In your response, you should:

- Make suggestions for an emergency plan.

- Include reasons from the article.

- Use at least one word from the Word Bank.

- Use correct grammar, usage, and mechanics.

Writing Prompt

Imagine that your town wants to make an emergency plan for an outbreak of bird flu. Write suggestions that town leaders can use in their plan. Include ideas from the article and at least one word from the Word Bank.

debate • emphasis • progress • radical • struggle

Prewrite It

Once you are sure you understand the prompt, plan what you want to say.

1. Review your notes from the class discussion. Are there ideas you can use when you write your suggestions? Jot them down on your organizer.

2. Reread the article. Look for other ideas you can use. Add them to your organizer.

3. Review the ideas on your organizer. Decide which you will use in your suggestions, and underline them.

Flu Outbreak Plan

Things We Should Do	Reasons Why

Draft It

Now use your organizer to draft, or write, your suggestions.
The writing frame below will help you.

1. Read the first sentence. It states the main idea. Then complete the
sentence starters by giving a suggestion and a reason why it is a
good idea.

2. Follow up with another suggestion and reason. Be sure to use ideas
from the article.

Do a "reality check" with a
partner. Read each other's
suggestions as if your town
actually faced a flu outbreak.
Could they be put into
practice? If not, discuss how
to revise them.

Flu Emergency Do's

Here are some things our town might do if there is an outbreak

of the bird flu. My first suggestion is to ________________________

____.

This is a good idea because ___________________________________

____

____.

Another suggestion is to ______________________________________

____.

This is a good idea because ___________________________________

____

____.

Check It and Fix It

After you have written your suggestions, check your work. Could you
present them to your town leaders?

1. Is everything written clearly and correctly? Use the checklist on the
right to see.

2. Trade your written suggestions with a classmate. Discuss ways you
might improve them. Use the ideas to make revisions.

3. For help with grammar, usage, and mechanics, go to the Handbook
on pages 189–231.

✔ **CHECKLIST**

Evaluate your writing.
A score of "5" is excellent.
A score of "1" means you
need to do more work.
Then ask a partner to rate
your writing.

**1. Are the suggestions clear
and practical?**

Me: 1 2 3 4 5
Partner: 1 2 3 4 5

**2. Are suggestions
supported by reasons
from the article?**

Me: 1 2 3 4 5
Partner: 1 2 3 4 5

**3. Is there at least one word
from the Word Bank?**

Me: 1 2 3 4 5
Partner: 1 2 3 4 5

**4. Are grammar, usage, and
mechanics correct?**

Me: 1 2 3 4 5
Partner: 1 2 3 4 5

Vocabulary Workshop

Add these words to your personal word bank by practicing them.

debate • emphasis • progress • radical • struggle

Define It

Fill in the chart. In the center oval, write two or three subjects you could write about using the Word Bank words. Use the examples as models.

debate		
What It Means	**What It Means**	**What It Means**
a discussion of arguments in favor of or against something		

Subjects

social studies: might have a debate about a current event

What It Means		**What It Means**

Your Choice

What other new words in the article would you like to remember? List them.

____

____

____

Think about how you or a teacher might use Word Bank words in class. If you think of everyday ways to use the words, you will remember them longer.

Show You Know

Write a dialogue, or conversation between people, in the space below. Use all the Word Bank words in a way that shows you understand their meanings.

________________ : ________________________________

____

________________ : ________________________________

____

________________ : ________________________________

____

________________ : ________________________________

____

Read your dialogue aloud with a partner. If the word meanings are unclear, ask for suggestions on how to rewrite them. Then make the changes.

Context Clues

Sometimes you can figure out what an unfamiliar word means by using context clues. What clue or clues tell you what the Word Bank word *radical* means in the sentence below?

- His **radical** views were very far to the right.

From "very far to the right," you can guess that *radical* means "far to one side" or "extreme."

Underline the context clues that tell you what each boldface Word Bank word means.

1. We practiced our arguments for tomorrow's face-off against the other team in the **debate**.

____

2. By stressing every word, Mom put **emphasis** on the importance of Maria's cleaning her room.

____

3. If you want to make **progress** in reaching your goal, each step will have to bring you closer.

____

4. Fighting against his severe illness was a **struggle**, but Phil would not quit.

____

The Development Debate

Write About It!

You have read an article about conflicts over land development. Now you will write about the topic. Read the writing prompt. It gives your writing assignment.

In your response, you should:

- Give pros and cons of development and draw a conclusion.

- Include information and arguments from the article.

- Use at least one word from the Word Bank.

- Use correct grammar, usage, and mechanics.

Writing Prompt

After reading "The Development Debate," what do you think are the advantages and disadvantages of building on open space? Explain these development pros and cons and draw a conclusion from them in a speech for a city council hearing. Use information from the article and at least one word from the Word Bank.

motive • negotiate • resolve • unify

Prewrite It

Once you are sure you understand the prompt, plan what you want to say.

1. Review your notes from the class discussion. On the organizer on the right, jot down ideas you might use in your speech.

2. Reread the article. Look for other information or arguments you might include in your speech. Add those to your organizer.

3. Take another look at your organizer. Read all the arguments you have included. If any are weak, think about ways to make them stronger. Is your conclusion persuasive? If not, revise it.

A Two-Sided Issue

Pros	Cons

My Conclusion:

Here, tell what you think of land development based on the pros and cons.

Draft It

Now use your organizer to draft, or write, your speech. The writing frame below will help you.

1. Read the first sentence. Then finish the sentence starter by adding an advantage.

2. Then add a disadvantage and a conclusion. Be sure to use ideas from the article.

Ladies and Gentlemen of the Council, Fellow Citizens:

There are advantages and disadvantages to further land

development in our town. A main advantage is ___________________

____

____

____

____.

A main disadvantage is _____________________________________

____

____.

Given these pros and cons, I conclude that we should

____

____.

Check It and Fix It

After you have written your speech, check your work. Try to read it as if you were another citizen at the city council hearing.

1. Is everything written clearly and correctly? Use the checklist on the right to see.

2. Trade speeches with a classmate. Discuss ways you might make your speeches more informative and interesting. Use the ideas to improve your work.

3. For help with grammar, usage, and mechanics, go to the Handbook on pages 189–231.

Deliver your speech aloud to a partner. It should sound natural and should be easy to read. If it does not sound right to you, ask your partner for suggestions on how to reword your ideas.

✔ CHECKLIST

Evaluate your writing. A score of "5" is excellent. A score of "1" means you need to do more work. Then ask a partner to rate your writing.

1. Does the speech give pros, cons, and a conclusion?

Me: 1 2 3 4 5
Partner: 1 2 3 4 5

2. Does the speech include ideas from the article?

Me: 1 2 3 4 5
Partner: 1 2 3 4 5

3. Is there at least one word from the Word Bank?

Me: 1 2 3 4 5
Partner: 1 2 3 4 5

4. Are grammar, usage, and mechanics correct?

Me: 1 2 3 4 5
Partner: 1 2 3 4 5

Vocabulary Workshop

Add these words to your personal word bank by
practicing them.

Define It

For each set of boxes below, do as follows. Choose two words
from the Word Bank and write them in the small boxes. In the
Connection box, describe how the two are connected.

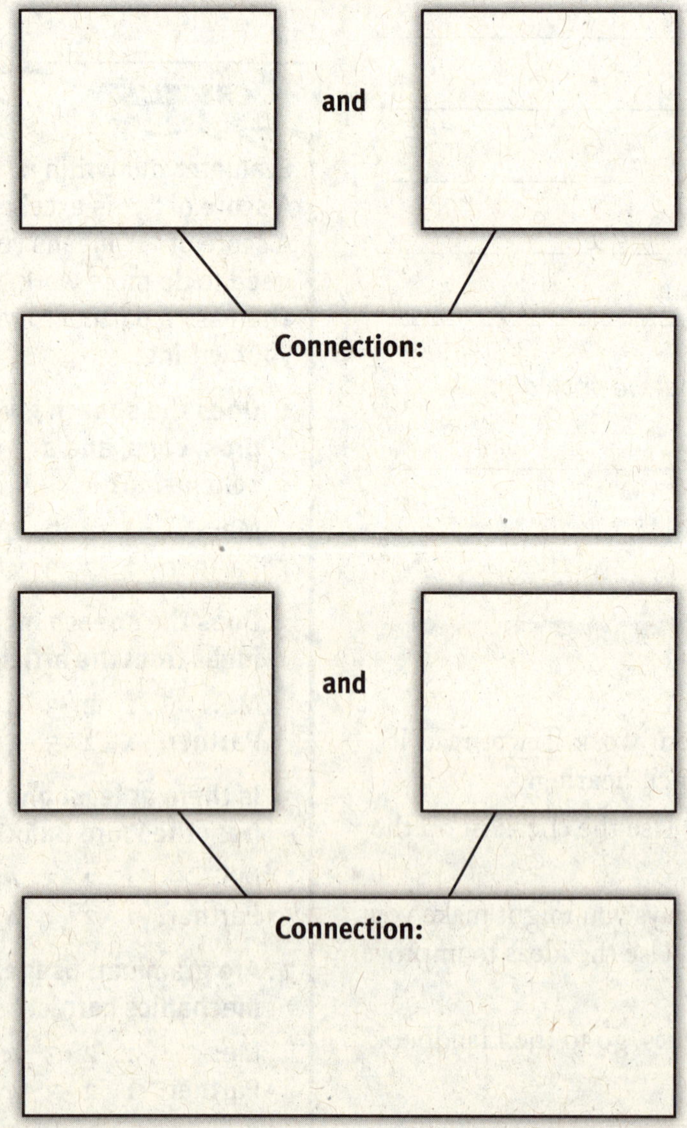

What other new words in
the article would you like
to remember? List them.

____

____

____

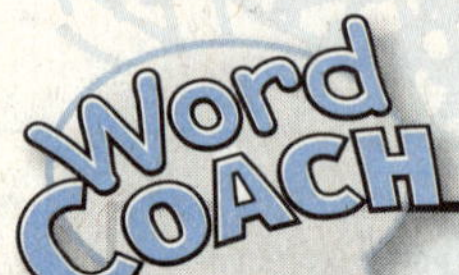

When you understand
how words are connected,
you can use them in
more meaningful ways.
Combining new words in
sentences will help you
remember them.

Show You Know

To show that you understand the Word Bank words, write a clue for each word. Exchange clues with a partner. See whether your partner can identify the correct word for each clue.

1. ____

2. ____

3. ____

4. ____

5. ____

If any of your sentences are too hard or confusing for your partner to guess, ask him or her for tips on how to make them clearer. Then revise them.

Suffixes That Mean "Produce": *-fy, -ify*

- The suffixes *-fy* or *-ify* mean "to produce, do, make, cause, or make similar to." When you add the *-fy* or *-ify* ending to a word, the new word becomes a verb.

  Noun: The army **unit** might join other forces.

  Verb: They will **unify** their troops.

  Adjective: Those statements are **false.**

  Verb: Did the criminal **falsify** the documents?

Complete each sentence below by underlining the correct form of the word in parentheses.

Each group of science students formed its own study (unit, unify). They wanted to find out if an (acid, acidify) can be made from something else. First, the members of each group had to (unit, unify) their efforts. They discussed how to (pure, purify) their equipment. Then they added a (pure, purify) form of one liquid to another. The mixture had a (horrid, horrify) smell! Though the process might (horrid, horrify) anyone walking past the lab, the students did indeed find that the ingredients began to (acid, acidify).

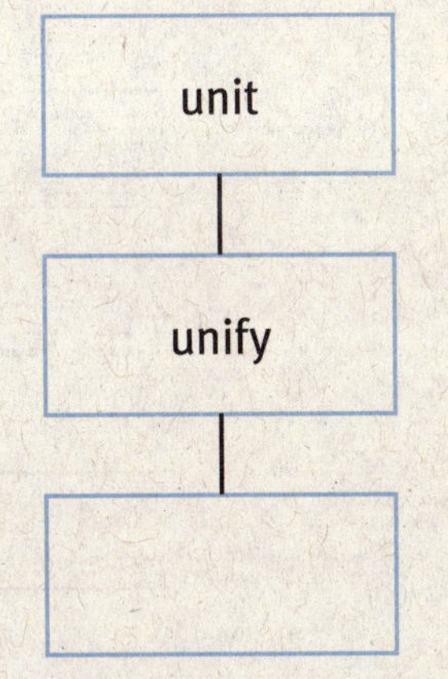

The following words are in the same word family. What are some other words that have a form of the word *unit* in them? Add one to the list.

unit
unify

Writing Reflection

Can progress be made without conflict?

Look through your writing from this unit and choose the best piece.
Reflect on this piece of writing by completing each sentence below.

My best piece of writing from this unit is _______________________

____

I chose this piece because _______________________________________

____

____

While I was writing, one goal I had was _____________________________

____

I accomplished this goal by _______________________________________

____

____

This writing helped me think more about the Big Question because

____

____

One thing I learned while writing that can help me in the future is

____

____

What kind of knowledge changes our lives?

Write About It!

You have read an article about the sixth sense. Now you will write about the topic. Read the writing prompt. It gives your writing assignment.

In your response, you should:

- Describe what you believe about the sixth sense.

- Support your beliefs with information from the article.

- Use at least one word from the Word Bank.

- Use correct grammar, usage, and mechanics.

Writing Prompt

Write a handout for a science fair presentation on the sixth sense. Describe what you believe about the sixth sense and whether science has proven that it exists. Use ideas from the article and at least one word from the Word Bank.

awareness • distinguish • evolve • insight • reaction

Prewrite It

Once you are sure you understand the prompt, plan what you want to say.

1. Review your notes from the class discussion. Use the organizer on the right to jot down your thoughts.

2. Reread the article. Look for scientific evidence to support or explain your beliefs. Add it to your organizer.

3. Take another look at your beliefs. Do you need to change them in any way after rereading the article? If so, make the changes.

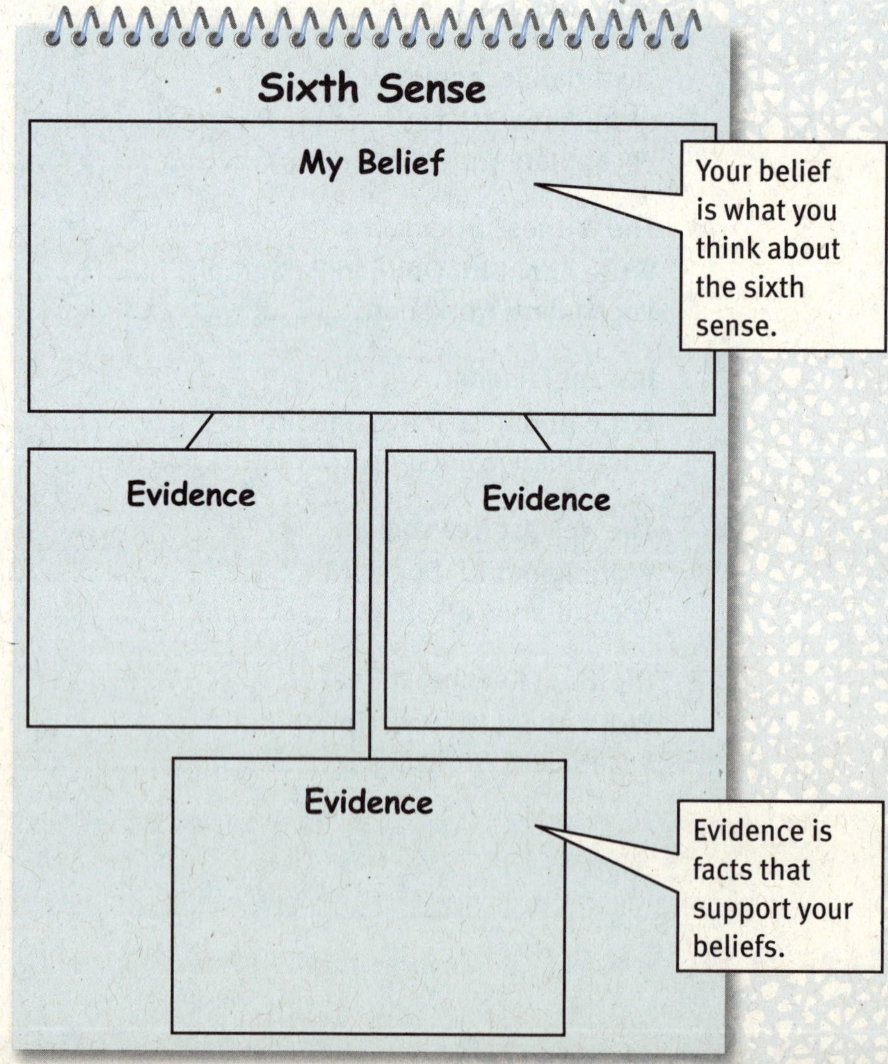

Draft It

Now use your organizer to draft, or write, your handout. The writing frame below will help you.

1. Start by stating your belief. You have three choices. Underline your choice.

2. Then give your scientific evidence. Read the second sentence below. Finish the sentence starter by giving facts that support your belief. Make sure you include information from the article.

Do You Have a Sixth Sense?

There is (a lot of evidence, some evidence, little evidence) to

suggest that humans have a sixth sense. I say this because ______

____

____

____

____

____

____

____

____

If you have trouble deciding what you believe about the sixth sense, work with a partner. Tell your partner what you know about the sixth sense. Ask your partner to take notes for you. Discuss the notes with your partner, and use them to state your beliefs.

Check It and Fix It

After you have written your handout, check your work. Try to read it with a "fresh eye." Imagine that you are a judge at the science fair reading the handout.

1. Is everything written clearly and correctly? Use the checklist on the right to decide.

2. Then trade handouts with a classmate. Talk over ways you both might improve your handouts. Use the ideas to revise your work.

3. For help with grammar, usage, and mechanics, go to the Handbook on pages 189–231.

✔ CHECKLIST

Evaluate your writing. A score of "5" is excellent. A score of "1" means you need to do more work. Then ask a partner to rate your writing.

1. **Does the handout state a clear belief about the sixth sense?**

   Me: 1 2 3 4 5
   Partner: 1 2 3 4 5

2. **Is there scientific evidence to support the belief?**

   Me: 1 2 3 4 5
   Partner: 1 2 3 4 5

3. **Is there at least one word from the Word Bank?**

   Me: 1 2 3 4 5
   Partner: 1 2 3 4 5

4. **Are grammar, usage, and mechanics correct?**

   Me: 1 2 3 4 5
   Partner: 1 2 3 4 5

Vocabulary Workshop

Add these words to your personal word bank by practicing them.

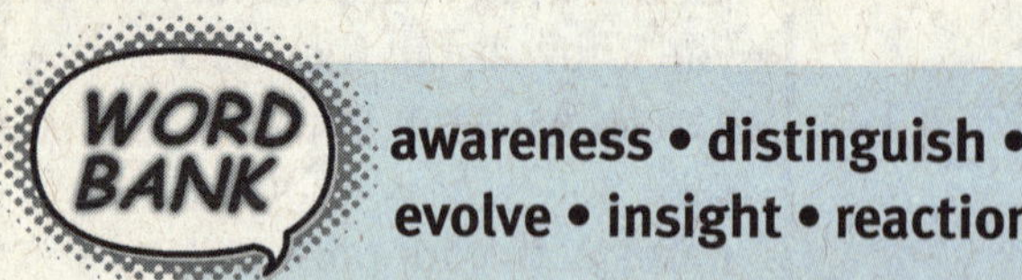

Your Choice

What other new words in the article would you like to remember? List them.

____

____

____

Define It

Complete the chart below. In the first column, write each word in the Word Bank. In the second column, write the meaning of each word. In the last column, write clues from the article that help you understand the word's meaning. The first row is done for you as a guide.

Word	What It Means	Clues from Text
awareness	knowing about something that exists or happens	" . . . it was important that people be aware of even small movements and sounds."

Show You Know

To show that you understand the Word Bank words, write a clue for each word. Exchange clues with a partner. See whether your partner can identify the correct word for each clue. Use the clue for *awareness,* below, as a model.

- If you have this, you realize that something exists.

1. ____

2. ____

3. ____

4. ____

5. ____

Suffixes That Mean "State Of": *-ness, -tion*

- The suffix *-ness* means "state of being." When you add the suffix to an adjective, the new word you create is a noun.

  Adjective: I was **aware** of a person standing in the shadows.

  Noun: My **awareness** of the person protected me.

- The suffix *-tion* means "state of doing." When you add the suffix to a verb, the new word you create is a noun.

  Verb: Scientists study how quickly people **react** to danger.

  Noun: My **reaction** to the scary movie was fear.

Complete each sentence by underlining the right form of the word in parentheses.

For my science report, I plan to (investigate, investigation) how quickly people (react, reaction) when playing a video game. I will use a common (distract, distraction), such as (loud, loudness) sounds to test the players' (aware, awareness) of the game. I will make a (predict, prediction) that people will do better in a (quiet, quietness) environment.

Many words belong to the *react* word family. Find two other variations of the word *react* in the article, and write them in the boxes below.

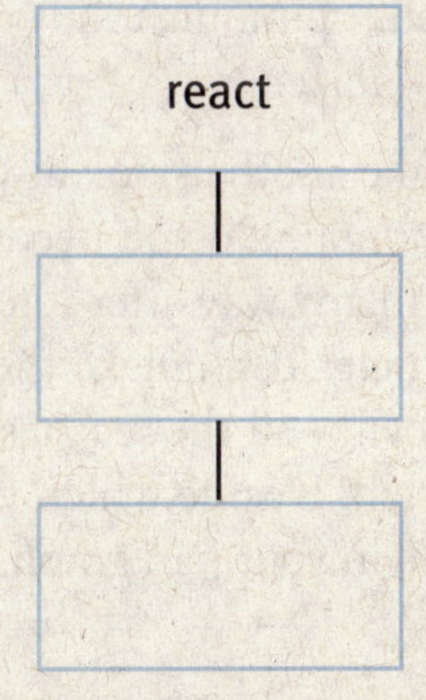

Write About It!

You have read an article about GPS technology. Now you will write about the topic. Read the writing prompt. It gives your writing assignment.

Writing Prompt

After reading "Looking over Your Shoulder," do you think GPS technology protects people, invades their privacy, or does a little of both? Write a paragraph stating your opinion. Use ideas from the article and at least one word from the Word Bank.

growth • ignorance • modified • revise • technique

WRITING RUBRIC

In your response, you should:

- Write a paragraph stating your opinion.

- Support your opinion with ideas from the article.

- Use at least one word from the Word Bank.

- Use correct grammar, usage, and mechanics.

Prewrite It

Once you are sure you understand the prompt, plan what you want to say.

1. Review your notes from the class discussion. Use the organizer on the right to jot down your thoughts.

2. Reread the article. Look for additional information that supports or explains your opinion. Add it to your organizer.

3. Take another look at your opinion. Do you need to change it in any way after rereading the article? If so, make the changes. Review all the reasons you have listed. Decide which you will use in your paragraph.

The Use of GPS Today

My Opinion

Your opinion is what you believe about GPS.

My Reasons

Your reasons explain why you hold the opinion.

Draft It

Now use your organizer to draft, or write, your paragraph.
The writing frame below will help you.

1. Start by stating your opinion. You have three choices of opinion. Underline your choice.

2. Then give your reasons. Read the second sentence below. Finish the sentence starter by giving a reason for your opinion. Make sure you explain your reason with ideas from the article.

GPS: Friend or Enemy?

The use of GPS technology today (mostly invades our privacy, mostly protects us, both protects us and invades our privacy). I think this because ___________________________________

____

____

____

____

____

____

____

____

____

Check It and Fix It

After you have written your paragraph, check your work. Try to read it with a "fresh eye." Imagine that you are reading about the use of GPS for the first time.

1. Is everything written clearly and correctly? Use the checklist on the right to decide.

2. Then trade paragraphs with a classmate. Talk over ways you might improve your paragraphs. Use the ideas to revise your work.

3. For help with grammar, usage, and mechanics, go to the Handbook on pages 189–231.

Writing COACH

If you have trouble supporting your opinion, work with a partner. Tell your partner your opinion. Ask your partner to write down reasons from the article that support your opinion. Use your partner's notes to write.

✔ CHECKLIST

Evaluate your writing. A score of "5" is excellent. A score of "1" means you need to do more work. Then ask a partner to rate your writing.

1. Does the paragraph state a clear opinion about GPS?

Me: 1   2   3   4   5
Partner: 1   2   3   4   5

2. Is the opinion supported by reasons or examples from the article?

Me: 1   2   3   4   5
Partner: 1   2   3   4   5

3. Is there at least one word from the Word Bank?

Me: 1   2   3   4   5
Partner: 1   2   3   4   5

4. Are grammar, usage, and mechanics correct?

Me: 1   2   3   4   5
Partner: 1   2   3   4   5

Vocabulary Workshop

Add these words to your personal word bank by
practicing them.

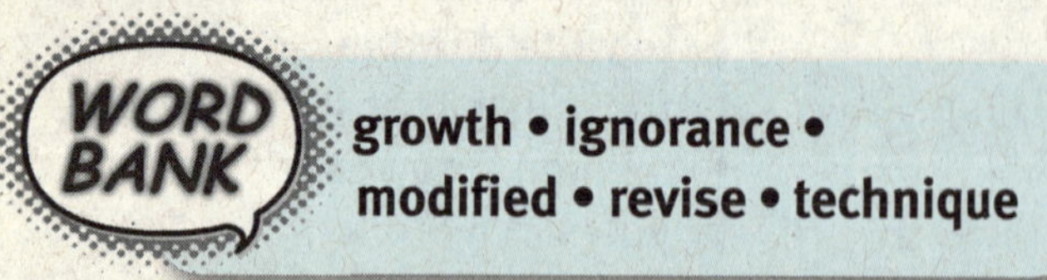

Define It

For each set of boxes below, do as follows. Choose two words from
the Word Bank and write them in the small boxes. (One word will
appear twice.) In the Connection box, describe how the two are
connected. Use the example as a guide.

modified	**and**	revise

Connection:
When you revise writing, it is modified, because
you have made changes to it.

	and	

Connection:

	and	

Connection:

Your Choice

What other new words in
the article would you like
to remember? List them.

____

____

____

To remember a new word,
try linking it to a real or
imagined picture. For
example, you might link
technique to a picture of
someone using a cooking
technique in the kitchen or
a dancing technique on the
dance floor.

Show You Know

Write a comic strip in the space below. Use all the Word Bank
words in a way that shows you understand their meanings.

A Suffix That Forms Adjectives: *-ed*

- You probably know that the word ending *-ed* can be added to
  many verbs to make them past tense. The *-ed* ending can also
  be used to turn a verb into an adjective.

  Verb: I **modified** my report to include charts.

  Adjective: My teacher liked my **modified** report.

  In the first sentence, *modified* is a verb expressing an action done
  in the past. In the second sentence, *modified* describes the noun
  report, so *modified* is an adjective.

Tell whether each boldface word below is a verb or an adjective.

1. The **preferred** way of treating many diseases has changed.

2. Parents **supervised** the teenagers at the dance.

3. In class, we write the **corrected** sentences on the board.

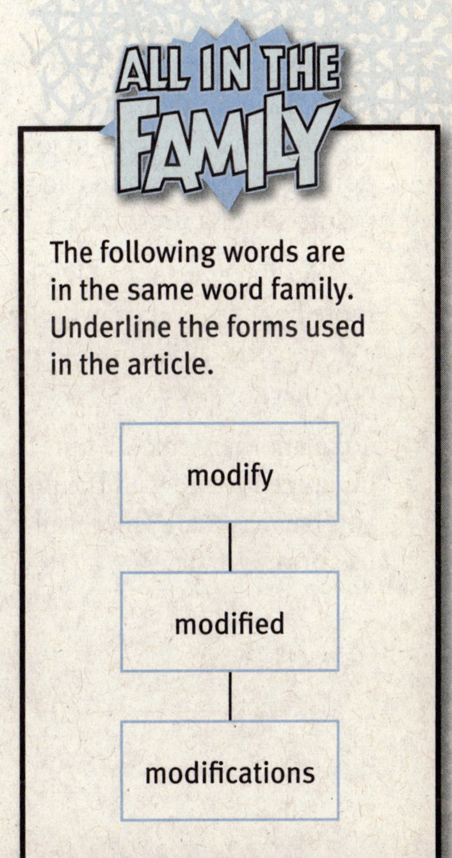

Looking over Your Shoulder   **77**

Write About It!

You have read an article about school dress codes. Now you will write about the topic. Read the writing prompt. It gives your writing assignment.

In your response, you should:

- Write an article for your school newspaper.

- Name positive and negative aspects of a dress code.

- Use at least one word from the Word Bank.

- Use correct grammar, usage, and mechanics.

Writing Prompt

Imagine that you are writing an article about dress codes for your school newspaper. Describe the positive and negative aspects of a dress code for your school. Use ideas from the article and at least one word from the Word Bank.

influence • process • question • reflect • statement

Prewrite It

Once you are sure you understand the prompt, plan what you want to say.

1. Review your notes from the class discussion. Use the organizer on the right to jot down good points and bad points about a dress code.

2. Reread the article. Look for more benefits and drawbacks of a dress code. Add those to your organizer.

3. Take another look at your organizer. Review all the points you have listed. Which will you use in your article?

School Dress Codes

Benefits	Drawbacks

Draft It

Now use your organizer to draft, or write, an article. The writing frame below will help you.

1. Start by describing the benefits of a school dress code. Read the first sentence. Then complete the sentence starter by stating positive aspects of a dress code. Make sure you explain why these aspects are positive.

2. Then state some negative aspects of a school dress code. Explain why these aspects are negative. Be sure to use information from the article.

Work with a partner to make sure you have correctly identified good points and bad points about dress codes. Read your lists to each other. Discuss any ideas that you are unsure about.

THIS JUST IN

Do Schools Need Dress Codes?

Today, about half of all schools have a dress code. Some of the benefits of having a school dress code are ________________________

____

____

____ .

There are also drawbacks to having a school dress code. These include ____

____

____

____

____ .

Evaluate your writing. A score of "5" is excellent. A score of "1" means you need to do more work. Then ask a partner to rate your writing.

1. **Does the article present positive and negative aspects of dress codes?**

   Me: 1 2 3 4 5
   Partner: 1 2 3 4 5

2. **Are there ideas from the article to explain the positives and negatives?**

   Me: 1 2 3 4 5
   Partner: 1 2 3 4 5

3. **Is there at least one word from the Word Bank?**

   Me: 1 2 3 4 5
   Partner: 1 2 3 4 5

4. **Are grammar, usage, and mechanics correct?**

   Me: 1 2 3 4 5
   Partner: 1 2 3 4 5

Check It and Fix It

After you have written your article, check your work. Imagine that you are a student reading the article for the first time.

1. Is everything written clearly and correctly? Use the checklist on the right to decide.

2. Then trade articles with a classmate. Talk over ways you might improve your articles. Use the ideas to revise your work.

3. For help with grammar, usage, and mechanics, go to the Handbook on pages 189–231.

Vocabulary Workshop

Add these words to your personal word bank by
practicing them.

influence • process •
question • reflect • statement

Define It

Fill in the chart. In the center oval, write two or three subjects you
could write about using the Word Bank words. Use the examples
as a model.

Your Choice

What other new words in
the article would you like
to remember? List them.

____

____

____

influence		
What It Means	**What It Means**	**What It Means**
to have an effect on		

Subjects

Science: might write
about the influence
of fossil fuels on the
atmosphere

What It Means

What It Means

Show You Know

In the space below, write a short, short story (just a paragraph!) using the Word Bank words. Be sure that your sentences show that you understand the meanings of the words.

Once upon a time, _______________________________________

____

____

____

____

____

____

Multiple-Meaning Words

When you use a dictionary to find the meaning of a word, you often find more than one definition. How can you tell which is the right one? Look at how the word is used in the context of a sentence. Then choose the definition that makes sense for that context. For example, which definition for *reflect* makes sense below?

- Many people **reflect** on the past year on New Year's Eve.

  reflect (a) to bounce light back, as a mirror; (b) to think quietly and calmly.

  If you chose definition (b), you are right! That definition makes sense in the sentence.

For each sentence below, underline the right definition of the boldface word.

1. The **process** for getting a driver's license includes passing a test.

  process: (a) a series of steps taken to meet a goal; (b) to put through a special procedure or treatment.

2. Role models can **influence** children's lives in a positive way.

  influence: (a) the act of producing an effect on something; (b) to have an effect on something.

Write About It!

You have read an article about electronic textbooks. Now you will write about the topic. Read the writing prompt. It gives your writing assignment.

In your response, you should:

- Write a letter to your principal with your advice.

- Give reasons for your advice that are based on the article.

- Use at least one word from the Word Bank.

- Use correct grammar, usage, and mechanics.

Writing Prompt

After reading "Textbook Technology," what do you think about using electronic textbooks? Write a letter to your principal. Tell the principal whether you think your school should switch to electronic textbooks and why. Use ideas from the article and at least one word from the Word Bank.

adapt • enlighten • history • subject • understanding

Prewrite It

Once you are sure you understand the prompt, plan what you want to say.

1. Review your notes from the class discussion. Use the organizer on the right to jot down your thoughts.

2. Reread the article. Look for reasons and examples that support your advice. Add those to your organizer.

3. Take another look at your advice. Do you need to change it in any way after rereading the article? If so, make the changes. Read through the reasons you have listed and the support you give. Which are the strongest? Cross out the reasons that are not as strong.

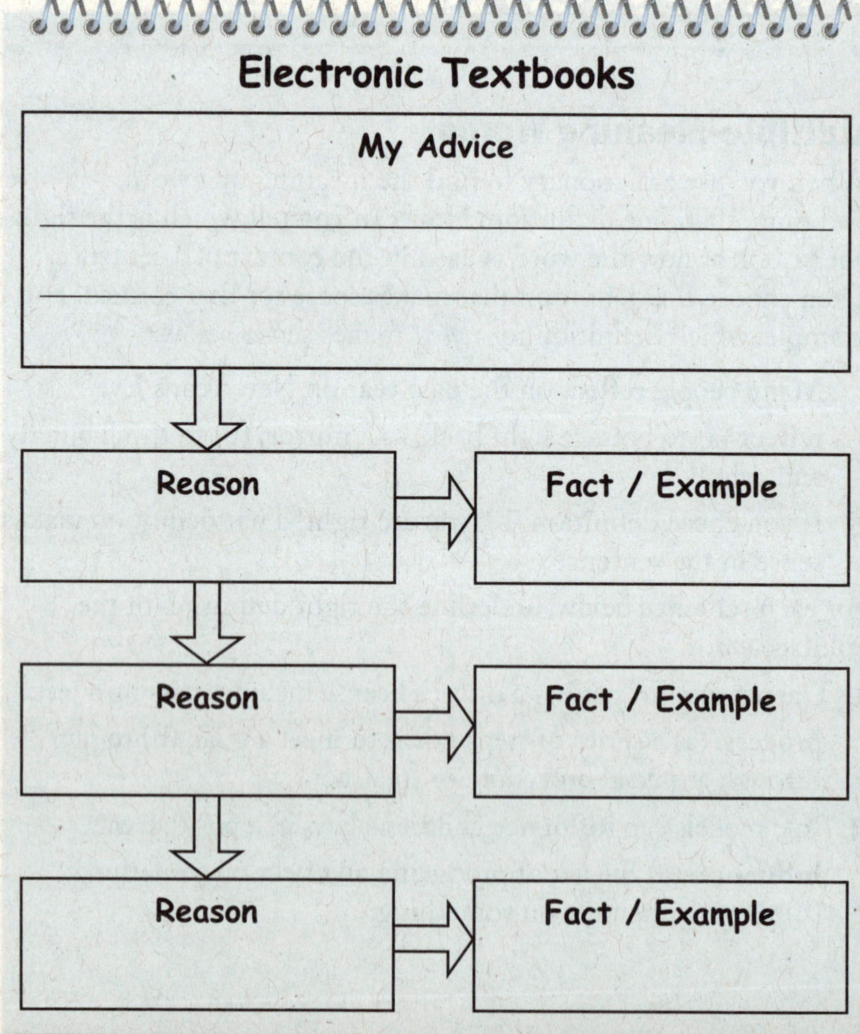

Draft It

Now use your organizer to draft, or write, a letter of advice.
The writing frame below will help you.

1. Start by filling in your principal's name. Then give your advice. You have two choices. Underline your choice.

2. Then read the second sentence below. Finish the sentence starter by giving a reason for your advice. Make sure you explain your reasons with examples from the article.

Think about your audience when you write. What kind of language should you use in your letter: casual or formal? How should your letter sound? Discuss these questions with a partner. Then use your answers to guide your writing.

Dear Principal ____ :

    Our school (should, should not) switch to electronic textbooks.

I think this because ____

____

____

____

____

____

____

____

____

____

____

Check It and Fix It

After you have written your letter, check your work. Imagine that you are the principal reading the letter.

1. Is everything written clearly and correctly? Use the checklist on the right to decide.

2. Then trade letters with a classmate. Talk over ways you might improve your letters. Use the ideas to revise your work.

3. For help with grammar, usage, and mechanics, go to the Handbook on pages 189–231.

✔ **CHECKLIST**

Evaluate your writing. A score of "5" is excellent. A score of "1" means you need to do more work. Then ask a partner to rate your writing.

1. Does the letter give the principal clear advice?

Me: 1 2 3 4 5
Partner: 1 2 3 4 5

2. Are there facts and examples from the article to support the advice?

Me: 1 2 3 4 5
Partner: 1 2 3 4 5

3. Is there at least one word from the Word Bank?

Me: 1 2 3 4 5
Partner: 1 2 3 4 5

4. Are grammar, usage, and mechanics correct?

Me: 1 2 3 4 5
Partner: 1 2 3 4 5

Vocabulary Workshop

Add these words to your personal word bank by practicing them.

adapt • enlighten • history • subject • understanding

Define It

For each organizer below, do the following. Choose two words from the Word Bank and write them on either side of the triangle. (One word will appear twice.) On the blank "because" lines, tell why the two words are connected. Use the examples as a guide.

history — **is connected to** — subject

because: history is a subject that we study in school.

is connected to

because: ___________________

is connected to

because: ___________________

Your Choice

What other new words in the article would you like to remember? List them.

____

____

____

Word COACH

One way to remember new words is to use them often. Try to use a new word three times in a day. Write a sentence with it, use it when you talk, and think of what it reminds you of.

Show You Know

To show that you understand the Word Bank words, write three sentences. In each sentence, use and highlight two of the words. (You will use one word twice.) Use the example as a model.

- I have a better understanding of American history after visiting the Civil War battlefield.

1. ____

   ____

2. ____

   ____

3. ____

   ____

Trade sentences with a partner. Check each other's sentences. If something needs to be fixed, talk over how to fix it. Then make corrections.

A Suffix That Forms Nouns: -ing

- You can use the -ing suffix to change verbs into nouns.
  Verb: Our teacher helped us to **understand** chemistry.
  Noun: Our **understanding** of science has increased greatly.

Complete each sentence by underlining the correct word in parentheses.

I read a book about how animals (adapt, adapting) to their environment. For example, chameleons (change, changing) their color. (Blend, Blending) in with plants helps them stay safe. This way of (hide, hiding) is like camouflage clothing that military people wear. The difference is that chameleons do not (have, having) to wear clothes.

There are many words in the family built around the word *understand*. What other words can you create by adding prefixes or suffixes to *understand*? Add two other words to the list.

understand

The Witness Dilemma

Write About It!

You have read an article about witnessing a crime. Now you will write about the topic. Read the writing prompt. It gives your writing assignment.

In your response, you should:

- Write a paragraph stating your opinion.

- Support your opinion with ideas from the article.

- Use at least one word from the Word Bank.

- Use correct grammar, usage, and mechanics.

Writing Prompt

After reading "The Witness Dilemma," do you think there are situations in which witnesses should not be required to testify in court? Write a paragraph giving your opinion and supporting it. Use ideas from the article and at least one word from the Word Bank.

empathy • evolve • question • represent • revise

Prewrite It

Once you are sure you understand the prompt, plan what you want to say.

1. Review your notes from the class discussion. Use the organizer on the right to jot down your thoughts.

2. Reread the article with your opinion in mind. Look for examples and reasons that explain your opinion. Add those to your organizer.

3. Take another look at your organizer. Do you need to revise your opinion after rereading the article? If so, make the change. Then reread the reasons you have listed. Which are the strongest? Cross out the reasons that are not as strong.

Paragraph Organizer

My Opinion:

Reason and Example:

The examples are situations you read about that helped you form your opinion.

Reason and Example:

Draft It

Now use your organizer to draft, or write, a paragraph. The writing frame below will help you.

1. Start by stating your opinion. Read the first sentence, and underline your choice. Then finish the sentence starter by giving a reason for your opinion.

2. Follow up by giving an example of a situation that explains your reason. Then add another reason and example if you wish. Be sure to use ideas from the article.

Reasons are your "whys," or your rationales for holding a particular opinion. Examples are descriptions of real-life or imaginary situations. Examples help explain reasons. If you need help finding or wording reasons and examples, work with a partner.

Witnesses on Trial

In my opinion, there (are, are not) situations in which a witness to

a crime should be required to testify. I feel this way because ______

____

____

____

____

____ .

For example, _______________________________

____

____

____

____

____

____

Check It and Fix It

After you have written your paragraph, check your work. Try to read it with a "fresh eye," as if you have never before seen the paragraph.

1. Is everything written clearly and correctly? Use the checklist on the right to decide.

2. Then trade paragraphs with a classmate. Talk over ways you both might improve your paragraphs. Use the ideas to revise your work.

3. For help with grammar, usage, and mechanics, go to the Handbook on pages 189–231.

✔ CHECKLIST

Evaluate your writing. A score of "5" is excellent. A score of "1" means you need to do more work. Then ask a partner to rate your writing.

1. **Does the paragraph state an opinion and support it with a reason?**

   Me: 1 2 3 4 5
   Partner: 1 2 3 4 5

2. **Does an example from the article explain the reason?**

   Me: 1 2 3 4 5
   Partner: 1 2 3 4 5

3. **Is there at least one word from the Word Bank?**

   Me: 1 2 3 4 5
   Partner: 1 2 3 4 5

4. **Are grammar, usage, and mechanics correct?**

   Me: 1 2 3 4 5
   Partner: 1 2 3 4 5

Vocabulary Workshop

Add these words to your personal word bank by
practicing them.

**empathy • evolve • question •
represent • revise**

Define It

Complete the chart below using the Word Bank words. First, tell
what the word means. Then tell what the word does not mean.
Use the example as a guide.

Word	What It Is	What It Is Not
empathy	sympathy for how someone else is feeling	being cold or uncaring toward someone else

Your Choice

What other new words in
the article would you like
to remember? List them.

____

____

____

To help yourself remember
a new word, try to think of
a familiar word that means
the opposite. Then use the
new word and its opposite
in a sentence, like this:
I could not be **uncaring**
because I felt too much
empathy for him.

Show You Know

Answer the questions below to show you know the meaning of each Word Bank word.

1. How might you show **empathy** for someone else?

____

____

2. What is a way you wish computers would **evolve** in the future?

____

____

3. When might you **question** a statistic?

____

____

4. How would you **represent** your class if you were president?

____

____

5. What is something that you might fix when you **revise** a paper?

____

____

A Combining Form That Means "Feeling": *-pathy*

- You can form many words with *-pathy* by adding prefixes.

Prefix	Word and Definition
a- = not; without	**apathy** = lack of feeling
anti- = against	**antipathy** = dislike of or feeling against

Write a sentence using each of the words.

1. ____

2. ____

Instant Friends

Write About It!

You have read an article about online friendships. Now you will write about the topic. Read the writing prompt. It gives your writing assignment.

Writing Prompt

After reading "Instant Friends," what do you think is the best way to communicate with friends? Write a feature article for a teen magazine. In your article, describe ways that teenagers like to communicate with friends. Explain which way you prefer and why. Use ideas from the article and at least one word from the Word Bank.

concise • enlighten • history • insight • modified

In your response, you should:

- Write an article about the best way to communicate with friends.

- Describe advantages and disadvantages of different forms of communication, based on the article.

- Use at least one word from the Word Bank.

- Use correct grammar, usage, and mechanics.

Prewrite It

Once you are sure you understand the prompt, plan what you want to say.

1. Review your notes from the class discussion. Use the organizer on the right to jot down some benefits and drawbacks of different forms of communication.

2. Reread the article. Look for additional details about different forms of communication. Add those to your organizer.

3. Take another look at your organizer. After rereading the article, which form of communication with friends do you prefer? Focus on this form of communication when you write.

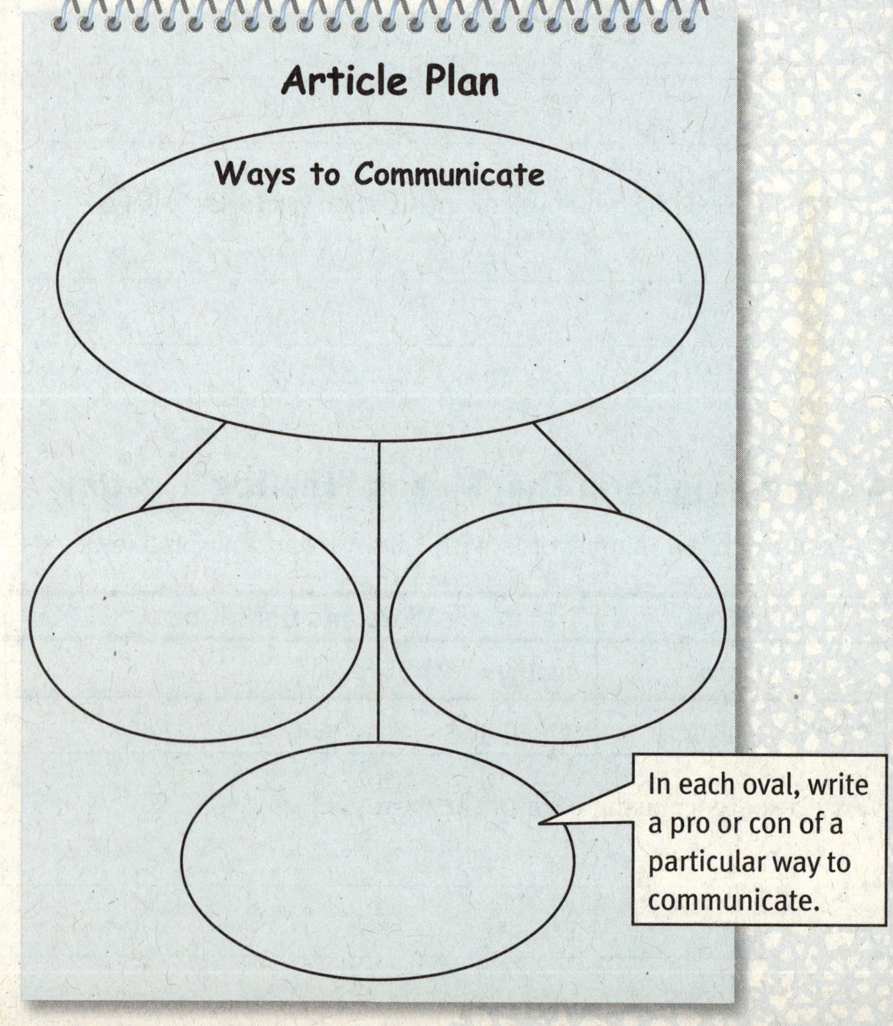

Draft It

Now use your organizer to draft, or write, your magazine article.
The writing frame below will help you.

1. Start by choosing the way you prefer to communicate. To do so,
read and complete the first sentence starter.

2. Then give a reason for your preference by finishing the second
sentence starter. Follow up by explaining your reason with ideas
from the article.

When you read magazine articles, what style of writing do you like: Casual? Formal? Made up only of sentences and paragraphs or made up of text with bulleted lists? As you write your article, try to copy the style you like.

THIS JUST IN

Communicate!

A great way to communicate with friends is _________________.

Many teens would agree that this is the best way to communicate

because ____

____

____

____

____

____

____

____

____

____.

Check It and Fix It

After you have written your article, check your work. Imagine that
you are a teenager reading the article for the first time.

1. Is everything written clearly and correctly? Use the checklist on the
right to decide.

2. Then trade articles with a classmate. Talk over ways you might
improve your articles. Use the ideas to revise your work.

3. For help with grammar, usage, and mechanics, go to the Handbook
on pages 189–231.

✔ CHECKLIST

Evaluate your writing.
A score of "5" is excellent.
A score of "1" means you
need to do more work.
Then ask a partner to rate
your writing.

1. Does the article state a preferred form of communication?

Me: 1 2 3 4 5
Partner: 1 2 3 4 5

2. Do ideas from the article explain the preference?

Me: 1 2 3 4 5
Partner: 1 2 3 4 5

3. Is there at least one word from the Word Bank?

Me: 1 2 3 4 5
Partner: 1 2 3 4 5

4. Are grammar, usage, and mechanics correct?

Me: 1 2 3 4 5
Partner: 1 2 3 4 5

Vocabulary Workshop

Add these words to your personal word bank by
practicing them.

concise • enlighten • history •
insight • modified

Your Choice

What other new words in
the article would you like
to remember? List them.

____

____

____

Define It

Complete the chart below using the Word Bank words. First, tell
what the word means. Then, tell what the word does not mean.

Word	What It Is	What It Is Not

Show You Know

Write a dialogue, or conversation between people, in the space below. Use all the Word Bank words in a way that shows you understand their meanings.

_______________ : _______________________________________

                  ____

_______________ : _______________________________________

                  ____

_______________ : _______________________________________

                  ____

_______________ : _______________________________________

                  ____

_______________ : _______________________________________

                  ____

With a partner, read your dialogue aloud. Check that the words are used correctly. If something needs to be fixed, talk over how to fix it. Then make corrections.

A Prefix That Means "Within" or "Not": *in-*

- If you know the meanings of common prefixes, you may be able to guess the meanings of unfamiliar words that begin with the prefixes. For example, if you know that *in-* can mean "within," you might be able to guess that the Word Bank word *insight* means "sight within," or "understanding."

The prefix *in-* can also mean "not." Study the following example.

- The puzzle was **incomplete** because some pieces were missing. *in-* + *complete* = *incomplete*, or "not complete."

Use your understanding of the prefix *in-* and the meaning of each sentence to choose the correct meaning in parentheses. Underline your answers.

1. The **incoming (not coming, coming in)** freshman class at our high school has to attend a special assembly.

2. Joe gained weight when he was **inactive (not active, active within).**

3. You should always **inspect (not look at, look carefully into)** a used car before buying it.

The Newest Newcomers

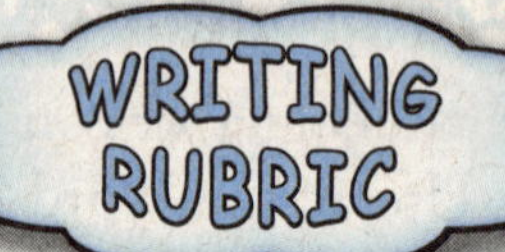

Write About It!

You have read an article about immigrants to the United States. Now you will write about the topic. Read the writing prompt. It gives your writing assignment.

Writing Prompt

After reading "The Newest Newcomers," what do you think the United States offers to immigrants today? Write a speech for a school assembly about the most important American freedoms. Use ideas from the article and at least one word from the Word Bank.

adapt • argument • empathy • ignorance • understanding

In your response, you should:

- Write a speech describing the most important freedoms for immigrants.

- Include information and examples from the article.

- Use at least one word from the Word Bank.

- Use correct grammar, usage, and mechanics.

Prewrite It

Once you are sure you understand the prompt, plan what you want to say.

1. Review your notes from the class discussion. Use the organizer on the right to jot down your thoughts.

2. Reread the article. Look for additional information and examples of the different freedoms offered in the United States. Add those to your organizer.

3. Take another look at your organizer. Use the center circle to describe the most important freedom, or the main idea of your speech. Review what you have written about the freedoms. Which are the most important? Use them in your speech.

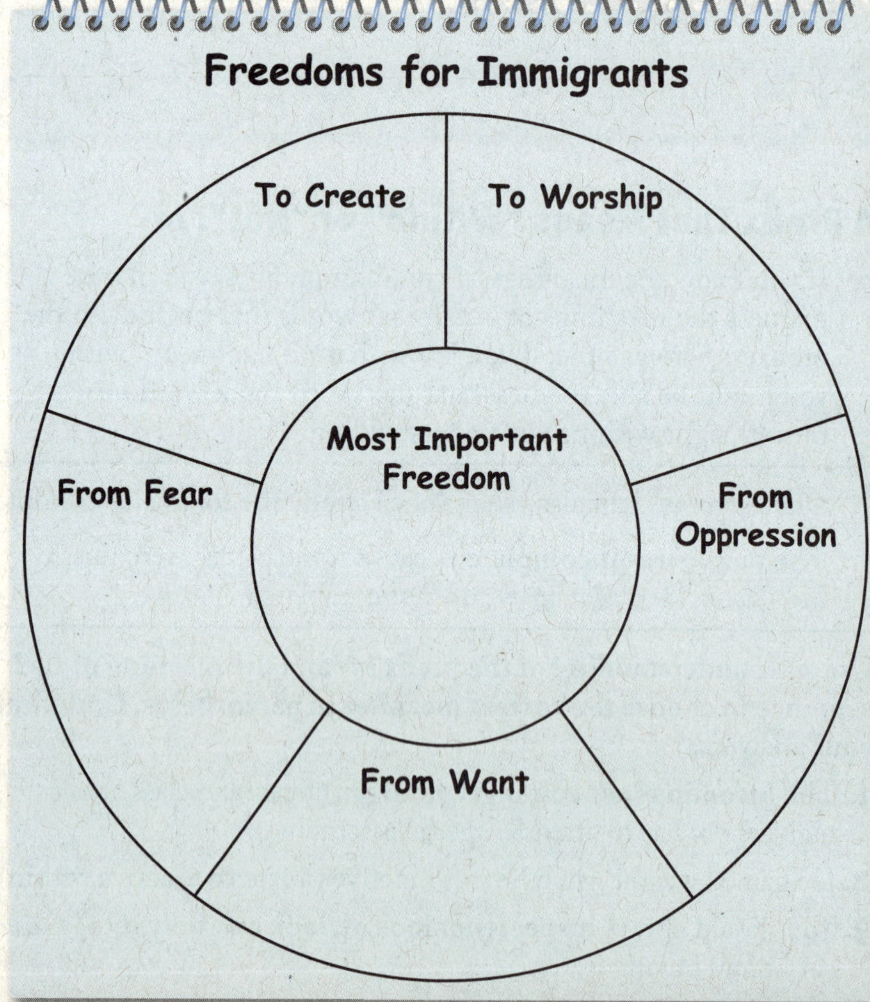

Draft It

Now use your organizer to draft, or write, a speech. The writing frame below will help you.

1. Read the first sentence. Then, in the second sentence, state your main idea, or the freedom you believe is the most important.

2. Last, finish the final sentence starter by explaining why the freedom is important to immigrants. Make sure you support your explanation with ideas or examples from the article.

Speeches should be easy to read or say. Try reading your speech aloud to a small group of classmates. If something in your speech does not sound right to you or them, consider revising it.

Freedom!

America offers many freedoms to immigrants. I believe that the

most important freedom is ________________________________.

This is the most important freedom because ________________

____

____

____

____

____

____

____

____

____

____.

Check It and Fix It

After you have written your speech, check your work. Imagine that you are a student in the audience hearing the speech.

1. Is everything written clearly and correctly? Use the checklist on the right to decide.

2. Then take turns reading speeches with a classmate. Talk over ways you both might improve your speeches. Use the ideas to revise your work.

3. For help with grammar, usage, and mechanics, go to the Handbook on pages 189–231.

✔ CHECKLIST

Evaluate your writing. A score of "5" is excellent. A score of "1" means you need to do more work. Then ask a partner to rate your writing.

1. Does the speech include a clear statement of which freedom is most important?

Me: 1 2 3 4 5
Partner: 1 2 3 4 5

2. Are there examples from the article to describe the freedom?

Me: 1 2 3 4 5
Partner: 1 2 3 4 5

3. Is there at least one word from the Word Bank?

Me: 1 2 3 4 5
Partner: 1 2 3 4 5

4. Are grammar, usage, and mechanics correct?

Me: 1 2 3 4 5
Partner: 1 2 3 4 5

Vocabulary Workshop

Add these words to your personal word bank by practicing them.

adapt • argument • empathy • ignorance • understanding

What other new words in the article would you like to remember? List them.

____

____

____

Define It

Fill in the chart with the Word Bank words. In your own words, tell what each word means. Then circle the number that tells how well you understand each word. Circle "4" if you understand it completely. Circle "1" if you are not sure you understand the word at all.

What It Means	adapt
to change to fit in better in a new place or situation	**How Well I Understand It** 1 2 ③ 4
What It Means	
	How Well I Understand It 1 2 3 4
What It Means	
	How Well I Understand It 1 2 3 4
What It Means	
	How Well I Understand It 1 2 3 4
What It Means	
	How Well I Understand It 1 2 3 4

Show You Know

To show that you understand the Word Bank words, write a clue for each word. Exchange clues with a partner. See whether your partner can identify the correct word for each clue.

1. ____

2. ____

3. ____

4. ____

5. ____

It's Academic

Did you notice that some of the Word Bank words are academic vocabulary? These are words you may use—or hear your teacher use—in your classes. For example, a teacher might ask you your **understanding** of what a poem means, or you might solve a math problem to show your **understanding** of an equation.

Write three sentences to show how you might use the academic vocabulary word *argument* in three different classes.

1. ____

____

2. ____

____

3. ____

____

The following words are in the same word family. What are some other words that have the word *argue* in them? Add two to the list.

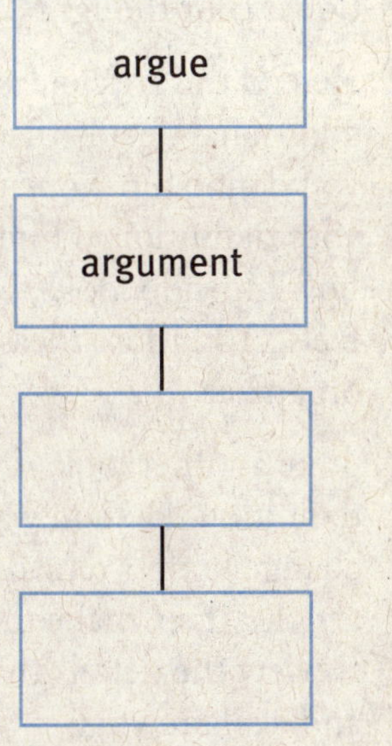

Write About It!

You have read an article about hip-hop. Now you will write about the topic. Read the writing prompt. It gives your writing assignment.

Writing Prompt

What do you think makes hip-hop the real deal? Imagine that you and other teens are meeting with advertising executives to discuss this question. For the meeting, write a description of hip-hop that answers the question. Use ideas from the article and at least one word from the Word Bank.

awareness • growth • imitate • influence • reflect

Prewrite It

Once you are sure you understand the prompt, plan what you want to say.

1. Review your notes from the class discussion. Use the organizer on the right to jot down your thoughts.

2. Reread the article. Look for additional details that will help you define hip-hop and explain your definition. Think about how hip-hop looks, sounds, and feels. Add those ideas to your organizer.

3. Take another look at your definition. Do you want to change it after rereading the article? If so, make the changes. Review the details that describe and explain what hip-hop really is. Which are the strongest? Use them when you write.

Writing Rubric

In your response, you should:

- Define what you think hip-hop really is.

- Support your definition of hip-hop with ideas from the article.

- Use at least one word from the Word Bank.

- Use correct grammar, usage, and mechanics.

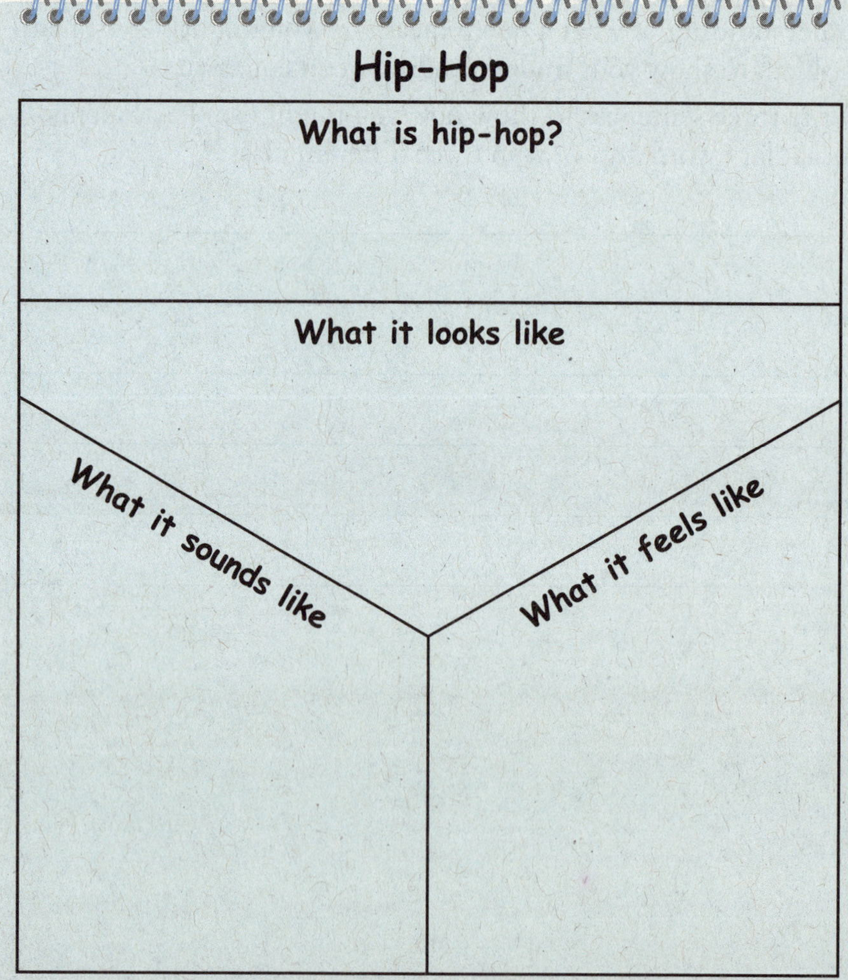

Draft It

Now use your organizer to draft, or write, your meeting presentation. The writing frame below will help you.

1. Start by giving your definition of hip-hop. Complete the first sentence starter.

2. Then give your description of hip-hop. Start by telling how hip-hop looks, sounds, or feels. Underline your choice. Finish the thought by giving your description. Make sure you use ideas from the article.

For help finding examples in the article, work with a partner. Together, look for examples of what hip-hop does and does not look, sound, and feel like. Use your notes to write.

Keeping It Real

Real hip-hop is ___________________________

____

____

____.

To me, real hip-hop (looks, sounds, feels) like ___________________

____

____

____.

Some examples of this are ___________________

____

____

____.

✔ CHECKLIST

Evaluate your writing. A score of "5" is excellent. A score of "1" means you need to do more work. Then ask a partner to rate your writing.

1. Does the presentation define what real hip-hop is?

Me: 1 2 3 4 5
Partner: 1 2 3 4 5

2. Is there a description of hip-hop and examples from the article to support the description?

Me: 1 2 3 4 5
Partner: 1 2 3 4 5

3. Is there at least one word from the Word Bank?

Me: 1 2 3 4 5
Partner: 1 2 3 4 5

4. Are grammar, usage, and mechanics correct?

Me: 1 2 3 4 5
Partner: 1 2 3 4 5

Check It and Fix It

After you have written your presentation, check your work. Try to read it as if you have never before seen it.

1. Is everything written clearly and correctly? Use the checklist on the right to decide.

2. Then take turns reading presentations with a classmate. Talk over ways you both might improve your presentations. Use the ideas to revise your work.

3. For help with grammar, usage, and mechanics, go to the Handbook on pages 189–231.

Vocabulary Workshop

Add these words to your personal word bank by practicing them.

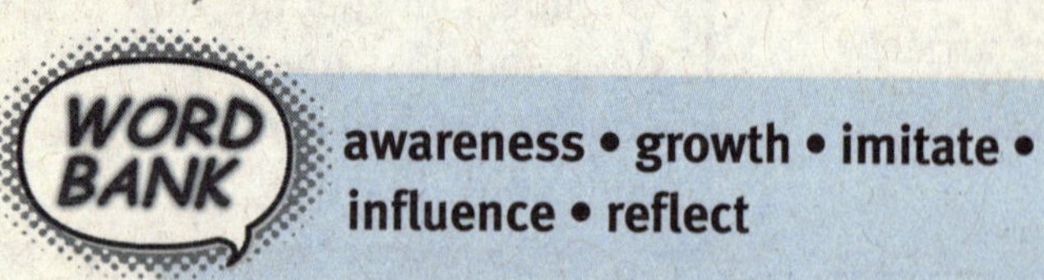

Define It

In your own words, write what each word in the Word Bank means. Then think of a word that has the same or a very similar meaning. Write that word as shown in the example below.

What It Means	imitate
to act like someone else or in some way try to be like the person	**A Word It Reminds Me Of** copy
What It Means	
	A Word It Reminds Me Of
What It Means	
	A Word It Reminds Me Of
What It Means	
	A Word It Reminds Me Of
What It Means	
	A Word It Reminds Me Of

Your Choice

What other new words in the article would you like to remember? List them.

For help learning new words, look for familiar word parts or think of other words that look similar. This can also help you understand what a word means.

Show You Know

In the space below, write a short, short story (just a paragraph!) using the Word Bank words. Be sure your sentences show that you understand the meanings of the words.

Once upon a time, ____

____

____

____

____

Partner Up

Trade stories with a partner. Check your partner's story to see whether all the Word Bank words are used correctly. If something needs to be fixed, discuss how to fix it. Then make corrections.

Context Clues

Sometimes, you can figure out what an unfamiliar word means by using context clues. The *context* of a word is the sentence in which the word appears and sometimes other nearby sentences. What clues tell what *distinctive* means in the sentence below?

- **Distinctive** fashion is a characteristic of the hip-hop culture. The best of hip-hop fashion gives wearers something called "flavor." Fashion flavor includes creative styles and colors.

From the clues "flavor," "various creative styles," and "colors," you might guess that *distinctive* means "unique" or "different."

Underline context clues that tell you what each boldface word means. Then use the clues to write a definition for the word.

1. Rap stars **promote** many products, from cars to shoes, and one soft drink company claims its rap advertising campaign increased sales by four times.

   ____

2. Some fans complain that hip-hop has become a marketing tool rather than a **genuine** youth culture.

   ____

3. Hip-hop started as the voice of **urban** youth, and many hip-hop performers are trying to "keep it real" by writing rap as a true expression of city life as young people live it.

   ____

Writing Reflection

What kind of knowledge changes our lives?

Look through your writing from this unit and choose the best piece. Reflect on this piece of writing by completing each sentence below.

My best piece of writing from this unit is _______________________________

____

I chose this piece because ____

____

____

While I was writing, one goal I had was ___________________________________

____

I accomplished this goal by ____

____

____

This writing helped me think more about the Big Question because

____

____

One thing I learned while writing that can help me in the future is

____

____

Does all communication serve a positive purpose?

Write About It!

You have read an article about horror movies of the past and present. Now you will write about the topic. Read the writing prompt. It gives your writing assignment.

In your response, you should:

- Tell whether you think past or present horror movies are better.

- Support your opinion with reasons and ideas from the article.

- Use at least one word from the Word Bank.

- Use correct grammar, usage, and mechanics.

Writing Prompt

After reading "Ooooh, Scary!" do you think today's horror movies are better than those of the past—or worse? Imagine that you are a critic for a teen movie magazine. Write a feature article giving your opinion about which type of horror movie is better and why. Use ideas from the article and at least one word from the Word Bank.

convey • emotion • isolation • pattern • self-expression

Prewrite It

Once you are sure you understand the prompt, plan what you want to say.

1. Review your notes from the class discussion. Jot down your thoughts on the organizer on the right.

2. Reread the article. Look for additional information about older and newer horror films and reasons that support your opinion. Add those to your organizer.

3. Take another look at your organizer. Read all the points you have listed. If you need to add, cut, or change any, do so.

Article Plan

Past	Present

My Opinion

Draft It

Now use your organizer to draft, or write, your magazine feature.
The writing frame below will help you.

1. Start by writing an introduction, or opening, for your article. Finish
   the first sentence starter. Which opinion matches yours? Underline
   that opinion. Then read the second sentence.

2. Finally, give reasons for your opinion. Be sure to include information
   and ideas from the article to support your view.

If you have trouble deciding
which kind of film you prefer,
discuss the topic with a
partner. Together, find
information in the article
that can help you write your
article.

THIS JUST IN

Horror Films Then and Now

If you are a fan of horror films, you may agree that scary

movies today are (better than, not as good as) those of old.

There are some important reasons that this is so.

The first reason is that _______________________________

____

____

____

____.

Another reason is that ________________________________

____

____

____

____.

Check It and Fix It

After you have written your feature article, check your work.
Try to read it objectively, as if you have never before seen it.

1. Is everything written clearly and correctly? Use the checklist on the
   right to find out.

2. Trade articles with a partner. Talk over ways you might make your
   articles more informative and convincing. Use helpful ideas from
   your partner to revise your work.

3. For help with grammar, usage, and mechanics, go to the Handbook
   on pages 189–231.

✔ CHECKLIST

Evaluate your writing.
A score of "5" is excellent.
A score of "1" means you
need to do more work.
Then ask a partner to rate
your writing.

1. **Does the article clearly
   state an opinion?**

   Me: 1 2 3 4 5
   Partner: 1 2 3 4 5

2. **Is the opinion supported
   by information from the
   article?**

   Me: 1 2 3 4 5
   Partner: 1 2 3 4 5

3. **Is there at least one word
   from the Word Bank?**

   Me: 1 2 3 4 5
   Partner: 1 2 3 4 5

4. **Are grammar, usage, and
   mechanics correct?**

   Me: 1 2 3 4 5
   Partner: 1 2 3 4 5

Vocabulary Workshop

Add these words to your personal word bank by practicing them.

WORD BANK convey • emotion • isolation • pattern • self-expression

Define It

Fill in the chart with the Word Bank words. In your own words, tell what each word means. Then circle the number that tells how well you understand each word. Circle "4" if you understand it completely. Circle "1" if you are not sure you understand the word at all. Use the example as a model.

What It Means	convey
to express an idea, usually in words or pictures	**How Well I Understand It** 1 2 3 ④
What It Means	
	How Well I Understand It 1 2 3 4
What It Means	
	How Well I Understand It 1 2 3 4
What It Means	
	How Well I Understand It 1 2 3 4
What It Means	
	How Well I Understand It 1 2 3 4

Your Choice

What other new words in the article would you like to remember? List them.

It is almost impossible to remember new words if you never use them. Next time you write about something in one of your classes, try to use some of the Word Bank words.

Show You Know

To show that you understand the Word Bank words, write a clue for each word. Exchange clues with a partner. See whether your partner can identify the correct word for each clue. Use the clue for *convey*, below, as a model.

- When you put your own feelings or thoughts into writing or art, you do this.

1. ____

2. ____

3. ____

4. ____

5. ____

A Prefix That Means "Done by Oneself": *self-*

- The prefix *self-* means "something that is done for, by, or to oneself." For example, self-expression is what you do when you convey *your own* feelings and thoughts. As the example shows, the prefix *self-* is added to whole words.

Use your understanding of the prefix *self-* to answer each of the following questions.

1. If someone is **self-employed,** is the person probably his or her own boss? Explain.

____

2. If someone is filled with **self-interest,** is the person selfish or unselfish? Explain.

____

3. How do you feel about yourself if you have **self-respect**?

____

____

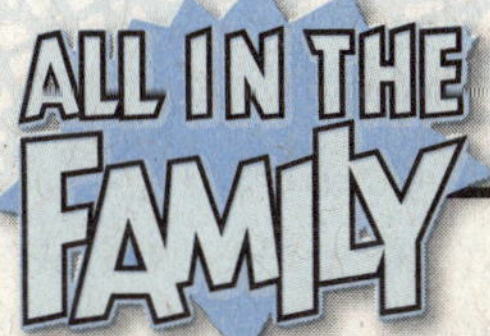

The following words are in the same word family. What are some other words that have *express* in them? Add one to the list.

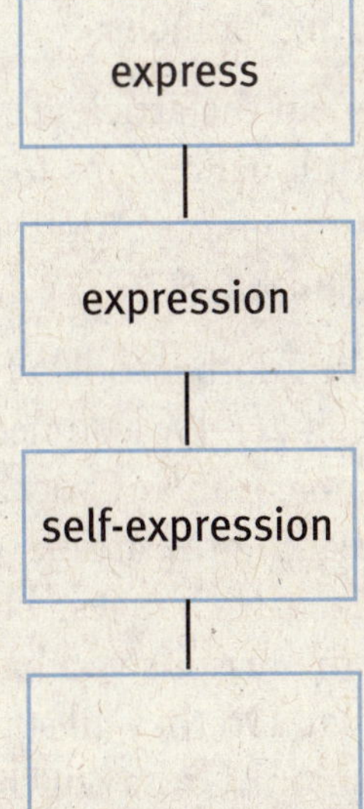

Write About It!

You have read an article about a woman who lived in a tree to keep it from being chopped down. Now you will write about the topic. Read the writing prompt. It gives your writing assignment.

Writing Prompt

After reading "Up a Tree," do you agree with Julia Butterfly Hill's method of protesting? Write a paragraph stating your opinion and supporting it with reasons. Use ideas from the article and at least one word from the Word Bank.

connection • define • discourse • frequently

WRITING RUBRIC

In your response, you should:

- Tell whether you agree with Hill's protest methods.
- Include reasons and ideas from the article.
- Use at least one word from the Word Bank.
- Use correct grammar, usage, and mechanics.

Prewrite It

Once you are sure you understand the prompt, plan what you want to say.

1. Review your notes from the class discussion. Then jot down your thoughts. Write your opinion in the "trunk" of the organizer on the right. Then, using key words, write reasons on the "branches."

2. Reread the article. Look for additional reasons to support your opinion. Add those to your organizer.

3. Take another look at your organizer. Do you need to change it in any way after rereading the article? If so, make the changes. Then read all the reasons you have jotted down. Do they all support your opinion? Cross out those that do not.

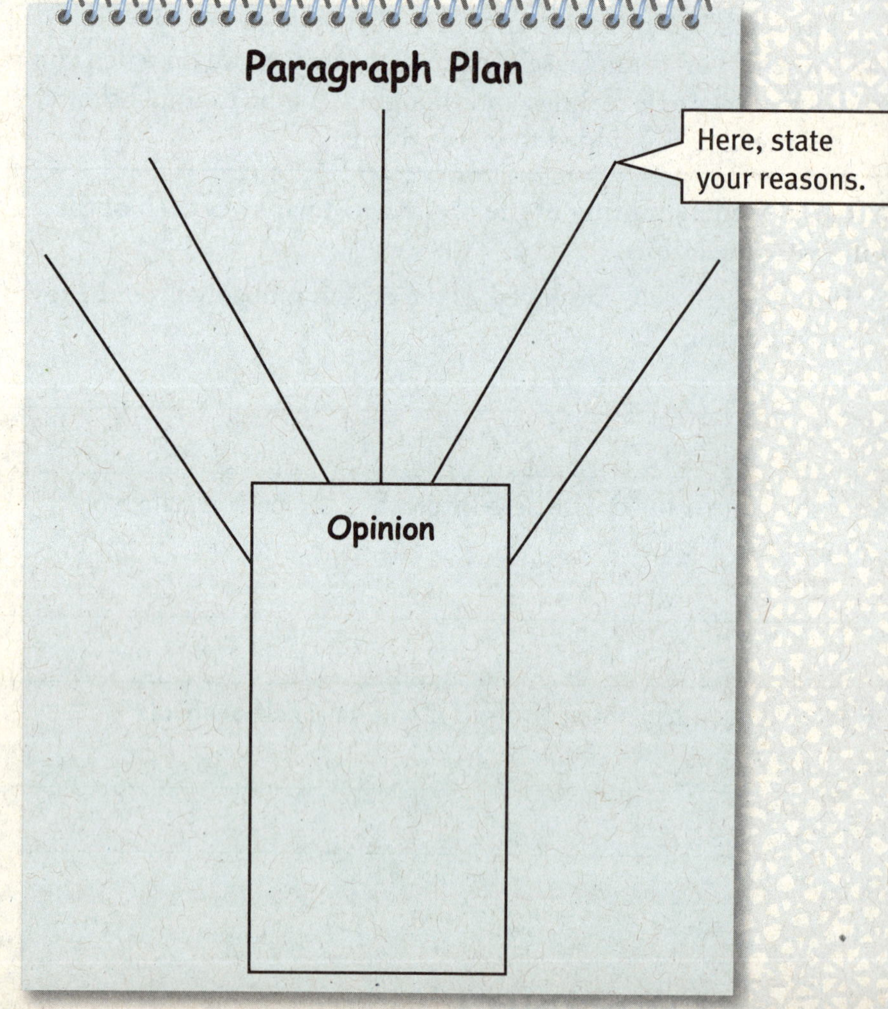

Draft It

Now use your organizer to draft, or write, your opinion paragraph.
The writing frame below will help you.

1. Start by writing a title for your paragraph. The title should state
the topic, or subject, of your paragraph in an interesting way. Then
finish the first sentence starter at the beginning of the paragraph by
underlining your opinion of Hill's "tree-sitting" protest.

2. Next, briefly describe Hill's protest. Imagine that your readers do
not know what Hill did. Summarize her actions in a few sentences.

3. Finally, support your opinion. Finish the last sentence starter by
giving a reason for your opinion. Include ideas from the article.

My title: ________________________________

I think Julia Butterfly Hill (helped, hurt) her cause by "tree-sitting."

To keep loggers from cutting down a very old redwood tree, she

____

____

____

____

____

In my judgment, Hill _________________________

____

____

____

Check It and Fix It

After you have written your opinion paragraph, check your work.
Read it as if you were hearing about Hill's protest for the first time.

1. Is everything written clearly and correctly? Use the checklist on the
right to find out.

2. Trade paragraphs with a partner. Talk over ways you both might
improve your paragraphs. Use each other's ideas to revise your work.

3. For help with grammar, usage, and mechanics, go to the Handbook
on pages 189–231.

If you are not sure how to sum
up what Hill did, begin by
answering the questions that
newspaper reporters use:
*Who? What? Where? When?
Why? How?* Then discuss your
answers with a classmate.
Together, write a one- or
two-sentence summary of
Hill's actions.

✔ **CHECKLIST**

Evaluate your writing.
A score of "5" is excellent.
A score of "1" means you
need to do more work.
Then ask a partner to rate
your writing.

**1. Does the opinion
paragraph explain
the protest and give
an opinion about it?**

Me: 1 2 3 4 5
Partner: 1 2 3 4 5

**2. Does the paragraph
contain reasons based
on information from the
article?**

Me: 1 2 3 4 5
Partner: 1 2 3 4 5

**3. Is there at least one word
from the Word Bank?**

Me: 1 2 3 4 5
Partner: 1 2 3 4 5

**4. Are grammar, usage, and
mechanics correct?**

Me: 1 2 3 4 5
Partner: 1 2 3 4 5

Vocabulary Workshop

Add these words to your personal word bank by practicing them.

connection • define • discourse • frequently

Define It

Complete the chart below using the Word Bank words. First, tell what the word means. Then tell what the word does not mean. Use the example as a guide.

Word	What It Is	What It Is Not
connection	something that links things together	something that tears things apart

What other new words in the article would you like to remember? List them.

____

____

____

Look in a thesaurus if you cannot think of a synonym (similar word) or antonym (opposite word) for a new word. Check a print thesaurus or an electronic, on-line thesaurus. To use an on-line thesaurus, type the new word in the search box.

Show You Know

Answer the questions below to show you know the meaning of each
Word Bank word.

1. In which of your classes might you have a **discourse** and about what? _______________

____

2. If a quiz-show host asks a contestant to **define** the word *bugaboo*, what does the contestant have to do?

____

____

3. If you **frequently** visit the library, how often do you think you go each week and why? _______________

____

4. If you make a **connection** with a character in a story or movie, what do you do? _______________

____

A Suffix That Means "In the Manner Of": *-ly*

- When you add an *-ly* ending to an adjective, you change the
  word into an adverb—a word that tells how an action is done.

  Adjective: Frankie is known as a **frequent** flyer.

  Adverb: Frankie flies **frequently.**

Write the *-ly* adverb form of the adjectives below. Then write
a sentence for each.

1. weird + *ly* = _______________________________________

Sentence: _______________________________________

2. rapid + *ly* = _______________________________________

Sentence: _______________________________________

3. humorous + *ly* = _______________________________________

Sentence: _______________________________________

4. beautiful + *ly* = _______________________________________

Sentence: _______________________________________

As Big As All Outdoors

Write About It!

You have read an article about outdoor advertising. Now you will write about the topic. Read the writing prompt. It gives your writing assignment.

Writing Prompt

After reading "As Big As All Outdoors," do you think we should put limits on billboards and other large outdoor ads? Suppose a city near you is reviewing the issue. Write a speech to deliver at a city public hearing. In your speech, tell whether you are for or against stricter limits on outdoor ads. Use ideas from the article and at least one word from the Word Bank.

explanation • interact • respond • verbal

WRITING RUBRIC

In your response, you should:

- State your opinion about limits on outdoor advertising.

- Support your opinion with reasons based on the article.

- Use at least one word from the Word Bank.

- Use correct grammar, usage, and mechanics.

Prewrite It

Once you are sure you understand the prompt, plan what you want to say.

1. Review your notes from the class discussion. On the organizer on the right, jot down your opinion about whether to limit certain types of outdoor ads.

2. Reread the article. Look for information about different methods of outdoor advertising. In the bottom ovals, list a good point and bad point of each.

3. Take another look at your organizer. Read all the points you have included. If you need to add, cut, or change any, do so. Then decide which points you will use to write your speech.

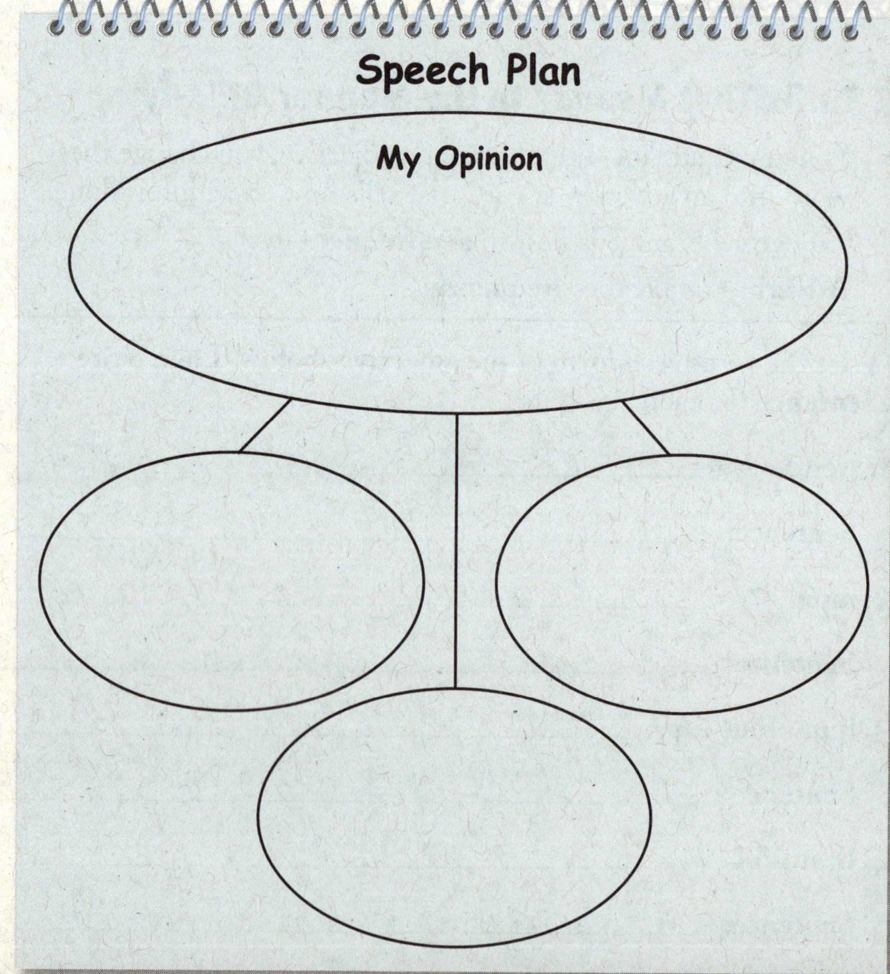

Draft It

Now use your organizer to draft, or write, your speech. The writing frame below will help you.

1. Start by briefly explaining the problem brought before the hearing.

2. State your recommendation by underlining your opinion on whether to put limits on various kinds of outdoor ads.

3. Then give reasons for your recommendation. Include good or bad points from your organizer and information from the article to support your view.

The purpose of your speech is to persuade the city council to agree with your opinion and take action. Therefore, your speech should sound serious and respectful. Ask a partner to evaluate the tone, or "sound," of your speech.

My Recommendation to the Council

Council members, I am here to speak about the outdoor advertising issue. In my opinion, we (should, should not) put stricter limits on outdoor ads. I feel this way because _______________

____

____

____

____

____

____

____

Check It and Fix It

After you have written your speech, check your work. Try to read it with a "fresh eye," as if you have never before seen it.

1. Is everything written clearly and correctly? Use the checklist on the right to find out.

2. Deliver your speech to a partner. Talk over ways you both might make your speeches clearer and more informative. Use the ideas to revise your work.

3. For help with grammar, usage, and mechanics, go to the Handbook on pages 189–231.

✔ CHECKLIST

Evaluate your writing. A score of "5" is excellent. A score of "1" means you need to do more work. Then ask a partner to rate your writing.

1. **Does the speech clearly state an opinion?**

   Me: 1 2 3 4 5
   Partner: 1 2 3 4 5

2. **Is the opinion supported by reasons and information from the article?**

   Me: 1 2 3 4 5
   Partner: 1 2 3 4 5

3. **Is there at least one word from the Word Bank?**

   Me: 1 2 3 4 5
   Partner: 1 2 3 4 5

4. **Are grammar, usage, and mechanics correct?**

   Me: 1 2 3 4 5
   Partner: 1 2 3 4 5

Vocabulary Workshop

Add these words to your personal word bank by
practicing them.

**explanation • interact •
respond • verbal**

Your Choice

What other new words in
the article would you like
to remember? List them.

____

____

____

Define It

Complete Venn diagrams to show how words are different and
alike. Choose a pair of words from the Word Bank. Write the
words on the lines inside the circles. On the sides of the circles,
tell how the two words are different. Where the circles overlap,
write how they are similar. The first pair is done for you as a model.
Do this for two more pairs of words.

respond — to answer or say back

Both have to do with acting or reacting.

interact — to do things or talk back and forth between people

Show You Know

Write a dialogue, or conversation between people, in the space below. In your conversation, use all the Word Bank words in a way that shows you understand their meanings.

_______________ : _________________________________

____

_______________ : _________________________________

____

_______________ : _________________________________

____

_______________ : _________________________________

____

A Prefix That Means "Between": *inter-*

- The prefix *inter-* is usually added to whole words. For example, the Word Bank word *interact* is made up of the word *act* and the prefix *inter-*. The prefix is used with many different kinds of words, including nouns, verbs, and adjectives.

Use your understanding of *inter-* to answer each question.

1. If two subjects are **interrelated,** are they connected or disconnected? Explain.

____

____

2. What do you do when you **intertwine** ribbon in a braid?

____

____

3. Does an **international** company do business in one country or more than one? How can you tell?

____

____

Put Me In, Coach!

Write About It!

You have read an article about life coaches. Now you will write about the topic. Read the writing prompt. It gives your writing assignment.

Writing Prompt

Do you think your school should hire life coaches to work with students? Should school funds be used to pay for them, or should school money be spent on other things? Write a memo to your principal explaining your position. Use ideas from the article and at least one word from the Word Bank.

confusion • emotion • isolation • self-expression

WRITING RUBRIC

In your response, you should:

- State whether you think school funds should be used to hire life coaches.

- Include information from the article to support your position.

- Use at least one word from the Word Bank.

- Use correct grammar, usage, and mechanics.

Prewrite It

Once you are sure you understand the prompt, plan what you want to say.

1. Review your notes from the class discussion. Use the organizer on the right to jot down your thoughts.

2. Reread the article. Look for other points about the benefits or drawbacks of life coaches. Add those to your organizer.

3. Take another look at your organizer. Review your position and the reasons you have listed. If you need to revise any points, make the revisions.

Hire Life Coaches?

My Position

My Reasons

Here, jot down whether you think school money should be spent on life coaches.

Draft It

Now use your organizer to draft, or write, a memo to your principal. The writing frame below will help you.

1. Start by filling in the blanks in the memo headings. Then read the first two sentences, and underline your opinion.

2. Follow up by finishing the "First of all" sentence starter with a reason for your opinion. Then finish the last sentence starter by stating another reason. Be sure to use ideas from the article in your reasons.

A memo is a written message that co-workers send to one another. Unlike letters, memos do not begin with "Dear _________," or end with a closing like "Sincerely yours." The headings at the top of the memo take their place. Likewise, memos are not usually signed, though some people do write their initials next to their names. Initial your memo if you wish.

To: Principal _______________________________________

From: _______________________________________

Subject: Hiring Life Coaches

Date: _______________________________________

I am writing to state my opinion about the school's proposal to hire life coaches. I (think, do not think) the proposal is a good idea. First of all, _______________

____

_______________________________________.

Also, _______________________________________

____

_______________________________________.

✔ CHECKLIST

Evaluate your writing. A score of "5" is excellent. A score of "1" means you need to do more work. Then ask a partner to rate your writing.

1. **Does the memo clearly state a position on the issue?**

   Me: 1 2 3 4 5
   Partner: 1 2 3 4 5

2. **Is the position supported by reasons based on the article?**

   Me: 1 2 3 4 5
   Partner: 1 2 3 4 5

3. **Is there at least one word from the Word Bank?**

   Me: 1 2 3 4 5
   Partner: 1 2 3 4 5

4. **Are grammar, usage, and mechanics correct?**

   Me: 1 2 3 4 5
   Partner: 1 2 3 4 5

Check It and Fix It

After you have written your memo, check your work. Read it as if you were the principal and had not yet made up your mind about the issue.

1. Is everything written clearly and correctly? Use the checklist on the right to see.

2. Trade memos with a classmate. Talk over ways you both might improve your memos. Use the ideas to revise your work.

3. For help with grammar, usage, and mechanics, go to the Handbook on pages 189–231.

Vocabulary Workshop

Add these words to your personal word bank by practicing them.

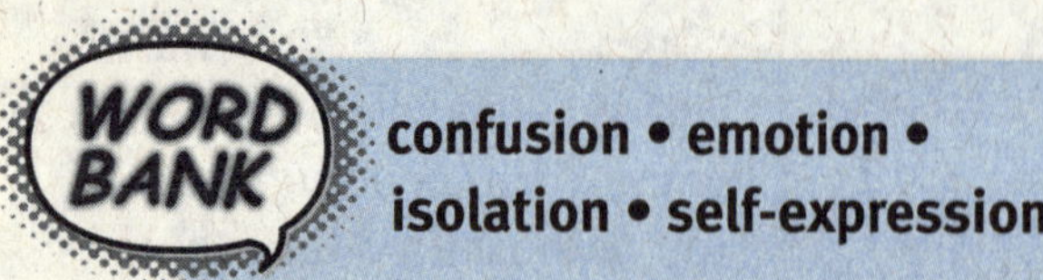

confusion • emotion • isolation • self-expression

Define It

Fill in the chart. In the center oval, write two or three subjects you could write about using the Word Bank words. Use the examples as a model.

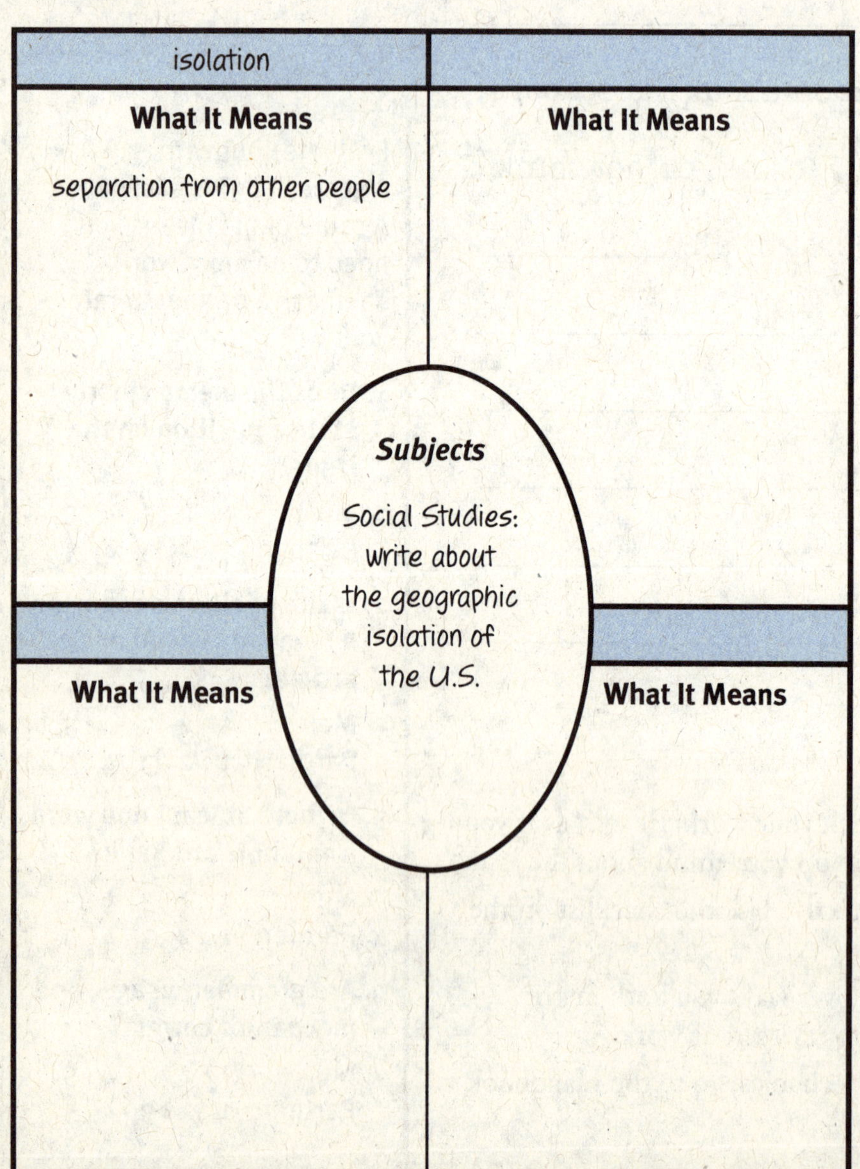

What other new words in the article would you like to remember? List them.

____

____

____

Word COACH

To find subjects you could write about using the Word Bank words, think about your classes. Have you or a teacher used any of the words in class? Can you think of a textbook you might see the words in?

Show You Know

Write a comic strip in the space below. Use all the Word Bank words in a way that shows you understand their meanings.

Context Clues

Sometimes, you can figure out what an unfamiliar word means by using context clues. The *context* of a word is the sentence in which the word appears and sometimes other nearby sentences. What clues tell what *emotion* means in the sentence below?

- My father did not mind showing **emotion,** so when he felt deeply about something, he cried.

From the clues "felt deeply" and "cried," you might guess that *emotion* means "a feeling, such as crying."

Underline context clues that tell you what each boldface word means. Then use the clues to write a definition for the word.

1. In Mexico, Carly was often lost and in a state of **confusion** because she did not understand Spanish.

Definition: _______________________________________

2. If you have a deadly disease others can catch, you may be set apart and put in **isolation.**

Definition: _______________________________________

3. Each dancer showed his or her feelings and personality in a dynamic form of **self-expression.**

Definition: _______________________________________

Write About It!

You have read an article about messages the sports media send about professional athletes. Now you will write about the topic. Read the writing prompt. It gives your writing assignment.

Writing Prompt

After reading "Longing to Be Like Mike," do you think the media send the wrong message about sports careers? If this question were posted on an Internet blog, how would you respond? State and explain your point of view. Use ideas from the article and at least one word from the Word Bank.

connection • meaning • misinterpret • possible • respond

Prewrite It

Once you are sure you understand the prompt, plan what you want to say.

1. Review your notes from the class discussion. Use the organizer on the right to jot down your thoughts. State your view in the center oval and your reasons in the outside ovals.

2. Reread the article. Look for other ideas you might use in your blog posting. Add those to your organizer.

3. Review your organizer. Do you have enough reasons? Do all of them support your point of view? Cross out reasons you do not plan to use.

In your response, you should:

- Explain whether you think the media send the wrong message about sports careers.

- Support your viewpoint with reasons based on the article.

- Use at least one word from the Word Bank.

- Use correct grammar, usage, and mechanics.

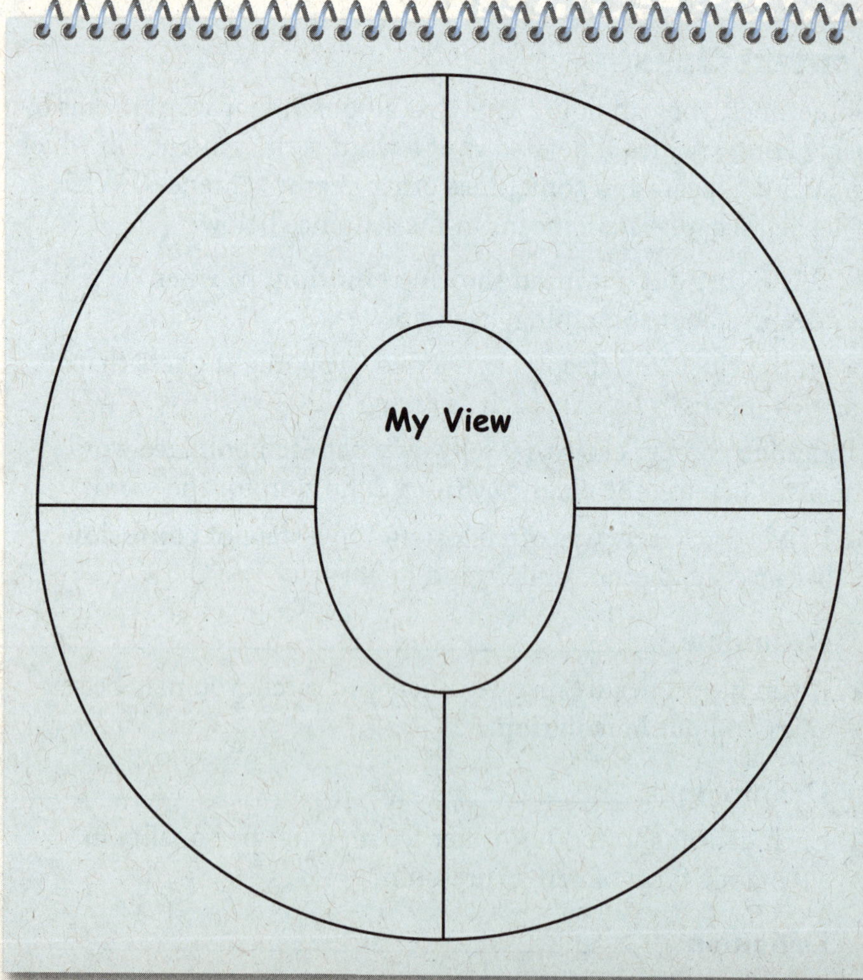

Draft It

Now use your organizer to draft, or write, your blog posting.
The writing frame below will help you.

1. Start by adding a title for your posting and your screen name.

2. Then underline your opinion in the first sentence. Follow up by giving your reasons. Back up your reasons with information from the article.

If you have trouble explaining your viewpoint, ask a partner to help you word your ideas. Tell your partner what you want to say, and ask him or her to take notes. Use the notes to write your blog posting.

Title: _______________________________

Posted By: _______________________________

I (agree, disagree) that the media communicate the

wrong message about sports careers. I say this because

____

____

____

____

____

____

____

_______________________________.

✔ CHECKLIST

Evaluate your writing.
A score of "5" is excellent.
A score of "1" means you need to do more work.
Then ask a partner to rate your writing.

1. **Does the blog posting clearly explain a viewpoint?**

   Me: 1   2   3   4   5
   Partner: 1   2   3   4   5

2. **Is the viewpoint supported by information from the article?**

   Me: 1   2   3   4   5
   Partner: 1   2   3   4   5

3. **Is there at least one word from the Word Bank?**

   Me: 1   2   3   4   5
   Partner: 1   2   3   4   5

4. **Are grammar, usage, and mechanics correct?**

   Me: 1   2   3   4   5
   Partner: 1   2   3   4   5

Check It and Fix It

After you have written your blog posting, check your work. Read it as if you were surfing an Internet sports blog and did not know anything about the issue.

1. Is everything written clearly and correctly? Use the checklist on the right to find out.

2. Trade postings with a classmate. Talk over other ways you might support your views. Use each other's comments to revise your work if necessary.

3. For help with grammar, usage, and mechanics, go to the Handbook on pages 189–231.

Vocabulary Workshop

Add these words to your personal word bank by practicing them.

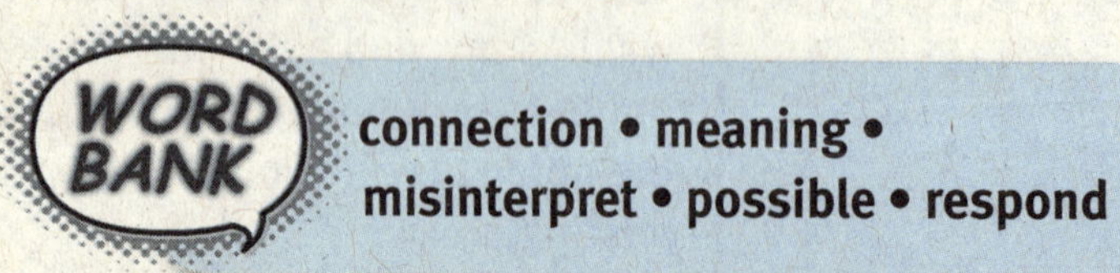

Define It

In your own words, write what each word in the Word Bank means. Then think of a word that has the same or a very similar meaning. Write that word as shown in the example below.

Your Choice

What other new words in the article would you like to remember? List them.

____

____

____

What It Means	misinterpret	
to mistakenly think or say something different from what a thing really means		**A Word It Reminds Me Of** misunderstand
What It Means		
		A Word It Reminds Me Of ___________
What It Means		
		A Word It Reminds Me Of ___________
What It Means		
		A Word It Reminds Me Of ___________
What It Means		
		A Word It Reminds Me Of ___________

Show You Know

In the space below, write a short, short story (just a paragraph!)
using the Word Bank words. Be sure your sentences show that
you understand the meanings of the words.

Once upon a time, ____

____

____

____

____

____

____

Word Sort

Sort the Word Bank words into the correct columns in the chart
below. Read through the article and add your own words to each
category. Use the examples as a guide.

Nouns	Verbs	Adjectives
connection	misinterpret	possible

Now that you have sorted your words, pick two from different
categories and combine them into a sentence. For a challenge,
pick more than two.

____

____

Write About It!

You have read an article about national service plans. Now you will write about the topic. Read the writing prompt. It gives your writing assignment.

Writing Prompt

After reading "Time to Serve," do you think all young Americans ages eighteen to forty-two should have to do volunteer service for their country? Write a letter to your Congressperson telling whether you think national service should be required and why. Include ideas from the article and at least one word from the Word Bank.

convey • discourse • interact • language

In your response, you should:

- Give your opinion about requiring young people to do national service.

- Give reasons for your opinion based on information in the article.

- Use at least one word from the Word Bank.

- Use correct grammar, usage, and mechanics.

Prewrite It

Once you are sure you understand the prompt, plan what you want to say.

1. Review your notes from the class discussion. Use the ladder organizer on the right to jot down your thoughts.

2. Reread the article. Look for reasons that support your viewpoint. Add them to your organizer.

3. Take another look at your organizer. Review all your reasons. Do they support your view? If not, revise them to make a stronger case.

Draft It

Now use your organizer to draft, or write, the letter to your Congressperson. The writing frame below will help you.

1. Start by giving your opinion. The sentence starter gives you two choices of opinion. Underline your choice.

2. Then finish the second starter by stating your supporting reasons. Be sure to use information from the article.

Dear Congressperson:

In my opinion, national service should be (voluntary, required).

I believe this because ____

____

____

____

____

____

____

____

____

____

____

Check It and Fix It

After you have written your letter, check your work. Read it as if you were a legislator who wants to know the views of the people he or she represents. Make sure the letter is respectful and persuasive.

1. Is everything written clearly and correctly? Use the checklist on the right to find out.

2. Trade letters with a classmate. Talk over other ways you both might make your opinions more convincing. Use each other's comments to revise your letters.

3. For help with grammar, usage, and mechanics, go to the Handbook on pages 189–231.

The purpose of your letter is to persuade your representative to agree with you. Do not just state your opinion; back up your opinion with reasons that are likely to matter to your representative. If you are not sure which reasons to include, talk them over with a partner or your teacher.

✔ **CHECKLIST**

Evaluate your writing. A score of "5" is excellent. A score of "1" means you need to do more work. Then ask a partner to rate your writing.

1. **Does the letter clearly explain an opinion?**

   Me: 1 2 3 4 5
   Partner: 1 2 3 4 5

2. **Are reasons from the article included in the letter?**

   Me: 1 2 3 4 5
   Partner: 1 2 3 4 5

3. **Is there at least one word from the Word Bank?**

   Me: 1 2 3 4 5
   Partner: 1 2 3 4 5

4. **Are grammar, usage, and mechanics correct?**

   Me: 1 2 3 4 5
   Partner: 1 2 3 4 5

Vocabulary Workshop

Add these words to your personal word bank by practicing them.

convey • discourse • interact • language

Define It

For each organizer below, do as follows. Choose two words from the Word Bank and write them on either side of the triangle. On the blank "because" lines, tell why the two words are connected. Use the example as a guide.

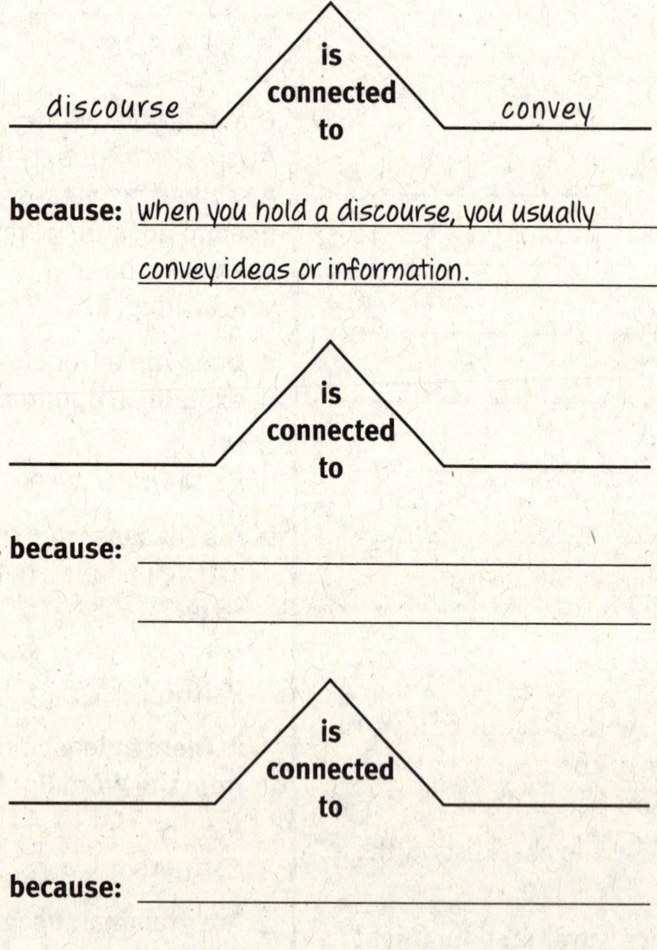

Your Choice

What other new words in the article would you like to remember? List them.

____

____

____

Word COACH

When you understand how words are connected, you can use them in more meaningful ways. Combining new words together in sentences will also help you use the words more precisely.

Show You Know

Answer the questions below to show you know the meaning of each
Word Bank word.

1. What is a way you might **convey** your feelings about something?

____

____

2. If you hold a **discourse** about something, what do you do?

____

____

3. What is a way you might **interact** with a friend who lives far away?

____

____

4. What is a way you might use **language** to express yourself?

____

____

Compare your answers with those of a classmate. Do your answers show that you understand the meanings of the words? If not, discuss how you might change your answers. Then make the changes.

It's Academic

Did you notice that some of the Word Bank words are academic
vocabulary? These are words you may use—or hear your teacher
use—in class. For example, a teacher might *convey* a math concept,
convey information about a period in history, *convey* new vocabulary
words, or *convey* details of a science experiment.

Use the Word Bank word *interact* to write three sentences. In each
sentence, show how you might use the word in a particular class.

1. ____

____

2. ____

____

3. ____

____

Write About It!

You have read an article on a debate about letting rap artists into the Rock and Roll Hall of Fame. Now you will write about the topic. Read the writing prompt. It gives your writing assignment.

Writing Prompt

Do you think rap singers and musicians should be allowed into the Rock and Roll Hall of Fame, or should they have their own hall of fame? Write a letter to the editor of a teen music magazine. In your letter, tell what you think and why. Include ideas from the article and at least one word from the Word Bank.

explanation • meaning • misinterpret • tone • verbal

Prewrite It

Once you are sure you understand the prompt, plan what you want to say.

1. Review your notes from the class discussion. Use the organizer on the right to jot down your thoughts.

2. Reread the article. Look for information and reasons that support your opinion. Add those to your organizer.

3. Take another look at your organizer. Read over your reasons. Do they all support your opinion? If not, revise them.

WRITING RUBRIC

In your response, you should:

- Tell whether you think rap artists should be part of the Rock and Roll Hall of Fame.

- Support your opinion with reasons based on the article.

- Use at least one word from the Word Bank.

- Use correct grammar, usage, and mechanics.

Hip-Hop and the Hall

My Opinion

Your opinion is what you believe about the issue.

My Reasons

Your reasons explain why you hold the opinion.

Draft It

Now use your organizer to draft, or write, your letter to the editor of the music magazine. The writing frame below will help you.

1. Read the first sentence. It introduces the topic of hip-hop and rap artists. Then finish the sentence starter by underlining the opinion that matches yours.

2. Finish the next sentence starter, at the beginning of the second paragraph, by giving a reason that supports your opinion. Then add another reason. Be sure to include information from the article.

Dear Editor:

    Hip-hop is an important part of American culture. For that reason and others, its greatest artists (should be part of the Rock and Roll Hall of Fame, should have their own hall of fame).

    Consider that _______________________________________

____

____

____

____ .

    Also, ____

____

____

____

____ .

Check It and Fix It

After you have written your letter to the editor, check your work.

1. Is everything written clearly and correctly? Use the checklist on the right to decide.

2. Trade letters with a classmate. Discuss whether your letters are effective. Talk over ways to improve your letters. Then use your ideas to revise your work.

3. For help with grammar, usage, and mechanics, go to the Handbook on pages 189–231.

The purpose of a letter to the editor is to persuade readers to agree with your opinion. Make sure you know the arguments of people who do not agree with you. Talk the issue over with classmates who think differently from you to get their opinions.

✔ CHECKLIST

Evaluate your writing. A score of "5" is excellent. A score of "1" means you need to do more work. Then ask a partner to rate your writing.

1. Does the letter clearly state an opinion?

Me: 1 2 3 4 5
Partner: 1 2 3 4 5

2. Are ideas from the article included in the letter?

Me: 1 2 3 4 5
Partner: 1 2 3 4 5

3. Is there at least one word from the Word Bank?

Me: 1 2 3 4 5
Partner: 1 2 3 4 5

4. Are grammar, usage, and mechanics correct?

Me: 1 2 3 4 5
Partner: 1 2 3 4 5

Vocabulary Workshop

Add these words to your personal word bank by
practicing them.

**explanation • meaning •
misinterpret • tone • verbal**

Define It

Fill in the chart. In the center oval, write two or three subjects you
could write about using the Word Bank words.

Your Choice

What other new words in
the article would you like
to remember? List them.

____

____

____

____

What It Means	What It Means	What It Means
	Subjects	
What It Means		**What It Means**

Show You Know

To show that you understand the Word Bank words, write three sentences. In each sentence, use and highlight two of the words. (You will use one word twice.) Use the example as a model.

* When you make a verbal expression of an idea, be sure your words convey the right tone.

1. ____

   ____

2. ____

   ____

3. ____

   ____

Exchange sentences with a partner and read them. Did you correctly use all the Word Bank words? If not, discuss ways to revise them. Then make the revisions.

A Suffix That Means "Related To": -al

* The suffix *-al,* which means "related to" or "marked by," appears at the end of the Word Bank word *verbal.* The root of this word—*verb*—means "word" in Latin. Therefore, the word *verbal* means "relating to words." A word ending with the *-al* suffix may be an adjective, like *verbal,* or a noun, like *rehearsal.*

Add *-al* to each word below. Then define the new word and use it in a sentence.

1. emotion + *-al* = ________________________________

   Sentence: ____

2. education + *-al* = ________________________________

   Sentence: ____

3. logic + *-al* = ________________________________

   Sentence: ____

4. comic + *-al* = ________________________________

   Sentence: ____

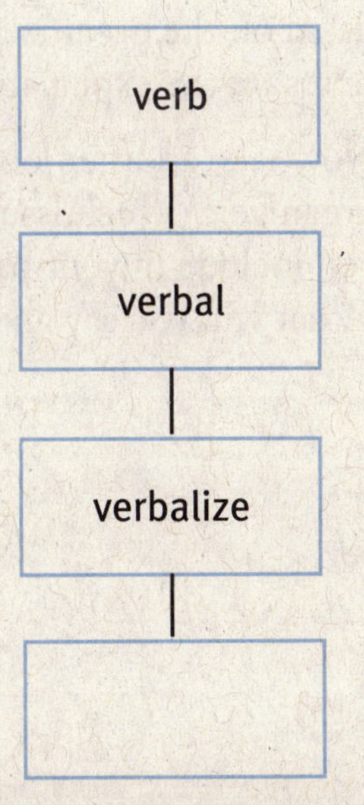

The following words are in the same word family. What are some other words that have *verb* in them? Add one to the list.

Hip-Hop into the Hall of Fame   **131**

Texting on Trial

Write About It!

You have read an article about text messaging and arguments in favor of and against it. Now you will write about the topic. Read the writing prompt. It gives your writing assignment.

Writing Prompt

After reading "Texting on Trial," do you think text messaging is harmful, safe and fun, or a little of both? If texting were on trial, would you defend it or speak out against it? Write a paragraph stating your opinion. Include ideas from the article and at least one word from the Word Bank.

confusion • continuum • frequently • language

In your response, you should:

- Write an opinion paragraph explaining whether you would be a text-messaging defender or prosecutor if it were on trial.

- Support your opinion with reasons from the article.

- Use at least one word from the Word Bank.

- Use correct grammar, usage, and mechanics.

Prewrite It

Once you are sure you understand the prompt, plan what you want to say.

1. Review your notes from the class discussion. Jot down your thoughts on the organizer on the right.

2. Reread the article. Look for explanations of the five issues listed on the organizer. Take notes on the explanations.

3. Now take another look at your organizer. Which issues will you include in your paragraph? What will you say about each?

Text Messaging

Text-Messaging Issues
1. Class Distractions
2. Sleep Loss
3. Cost
4. Writing Habits
5. Bullying

Draft It

Now use your organizer to draft, or write, your opinion paragraph.
The writing frame below will help you.

1. Start by giving your paragraph a title. Then finish the first sentence
   starter by underlining your opinion. Tell whether you would be on
   the defense team or the team for the prosecution.

2. Finally, finish the second starter by giving reasons to support
   your opinion.

My title: _______________________________

If text-messaging were on trial, I would have to side with the

(prosecution, defense). I feel this way because _______________

____

____

____

____

____

____

____ .

A title should state or hint at the topic of a piece of writing in an interesting way. If you are not sure how to write a title, review the titles of the articles in the book. Talk them over with a classmate, and see what he or she thinks.

Check It and Fix It

After you have written your opinion paragraph, check your work.
Try to read your paragraph with a "fresh eye," as if you have never
before seen it.

1. Is everything written clearly and correctly? Use the checklist on the
   right to find out.

2. Trade paragraphs with a classmate. Talk over how to make the
   arguments for your side stronger. Use each other's comments to
   revise your work.

3. For help with grammar, usage, and mechanics, go to the Handbook
   on pages 189–231.

✔ CHECKLIST

Evaluate your writing.
A score of "5" is excellent.
A score of "1" means you
need to do more work.
Then ask a partner to rate
your writing.

1. **Does the paragraph clearly explain which side the writer agrees with and why?**

   Me: 1 2 3 4 5
   Partner: 1 2 3 4 5

2. **Does the paragraph include reasons from the article?**

   Me: 1 2 3 4 5
   Partner: 1 2 3 4 5

3. **Is there at least one word from the Word Bank?**

   Me: 1 2 3 4 5
   Partner: 1 2 3 4 5

4. **Are grammar, usage, and mechanics correct?**

   Me: 1 2 3 4 5
   Partner: 1 2 3 4 5

Vocabulary Workshop

Add these words to your personal word bank by
practicing them.

**confusion • continuum •
frequently • language**

What other new words in
the article would you like
to remember? List them.

____

____

____

Define It

Fill in the chart with the Word Bank words. In your own words, tell
what each word means. Then circle the number that tells how well
you understand each word. Circle "4" if you understand it completely.
Circle "1" if you are not sure you understand the word at all.

What It Means	
	How Well I Understand It 1 2 3 4
What It Means	
	How Well I Understand It 1 2 3 4
What It Means	
	How Well I Understand It 1 2 3 4
What It Means	
	How Well I Understand It 1 2 3 4

Show You Know

Write a dialogue, or conversation between people, in the space below. Use all the Word Bank words in a way that shows you understand their meanings.

______________ : ________________________________

____

______________ : ________________________________

____

______________ : ________________________________

____

______________ : ________________________________

____

Word Play

Using words with exact meanings can make your writing more lively and specific. In the chart below, list some words that mean the same or about the same as the Word Bank words. Think of words that have a precise meaning. Check a dictionary or thesaurus if you need to, and use the examples as models.

Word Bank Word	Words with Similar Meanings
confusion	misunderstanding, mix-up

Now try some of the words to see how they can make your writing more precise. Rewrite each of the sentences, substituting one of your words for the boldface word.

1. Is it better to use **language** or pictures to state a warning?

____

2. Do you **frequently** watch TV?

____

Writing Reflection

Does all communication serve a positive purpose?

Look through your writing from this unit and choose the best piece.
Reflect on this piece of writing by completing each sentence below.

My best piece of writing from this unit is __________________________

____

I chose this piece because ____

____

____

While I was writing, one goal I had was ____________________________

____

I accomplished this goal by ____

____

____

This writing helped me think more about the Big Question because

____

____

One thing I learned while writing that can help me in the future is

____

____

To what extent does experience determine what we perceive?

Write About It!

You have read an article about student protestors. Now you will write about the topic. Read the writing prompt. It gives your writing assignment.

Writing Prompt

After reading "Pros and Cons of Protest," how do you think college officials can protect the rights of both student protesters and non-protesters? Write a paragraph explaining and supporting your ideas. Use ideas from the article and at least one word from the Word Bank.

bias • expectations • perspective • universal

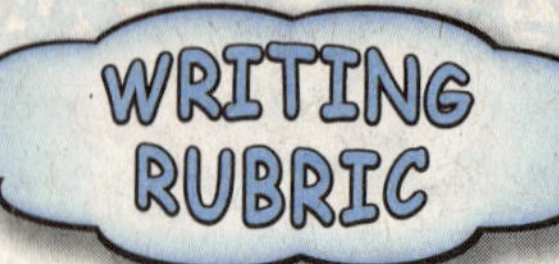

In your response, you should:

- Write a paragraph explaining how to protect protesters' and non-protesters' rights.

- Support your ideas with information from the article.

- Use at least one word from the Word Bank.

- Use correct grammar, usage, and mechanics.

Prewrite It

Once you are sure you understand the prompt, plan what you want to say.

1. Review your notes from the class discussion. Use the organizer on the right to jot down your thoughts.

2. Reread the article. Look for additional information that supports or explains your ideas. Add those to your organizer.

3. Take another look at your ideas and suggestions. Do you need to change them in any way after rereading the article? If so, make the changes. Do your ideas protect the rights of both protesters and non-protesters? If not, revise them.

Protecting Students' Rights

My Ideas:

How to Protect Protestors	How to Protect Non-Protestors

Draft It

Now use your organizer to draft, or write, your paragraph.
The writing frame below will help you.

1. First, read the first sentence starter and complete the thought by giving your suggestion.

2. Then explain how your suggestion protects both protesters and non-protesters. Read the second and third sentence starters below. Finish each sentence with your ideas. Make sure you explain your ideas with information from the article.

If you have trouble supporting your ideas, work with a partner. Tell your partner your suggestion for college officials. Ask your partner how your idea protects both protestors and non-protestors. Have your partner take notes, and use them to write your paragraph.

Protecting Students' Rights

One way for college officials to protect the rights of both

protestors and non-protestors is to ___________________________

____

____

This protects students' right to protest because ______________

____

____

____

It also protects the rights of non-protesters because __________

____

____

____

✔ CHECKLIST

Evaluate your writing. A score of "5" is excellent. A score of "1" means you need to do more work. Then ask a partner to rate your writing.

1. **Does the paragraph have a clear suggestion about what college officials can do?**

   Me: 1 2 3 4 5
   Partner: 1 2 3 4 5

2. **Are there ideas from the article to support the suggestion?**

   Me: 1 2 3 4 5
   Partner: 1 2 3 4 5

3. **Is there at least one word from the Word Bank?**

   Me: 1 2 3 4 5
   Partner: 1 2 3 4 5

4. **Are grammar, usage, and mechanics correct?**

   Me: 1 2 3 4 5
   Partner: 1 2 3 4 5

Check It and Fix It

After you have written your paragraph, check your work. Try to read it with a "fresh eye," as if you have never before read it.

1. Is everything written clearly and correctly? Use the checklist on the right to find out.

2. Then trade work with a classmate. Talk over ways you might improve your paragraphs. Use the ideas to revise your work.

3. For help with grammar, usage, and mechanics, go to the Handbook on pages 189–231.

Vocabulary Workshop

Add these words to your personal word bank by
practicing them.

bias • expectations •
perspective • universal

Define It

Complete the chart below using the Word Bank words. First, tell
what the word means. Then tell what the word does not mean.
Use the example as a guide.

Word	What It Is	What It Is Not
bias	feeling for or against something	being objective or having no opinion about something

Your Choice

What other new words in
the article would you like
to remember? List them.

____

____

____

To remember a new word,
use it in different ways. For
example, write a sentence
with the new word, draw
something that reminds
you of the word, and use
the word in a conversation.

Show You Know

Write a dialogue, or conversation between people, in the space below. In your conversation, use all the Word Bank words in a way that shows you understand their meanings.

__________ : __________________________

____

__________ : __________________________

____

__________ : __________________________

____

__________ : __________________________

____

A Prefix That Means "One": *uni-*

- If you remember that *uni-* means one, you have a head start on understanding unfamiliar words that begin with the *uni-* prefix. Here are some common words that contain *uni-* and the meanings of the words.

unicycle = one wheel   **uniform** = one form

unify = to join into one whole   **unison** = one sound

Complete each sentence by writing a word that begins with *uni-*. Use the list above for help.

1. At Andre's school, everyone must wear the same __________.

2. You must have good balance to ride a __________, because there are no handlebars.

3. The choir practiced each day so that the choir members could sing in __________.

Write About It!

You have read an article about celebrities and invasions of their privacy. Now you will write about the topic. Read the writing prompt. It gives your writing assignment.

Writing Prompt

After reading "Royal Rights to Privacy," do you think the public has the right to know about celebrities' private lives? Write a letter to the editor of a celebrity magazine. Tell the editor whether you think celebrities deserve privacy. Give reasons for your opinion. Use ideas from the article and at least one word from the Word Bank.

appropriate • background • discipline • identity • stereotype

WRITING RUBRIC

In your response, you should:

- Write a letter to the editor stating your opinion about privacy rights.

- Support your opinion with reasons based on the article.

- Use at least one word from the Word Bank.

- Use correct grammar, usage, and mechanics.

Prewrite It

Once you are sure you understand the prompt, plan what you want to say.

1. Review your notes from the class discussion. Use the organizer on the right to jot down your thoughts.

2. Reread the article. Look for additional reasons and examples that support or explain your opinion. Add those to your organizer.

3. Take another look at your opinion. Do you need to change it in any way after rereading the article? If so, make the changes. Read through all the reasons and examples you have listed. Which are the strongest? Cross out those that are not as strong.

Privacy for Celebrities

My Opinion

My Reasons and Examples

Draft It

Now use your organizer to draft, or write, a letter to the editor.
The writing frame below will help you.

1. Start by giving your opinion. Does the public have the right to
know about celebrities' private lives? Underline your choice.

2. Then give reasons for your opinion. Read the sentence starter in
the second sentence. Finish the thought by giving a reason for your
opinion. Explain your reason with ideas from the article.

Dear Editor:

    I think the public (does, does not) have the right to know about

the private lives of celebrities. I think this because _______________

____

____

____

____

____

____

____

____

____

____ .

In a letter to the editor, your
goal is to convince people
to agree with your opinion.
Talk over your opinion
and reasons with a few
classmates. Ask if your ideas
are persuasive and, if they
are not, ask how to improve
them.

✔ CHECKLIST

Evaluate your writing.
A score of "5" is excellent.
A score of "1" means you
need to do more work.
Then ask a partner to rate
your writing.

**1. Does the letter give
a clear opinion?**

Me: 1 2 3 4 5
Partner: 1 2 3 4 5

**2. Do reasons and ideas
from the article support
the opinion?**

Me: 1 2 3 4 5
Partner: 1 2 3 4 5

**3. Is there at least one word
from the Word Bank?**

Me: 1 2 3 4 5
Partner: 1 2 3 4 5

**4. Are grammar, usage, and
mechanics correct?**

Me: 1 2 3 4 5
Partner: 1 2 3 4 5

Check It and Fix It

After you have written your letter, check your work. Imagine that you
have never before read the letter.

1. Is everything written clearly and correctly? Use the checklist on the
right to find out.

2. Then trade work with a classmate. Talk over ways to improve your
letters. Use the ideas to revise your work.

3. For help with grammar, usage, and mechanics, go to the Handbook
on pages 189–231.

Vocabulary Workshop

Add these words to your personal word bank by practicing them.

appropriate • background • discipline • identity • stereotype

What other new words in the article would you like to remember? List them.

____

____

____

Define It

Fill in the chart with the Word Bank words. In your own words, tell what each word means. Then circle the number that tells how well you understand each word. Circle "4" if you understand it completely. Circle "1" if you are not sure you understand the word at all. Use the example as a model.

What It Means	appropriate
right for a particular situation	**How Well I Understand It** 1 2 ③ 4
What It Means	
	How Well I Understand It 1 2 3 4
What It Means	
	How Well I Understand It 1 2 3 4
What It Means	
	How Well I Understand It 1 2 3 4
What It Means	
	How Well I Understand It 1 2 3 4

Show You Know

Write a short, short story (just a paragraph!) using the Word Bank words. Be sure your sentences show that you understand the meanings of the words.

Once upon a time, ____________________________

____

____

____

____

____

____

____

Trade stories with a partner. Read each other's stories. Check to see if all the Word Bank words are used correctly. If not, make corrections.

Compound Words

A compound word is formed by joining two or more words. It is different from a word with a prefix or a suffix, because in a compound word, the parts are always complete words. You can often figure out the meaning of a compound word by looking at the words that form it. For example, the Word Bank word *background*, which is made up of the words *back* and *ground*, literally means "in the back of the ground," or "behind the scenes."

Use a word from each list to form a compound word. For each compound, write a sentence using the word. Some words can be used more than once.

down	town
home	stairs
class	field
ball	room
up	work

1. ____.

2. ____.

3. ____.

4. ____.

Write About It!

You have read an article about cliques. Now you will write about the topic. Read the writing prompt. It gives your writing assignment.

Writing Prompt

After reading "In or Out of the In Crowd," what advice would you give students who are about to start high school? Write a newspaper advice column for eighth-graders. In your column, define what cliques are, and tell students how to cope with them. Use ideas from the article and at least one word from the Word Bank.

consider • distortion • impression • individual • manipulate

Prewrite It

Once you are sure you understand the prompt, plan what you want to say.

1. Review your notes from the class discussion. Use the organizer on the right to jot down your thoughts.

2. Reread the article. Look for additional information about cliques and reasons that support your advice. Add those to your organizer.

3. Take another look at your description of cliques and your explanation of why they are a problem. Do you need to make any changes after rereading the article? Review your advice. Does it help solve the problem? If not, make changes.

WRITING RUBRIC

In your response, you should:

- Write a column defining cliques and advising how to cope with them.

- Explain your advice based on information from the article.

- Use at least one word from the Word Bank.

- Use correct grammar, usage, and mechanics.

Advice Column

Definition

What is a clique? ___________________________

Who joins? ___________________________

Why? ___________________________

Problems with Cliques

My Advice

Draft It

Now use your organizer to draft, or write, an advice column.
The writing frame below will help you.

1. Start by defining cliques. Complete the first sentence starter below with your definition.

2. Then complete the second sentence starter by describing why cliques may be a problem. Finally, complete the third sentence starter by giving advice on how to cope with cliques. Make sure you support your advice with information from the article.

Remember that you are writing to middle-school students. Do not assume that they already know all about high-school cliques. Talk over your ideas with a partner to make sure that they will be clear to middle-school students.

THIS JUST IN

Dear Eighth-Graders:

In high school, you will find many cliques, or _______________

____ .

As you may know, cliques can be a problem because _______________

____

____

____ .

My advice for dealing with cliques is _______________

____

____

____

____

____ .

Check It and Fix It

After you have written your advice column, check your work. Try to read it as if you have never before seen it. Imagine that you are about to enter high school and do not know much about cliques.

1. Is everything written clearly and correctly? Use the checklist on the right to find out.

2. Then trade advice columns with a classmate. Talk over ways you might improve your columns. Use the ideas to revise your work.

3. For help with grammar, usage, and mechanics, go to the Handbook on pages 189–231.

✔ CHECKLIST

Evaluate your writing. A score of "5" is excellent. A score of "1" means you need to do more work. Then ask a partner to rate your writing.

1. Does the column explain what cliques are and why they may be a problem?

Me: 1   2   3   4   5
Partner: 1   2   3   4   5

2. Does it give advice based on ideas from the article?

Me: 1   2   3   4   5
Partner: 1   2   3   4   5

3. Is there at least one word from the Word Bank?

Me: 1   2   3   4   5
Partner: 1   2   3   4   5

4. Are grammar, usage, and mechanics correct?

Me: 1   2   3   4   5
Partner: 1   2   3   4   5

Vocabulary Workshop

Add these words to your personal word bank by practicing them.

consider • distortion • impression • individual • manipulate

Define It

In your own words, write what each word in the Word Bank means. Then think of a word that has the same or a very similar meaning. Write that word as shown in the example below.

What It Means	consider	
to think carefully about something		**A Word It Reminds Me Of** ponder
What It Means		
		A Word It Reminds Me Of
What It Means		
		A Word It Reminds Me Of
What It Means		
		A Word It Reminds Me Of
What It Means		
		A Word It Reminds Me Of

Your Choice

What other new words in the article would you like to remember? List them.

Word COACH

When you come across an unfamiliar word while reading, look for synonyms and other context clues in the surrounding sentences. They can provide valuable clues to the meaning of the unfamiliar word.

Show You Know

To show that you understand the Word Bank words, write three sentences. In each sentence, use and highlight two of the words. (You will use one word twice.) Use the example as a model.

- An individual should try to make a good impression at a job interview.

1. ____

   ____

2. ____

   ____

3. ____

   ____

Trade sentences with a partner. Check each other's sentences to see if the Word Bank words are used correctly. Discuss how to fix any mistakes. Then fix them.

A Root That Means "Divide": *Divi*

- The root word *divi* comes from the Latin word *dividere*, meaning "to divide." You can use your knowledge of the root *divi* and other word parts it is combined with to figure out the meanings of other words. For example, analyze the parts of the Word Bank word *individual: in-* ("not") + *divi* ("divided") + *-al* ("characterized by") = "something that is not divided," or "a single person."

Complete each sentence by underlining the correct word in parentheses.

My neighbor got my (divided, undivided, individually) attention when he said that he was moving to Spain and wanted to (divvy, division, divisible) up his video games before he left. (Divide, Divisible, Division) has never been my favorite kind of math. Since there were four friends and nine games, the games were not evenly (divisible, indivisible, individual) among the friends. We decided that each (division, divvy, individual) would choose two games, and we would flip coins for the last one.

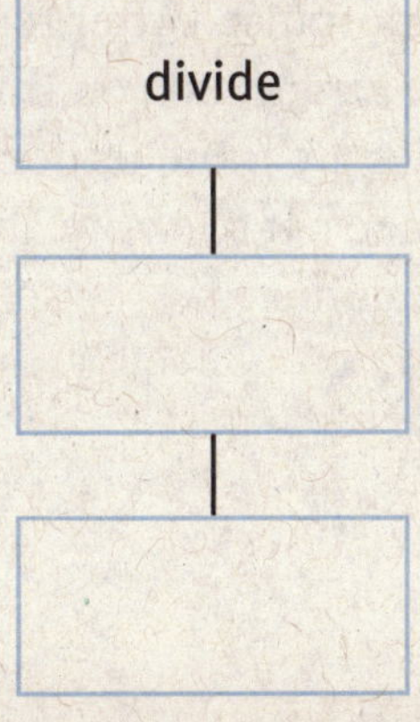

The word *divide* contains the root *divi*. Add a prefix or suffix to the root to make two other words in the same word family. Write the words in the boxes.

divide

The *Titanic* Tragedy

Write About It!

You have read an article about the sinking of the *Titanic*. Now you will write about the topic. Read the writing prompt. It gives your writing assignment.

Writing Prompt

After reading "The *Titanic* Tragedy," what have you learned about ship safety? Write a list of ship safety rules for crew members. Use ideas from the article and at least one word from the Word Bank.

anticipate • constant • interpretation • knowledge • presume

In your response, you should:

- Write a list of ship safety rules for crew members.

- Use information from the article to explain the importance of each rule.

- Use at least one word from the Word Bank.

- Use correct grammar, usage, and mechanics.

Prewrite It

Once you are sure you understand the prompt, plan what you want to say.

1. Review your notes from the class discussion. Use the organizer on the right to jot down your thoughts.

2. Reread the article. Look for additional rules that you can add to your list. Explain why each rule is important. Add that information to your organizer.

3. Rank the items on your list by importance. After rereading the article, do you think some rules are more important than others? If so, write about them first.

Safety Rules

Rank	Rule	Explanation

Draft It

Now use your organizer to draft, or write, a list of safety rules.
The writing frame below will help you.

1. Start by giving your most important safety rule first. Then briefly explain why it is important.

2. Continue by adding safety rules to your list in order of importance. Explain your rules with ideas from the article.

If you have trouble deciding which rule is the most important, work with a partner. Discuss which rule a crew member would have to know first and why. Use your discussion to rank the rules together.

Ship Safety Rules

Rule 1: ____

____.

This rule is important because _______________________________

____.

Rule 2: ____

____.

This rule is important because _______________________________

____.

Rule 3: ____

____.

This rule is important because _______________________________

____.

✔ CHECKLIST

Evaluate your writing.
A score of "5" is excellent.
A score of "1" means you need to do more work.
Then ask a partner to rate your writing.

1. **Does the list give clear and important safety rules?**

   Me: 1 2 3 4 5
   Partner: 1 2 3 4 5

2. **Are there ideas from the article to explain the rules?**

   Me: 1 2 3 4 5
   Partner: 1 2 3 4 5

3. **Is there at least one word from the Word Bank?**

   Me: 1 2 3 4 5
   Partner: 1 2 3 4 5

4. **Are grammar, usage, and mechanics correct?**

   Me: 1 2 3 4 5
   Partner: 1 2 3 4 5

Check It and Fix It

After you have written your list, check your work. Imagine that you are a crew member seeing the list for the first time.

1. Is everything written clearly and correctly? Use the checklist on the right to find out.

2. Then trade work with a classmate. Talk over ways you might improve your safety rules. Use the ideas to revise your work.

3. For help with grammar, usage, and mechanics, go to the Handbook on pages 189–231.

Vocabulary Workshop

Add these words to your personal word bank by
practicing them.

anticipate • constant • interpretation • knowledge • presume

Define It

For each set of boxes below, do as follows. Choose two words from
the Word Bank and write them in the small boxes. (One word will
appear twice.) In the Connection box, describe how the two are
connected. Use the examples as a guide.

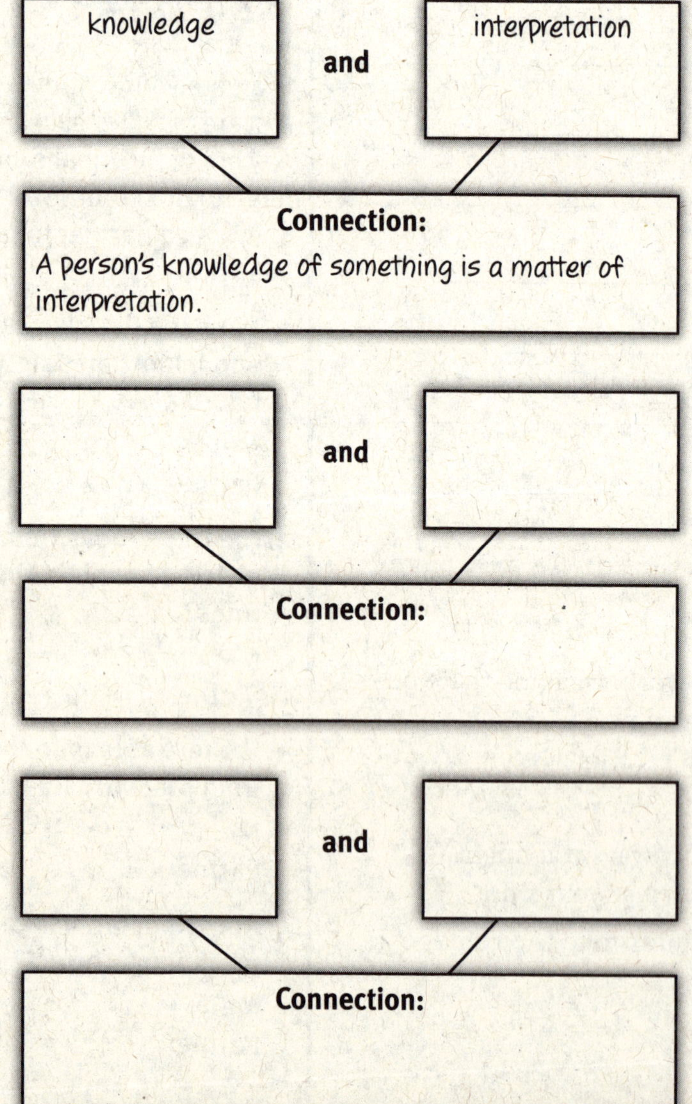

Your Choice

What other new words in
the article would you like
to remember? List them.

Word COACH

To remember new words,
think about them in
different ways. For example,
write a new word on an
index card. Then, on the
other side, list examples of
the word, name things the
word makes you think of,
and draw a picture that is
connected to the word.

Show You Know

To show that you understand the Word Bank words, write a clue for each word. Exchange clues with a partner. See whether your partner can identify the correct word for each clue. Use the clue for *anticipate*, below, as a model.

- Most students eagerly do this when they think of their summer vacation.

1. _______________________________________

____

2. _______________________________________

____

3. _______________________________________

____

4. _______________________________________

____

5. _______________________________________

____

Word Sort

Sort the Word Bank words into the correct columns in the chart below. Read the article and add your own words to each category. Use the examples as a guide.

Nouns	Verbs	Adjectives
interpretation	anticipate	

Writing Reflection

To what extent does experience determine what we perceive?

Look through your writing from this unit and choose the best piece.
Reflect on this piece of writing by completing each sentence below.

My best piece of writing from this unit is ________________________

____

I chose this piece because ________________________

____

____

While I was writing, one goal I had was ________________________

____

I accomplished this goal by ________________________

____

____

This writing helped me think more about the Big Question because

____

____

One thing I learned while writing that can help me in the future is

____

____

Can anyone be a hero?

Write About It!

You have read an article about the benefits and dangers of scientific advances. Now you will write about the topic. Read the writing prompt. It gives your writing assignment.

Writing Prompt

After reading "Science's Double-Edged Swords," do you think technological developments can be both positive *and* negative? Choose one of the developments described in the article and write a paragraph describing its benefits and dangers. Include ideas from the article and at least one word from the Word Bank.

attributes • conceive • determination • responsibility

WRITING RUBRIC

In your response, you should:

- Write a paragraph about the benefits and dangers of a technological development.

- Include ideas from the article.

- Use at least one word from the Word Bank.

- Use correct grammar, usage, and mechanics.

Prewrite It

Once you are sure you understand the prompt, plan what you want to say.

1. Review your notes from the class discussion. On the organizer on the right, jot down ideas you may be able to use in your paragraph.

2. Reread the article. Look for benefits and dangers of a scientific advancement you would like to write about. Take notes about them on the organizer.

3. Take another look at your organizer. Review all your notes. Which ideas will you include in your paragraph? Underline them.

Title: _______________

Benefits (+)	Dangers (−)

Write the name of the scientific advancement here.

Draft It

Now use your organizer to draft, or write, your paragraph.
The writing frame below will help you.

1. To begin, complete the first sentence starter by naming the scientific development you are writing about. Then complete the second sentence starter by describing benefits of the development.

2. Follow up by describing possible dangers of the development. Be sure to include ideas from the article.

Often, the main idea of a paragraph is stated in a topic sentence. Which sentence is the topic sentence of your paragraph? How can you tell? Talk it over with a partner.

A Double-Edged Sword

One technological development that can be seen as both positive

and negative is ____.

Its benefits are ____

____

____

____ .

Unfortunately, this technological development also involves possible

dangers, such as ____

____

____

____ .

✔ **CHECKLIST**

Evaluate your writing.
A score of "5" is excellent.
A score of "1" means you need to do more work.
Then ask a partner to rate your writing.

1. **Does the paragraph include both benefits and drawbacks?**

   Me: 1 2 3 4 5
   Partner: 1 2 3 4 5

2. **Does the paragraph contain ideas from the article?**

   Me: 1 2 3 4 5
   Partner: 1 2 3 4 5

3. **Is there at least one word from the Word Bank?**

   Me: 1 2 3 4 5
   Partner: 1 2 3 4 5

4. **Are grammar, usage, and mechanics correct?**

   Me: 1 2 3 4 5
   Partner: 1 2 3 4 5

Check It and Fix It

After you have written your paragraph, check your work. Read it as if you have not heard of the technological development before.

1. Is everything written clearly and correctly? Use the checklist on the right to decide.

2. Trade paragraphs with a partner. Talk over ways you might improve your paragraphs. Use the ideas to revise your work.

3. For help with grammar, usage, and mechanics, go to the Handbook on pages 189–231.

Vocabulary Workshop

Add these words to your personal word bank by practicing them.

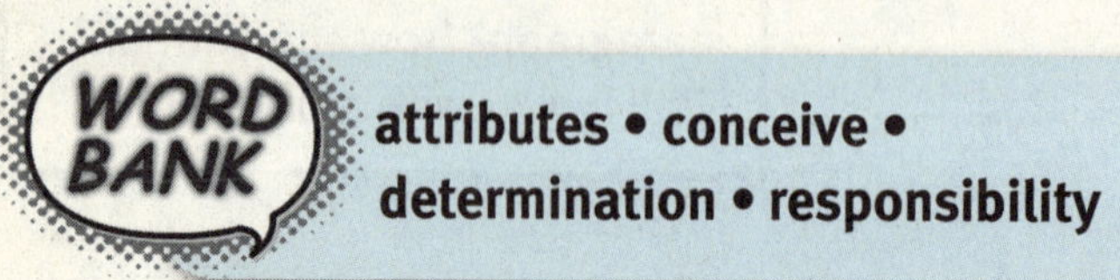

attributes • conceive • determination • responsibility

Define It

In your own words, write what each word in the Word Bank means. Then think of a word that has the same or a very similar meaning. Write the word as shown in the example below.

What It Means	attributes	
traits a person has, or the qualities of a thing		**A Word It Reminds Me Of** features
What It Means		
		A Word It Reminds Me Of
What It Means		
		A Word It Reminds Me Of
What It Means		
		A Word It Reminds Me Of

Your Choice

What other new words in the article would you like to remember? List them.

Word COACH

If you cannot think of a similar word for a Word Bank word, look in a print or electronic thesaurus. It lists synonyms, or words that mean about the same thing as other words.

Show You Know

Answer the questions below to show you know the meaning of each
Word Bank word.

1. When you do writing assignments, what are some ways you **conceive** of ideas to write about?

____

____

2. What are some ways teenagers can show **responsibility** as students?

____

____

3. What are two of your best **attributes**?

____

____

4. How might you show **determination** to do well in school?

____

____

Word Play

Using words with exact meanings can make your writing more lively
and specific. In the chart below, list some words that mean the same
or about the same as the Word Bank words. Think of words that
have a precise meaning. Check a dictionary or thesaurus for help if
you need to, and use the examples as models.

Word Bank Word	Words with Similar Meanings
attributes	qualities, traits, characteristics

Buffalo Battles

Write About It!

You have read an article about North America's bison. Now you will write about the topic. Read the writing prompt. It gives your writing assignment.

In your response, you should:

- Explain your point of view on the wild bison issue.

- Include information from the article.

- Use at least one word from the Word Bank.

- Use correct grammar, usage, and mechanics.

Writing Prompt

After reading "Buffalo Battles," do you think wild bison should be allowed to roam free, or should they be controlled to protect the rights of cattle ranchers? Write a letter to the director of the National Park Service expressing your point of view. Use ideas from the article and at least one word from the Word Bank.

character • integrity • purpose • resolute

Prewrite It

Once you are sure you understand the prompt, plan what you want to say.

1. Review your notes from the class discussion. Use the organizer to make notes about your viewpoint.

2. Reread the article. Look for facts and ideas that support your viewpoint. Add them to the organizer.

3. Take another look at your organizer. Review all your notes, and decide which facts and ideas you will include in your letter.

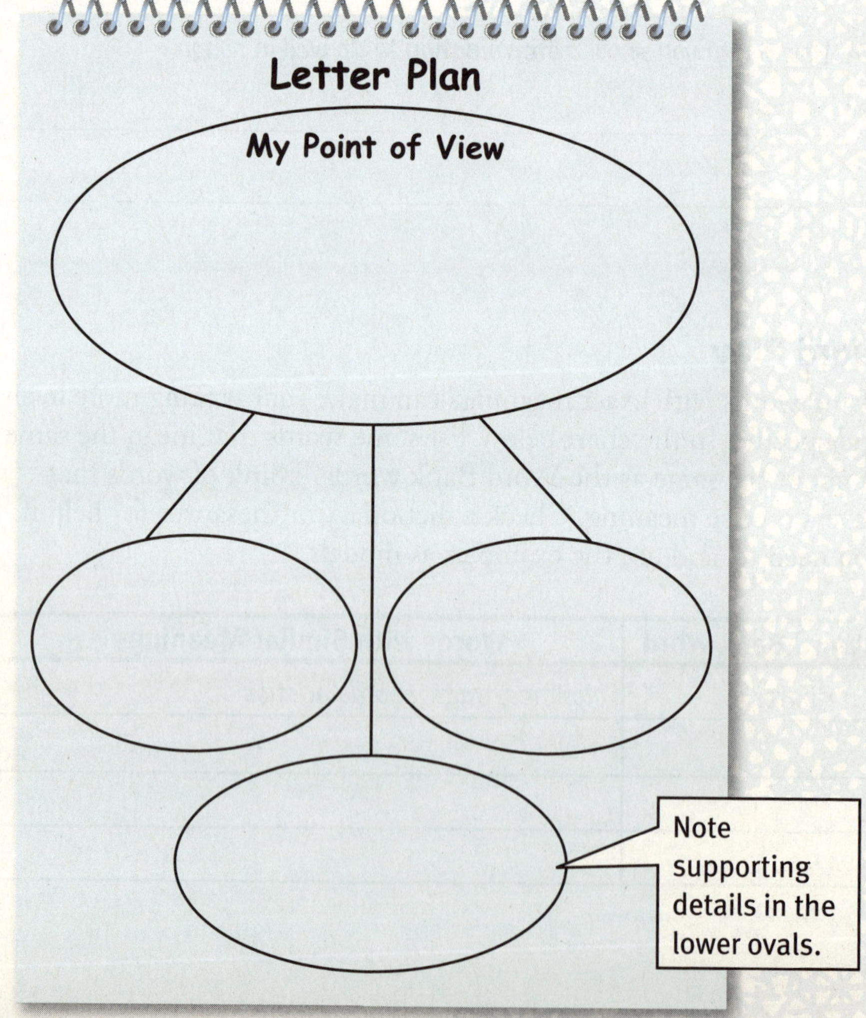

Draft It

Now use your organizer to draft, or write, your letter to the park service. The writing frame below will help you.

1. Start by stating your viewpoint. Complete the sentence starter by underlining the choice that best represents your viewpoint.

2. Continue your letter by explaining why you feel as you do. Be sure to support your viewpoint with facts and ideas from the article.

Dear Director:

   I believe that bison should be (allowed to roam, prevented from

grazing) on U.S. government lands. I feel this way because

____

____

____

____

____

____

____

____

____

____

____

Check It and Fix It

After you have written your letter, check your work. Read it as if you are the director who will receive it.

1. Is everything written clearly and correctly? Use the checklist on the right to decide.

2. Trade letters with a partner. Talk over ways you both might improve your letters. Use the ideas to revise your work.

3. For help with grammar, usage, and mechanics, go to the Handbook on pages 189–231.

If you are not sure how you feel, talk over the issue with a partner. Ask your partner to explain his or her viewpoint and the reasons behind it. Then decide whether you agree or disagree with your partner's viewpoint. Use the ideas to write about your own viewpoint.

✔ **CHECKLIST**

Evaluate your writing. A score of "5" is excellent. A score of "1" means you need to do more work. Then ask a partner to rate your writing.

1. **Does the letter clearly state a viewpoint on the bison issue?**

   Me: 1 2 3 4 5
   Partner: 1 2 3 4 5

2. **Does the letter include facts and ideas from the article?**

   Me: 1 2 3 4 5
   Partner: 1 2 3 4 5

3. **Is there at least one word from the Word Bank?**

   Me: 1 2 3 4 5
   Partner: 1 2 3 4 5

4. **Are grammar, usage, and mechanics correct?**

   Me: 1 2 3 4 5
   Partner: 1 2 3 4 5

Vocabulary Workshop

Add these words to your personal word bank by
practicing them.

**character • integrity •
purpose • resolute**

Your Choice

What other new words in
the article would you like
to remember? List them.

____

____

____

Define It

For each set of boxes below, do as follows. Choose two words
form the Word Bank and write them in the small boxes. In the
Connection box, describe how the two are connected. Use the
examples as a guide.

| purpose | and | resolute |

Connection:
Someone who is resolute may also have a strong sense of purpose.

| | and | |

Connection:

| | and | |

Connection:

Show You Know

Write a dialogue, or conversation between people, in the space below. In your conversation, use all the Word Bank words in a way that shows you understand their meanings.

It's Academic

Did you notice that some of the Word Bank words are academic vocabulary? These are words you may use—or hear your teacher use—in class.

For example, the **purpose** of a history unit may be to learn about the Civil War, and the **purpose** of a math assignment may be to find ratios.

Show how you might use the academic vocabulary word *character* in different classes. Write one sentence for each class.

1. ____

____

2. ____

____

3. ____

____

The Youngest Heroes

Write About It!

You have read an article about the importance of oral histories. Now you will write about the topic. Read the writing prompt. It gives your writing assignment.

Writing Prompt

Interview an older family member, teacher, or other trusted adult. Ask the person about a historical event he or she participated in, witnessed, or remembers. Take notes; then write a paragraph summing up the person's oral history. Use ideas from the article, if relevant, and at least one word from the Word Bank.

consult • courage • irony • persevere • sacrifice

In your response, you should:

- Write a brief oral history based on the memories of a trusted adult.

- Use ideas from the article if they relate to the oral history.

- Include at least one word from the Word Bank.

- Use correct grammar, usage, and mechanics.

Prewrite It

Once you are sure you understand the prompt, plan what you want to say.

1. Review your notes from the class discussion. On a separate piece of paper, jot down your thoughts about oral histories.

2. Reread the article. What insight does it give you into the importance of oral histories? Jot down your thoughts.

3. Read the questions on the organizer on the right. Use it to take notes during your interview. Are there other questions you would like to ask? Add them to your organizer. Then conduct the interview.

My Interview with ______________________

Question 1: What is the most important historical event that has taken place during your lifetime?

Answer: ________________________________

____

Question 2: Why do you think this event is the most important?

Answer: ________________________________

____

____

Question 3: What do you remember most about this event and why?

Answer: ________________________________

____

____

Draft It

Now use your organizer to draft, or write, a brief oral history.
The writing frame below will help you.

1. Begin by completing the title. What historical event are you writing
   about? Then complete the first sentence starter by filling in the date
   of the interview, the name of the person you interviewed, and the
   name of the historical event he or she discussed with you.

2. Follow up by describing the person's memories of the event.

An Oral History of _______________________

On ____________, I interviewed ____________ about ____________ .

Memories of this event include _______________________

____

____

____

____

____

____

____

____

____ .

Direct quotations make oral histories come alive. Try to include an interesting direct quotation or two in your oral history. If you are not sure which quotations to use, talk your choices over with a partner. Be sure to put quotation marks before and after any direct quotations you use.

✔ CHECKLIST

Evaluate your writing.
A score of "5" is excellent.
A score of "1" means you need to do more work.
Then ask a partner to rate your writing.

1. **Does the history identify and describe a historical event?**

   Me: 1 2 3 4 5
   Partner: 1 2 3 4 5

2. **Does the history include quotations or other interesting details?**

   Me: 1 2 3 4 5
   Partner: 1 2 3 4 5

3. **Is there at least one word from the Word Bank?**

   Me: 1 2 3 4 5
   Partner: 1 2 3 4 5

4. **Are grammar, usage, and mechanics correct?**

   Me: 1 2 3 4 5
   Partner: 1 2 3 4 5

Check It and Fix It

After you have written the oral history, check your work. Read it
as if you have never before seen it.

1. Is everything written clearly and correctly? Use the checklist on
   the right to decide.

2. Trade oral histories with a partner. Talk over ways you might
   improve your oral histories. Use the ideas to revise your work.

3. For help with grammar, usage, and mechanics, go to the Handbook
   on pages 189–231.

Vocabulary Workshop

Add these words to your personal word bank by practicing them.

consult • courage • irony • persevere • sacrifice

Define It

Fill in the chart. In the center oval, write two or three subjects you could write about using the Word Bank words. Use the examples as models.

courage		
What It Means	**What It Means**	**What It Means**
bravery		

Subjects:

English class: We might discuss the courage a character shows.

What It Means

What It Means

Word COACH

If you have trouble thinking of ways you might use a Word Bank word in class, talk it over with a student who takes the same classes as you.

Show You Know

To show that you understand all the Word Bank words, write three sentences. In each sentence, use and highlight two of the words. (You will use one word twice.) Use the example as a model.

- The sad irony of the soldier's sacrifice is that a truce was called just before he was injured.

1. ____

   ____

2. ____

   ____

3. ____

   ____

A Suffix That Means "State of": *-age*

- The base of the Word Bank word *courage* is the word *coeur*, which means "heart." Combined with the suffix *-age,* to form *courage,* the word literally means "the state of having heart," or "the state of being brave." Words that end with the *-age* suffix are usually nouns. When you add the *-age* suffix to a word that ends in *y,* change the *y* to an *i.*

Add the *-age* suffix to each word below. Then write a sentence using the new noun that you form.

1. break + *-age*: _______________________________________

Sentence: ____

____

2. marry + *-age*: _______________________________________

Sentence: ____

____

Exchange sentences with a partner. Are all the Word Bank words used correctly? If not, discuss how to revise the sentences; then revise.

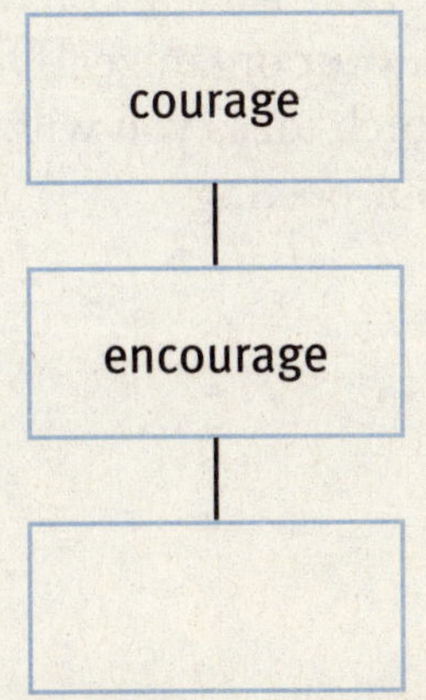

The following words are part of the same word family. What are some other words that have a form of the word *courage* in them? Add one to the list.

| courage |
| encourage |
| |

The Youngest Heroes   **167**

Write About It!

You have read an article about equal opportunities for women in sports. Now you will write about the topic. Read the writing prompt. It gives your writing assignment.

Writing Prompt

After reading "Equality on the Playing Field," do you think female athletes should be able to play on the same professional sports teams as males? Write your opinion in a message you can post on a sports blog, and support your opinion with reasons. Use ideas from the article and at least one word from the Word Bank.

inherent • integrity • resolute • selflessness

In your response, you should:

- State your opinion about men and women playing pro sports together.

- Support your opinion with ideas from the article.

- Use at least one word from the Word Bank.

- Use correct grammar, usage, and mechanics.

Prewrite It

Once you are sure you understand the prompt, plan what you want to say.

1. Review your notes from the class discussion. Use the organizer on the right to jot down your thoughts.

2. Reread the article. Look for reasons and examples that you can use to support your opinion. Add them to your organizer.

3. Review what you have written on your organizer. Decide which ideas you will use in your posting.

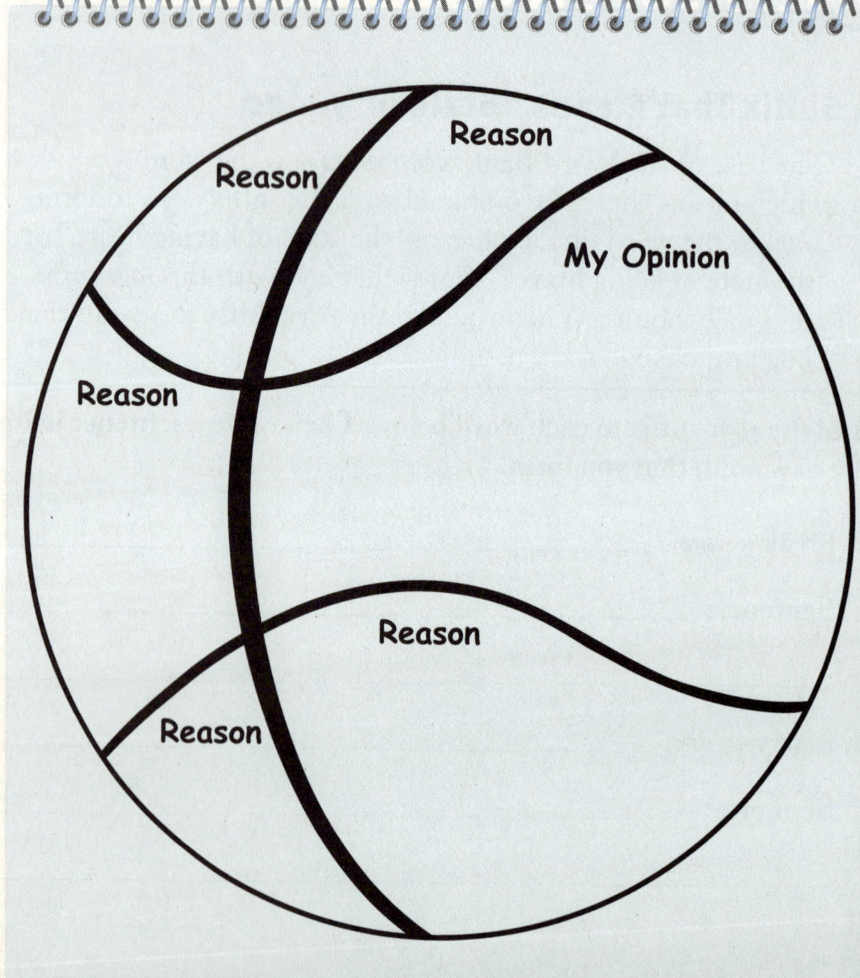

Draft It

Now use your organizer to draft, or write, your blog posting.
The writing frame below will help you.

1. Start by writing a title for your posting and your name. Then, in the first sentence, underline the choice that best represents your opinion.

2. Follow up by completing the first sentence starter. Give a reason for your opinion. Then complete the second sentence starter by giving an example that supports your reason. Be sure to use ideas from the article.

Blog postings are usually informal. It is OK to use casual language, but it is not OK to misspell words or make other mistakes. Leave your readers with a good impression of yourself by doing careful work.

✔ CHECKLIST

Evaluate your writing.
A score of "5" is excellent.
A score of "1" means you need to do more work.
Then ask a partner to rate your writing.

1. **Does the blog posting state and support an opinion?**

   Me: 1 2 3 4 5
   Partner: 1 2 3 4 5

2. **Does the posting include a reason or example from the article?**

   Me: 1 2 3 4 5
   Partner: 1 2 3 4 5

3. **Is there at least one word from the Word Bank?**

   Me: 1 2 3 4 5
   Partner: 1 2 3 4 5

4. **Are grammar, usage, and mechanics correct?**

   Me: 1 2 3 4 5
   Partner: 1 2 3 4 5

Check It and Fix It

After you have written your blog posting, check your work. Read it carefully to ensure that you find and correct any mistakes.

1. Is everything written clearly and correctly? Use the checklist on the right to decide.

2. Trade postings with a classmate. Talk over ways you might improve your postings. Use the ideas to revise your work.

3. For help with grammar, usage, and mechanics, go to the Handbook on pages 189–231.

Vocabulary Workshop

Add these words to your personal word bank by
practicing them.

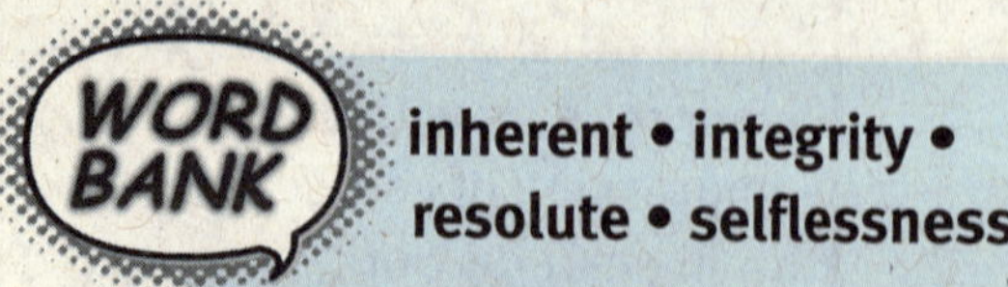

inherent • integrity •
resolute • selflessness

Your Choice

What other new words in
the article would you like
to remember? List them.

____

____

____

Define It

Fill in the chart with the Word Bank words. In your own words, tell
what each word means. Then circle the number that tells how well
you understand each word. Circle "4" if you understand it completely.
Circle "1" if you are not sure you understand the word at all. Use the
example as a model.

What It Means	inherent
a natural part of or built in	
	How Well I Understand It 1　2　③　4
What It Means	
	How Well I Understand It 1　2　3　4
What It Means	
	How Well I Understand It 1　2　3　4
What It Means	
	How Well I Understand It 1　2　3　4

Show You Know

To show that you understand the Word Bank words, write a clue for each word. Exchange clues with a partner. See whether your partner can identify the correct word for each clue. Use the clue for the word *resolute*, below, as a model.

If you are this, you will let nothing stand in your way of accomplishing a goal.

1. ____

2. ____

3. ____

4. ____

A Suffix That Means "Without": *-less*

- The word *selfless* means "without self," or "without thinking of oneself." Therefore, the Word Bank word *selflessness* means "the quality of not thinking of oneself." When you add *-less* to a verb or a noun, you create an adjective, or describing word.

Add the *-less* suffix to each word below. Then write a sentence using the new adjective that you form.

1. hair + *-less*: ____

Sentence: ____

2. hope + *-less*: ____

Sentence: ____

3. thought + *-less*: ____

Sentence: ____

The following words are part of the same word family. Find another word in the article that contains the word *self*, and add it to the list.

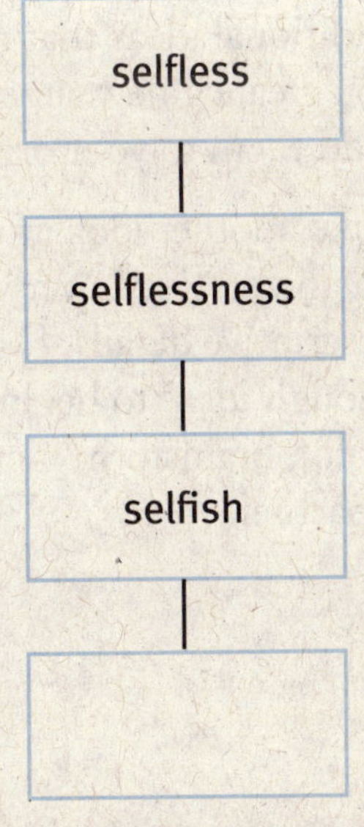

Equality on the Playing Field **171**

Write About It!

You have read an article about superheroes. Now you will write about the topic. Read the writing prompt. It gives your writing assignment.

Writing Prompt

After reading "Our Hero!" what kind of superhero would you create for kids today? Write a description of your modern superhero's characteristics and the kinds of superpowers he or she needs to conquer the problems of today's world. Include ideas from the article and at least one word from the Word Bank.

attributes • illustrate • legendary • selflessness

Prewrite It

Once you are sure you understand the prompt, plan what you want to say.

1. Review your notes from the class discussion. Use the organizer on the right to jot down your thoughts.

2. Reread the article. Look for additional ideas that might help you create a new superhero. Add them to your organizer.

3. Take another look at your organizer. Read over your descriptive details. Do you have enough ideas to begin writing? If not, brainstorm ideas with a partner.

My Hero

Possible Names:

Appearance:

Superpowers:

Importance to Today's Society:

How do your hero's superpowers help him or her face world challenges?

Draft It

Now use your organizer to draft, or write, your description of the superhero you invented. The writing frame below will help you.

1. Start by completing the first sentence starter with the name of your superhero. Then complete the second sentence starter by describing what your superhero looks like.

2. Follow up by describing your superhero's superpowers and a reason why they are important in today's world.

To make your writing more descriptive, ask a partner if it is easy to picture your superhero. If it is not, ask for suggestions on ways to describe your hero more vividly.

A Superhero for Today

Meet _____________, a superhero for today. You cannot miss

this superhero; just look for someone who is _______________

____

____

____.

This superhero's most important superpowers are _________

____

____

____.

These powers are important in today's world because _______

____

____

____.

Evaluate your writing. A score of "5" is excellent. A score of "1" means you need to do more work. Then ask a partner to rate your writing.

1. **Does the description name and clearly describe a new superhero?**

   Me: 1 2 3 4 5
   Partner: 1 2 3 4 5

2. **Does it explain why the hero's superpowers are important to today's world?**

   Me: 1 2 3 4 5
   Partner: 1 2 3 4 5

3. **Is there at least one word from the Word Bank?**

   Me: 1 2 3 4 5
   Partner: 1 2 3 4 5

4. **Are grammar, usage, and mechanics correct?**

   Me: 1 2 3 4 5
   Partner: 1 2 3 4 5

Check It and Fix It

After you have written your description, check your work. Read it as if you are planning a new graphic novel about this superhero and need to picture the character clearly.

1. Is everything written clearly and correctly? Use the checklist on the right to decide.

2. Trade descriptions with a classmate. Talk over other ways you might improve your descriptions. Use the ideas to revise your work.

3. For help with grammar, usage, and mechanics, go to the Handbook on pages 189–231.

Vocabulary Workshop

Add these words to your personal word bank by practicing them.

attributes • illustrate • legendary • selflessness

Define It

For each organizer below, do as follows. Choose two words from the Word Bank and write them on either side of the triangle. On the blank "because" lines, tell why the two words are connected. Use the example as a guide.

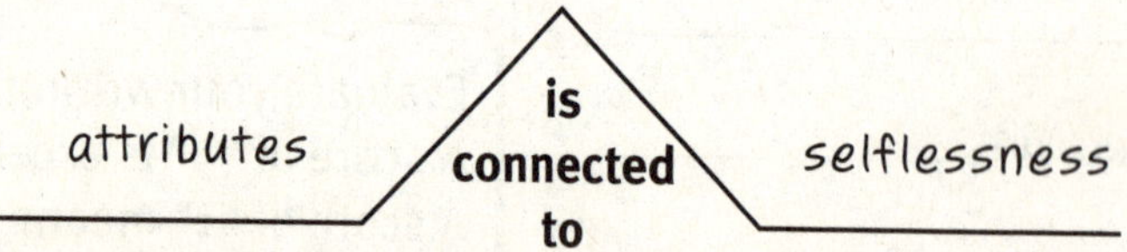

because: _selflessness is an attribute many people would like to have._

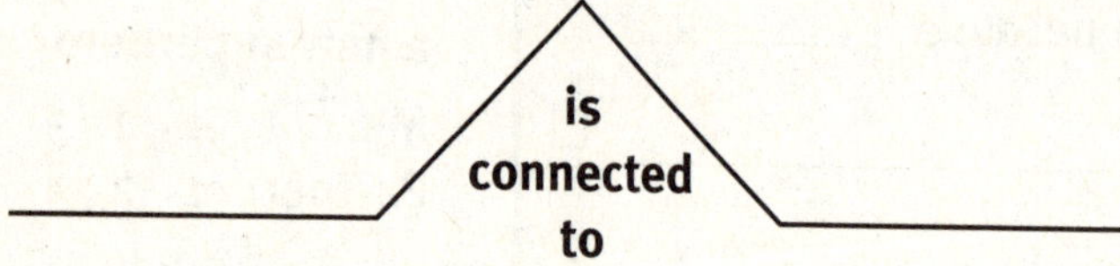

because: ___________________________

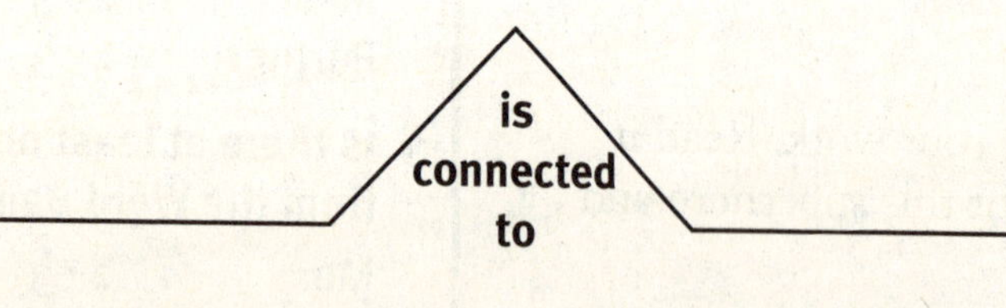

because: ___________________________

Your Choice

What other new words in the article would you like to remember? List them.

____

____

____

Word COACH

When you make connections between new words, you can better understand their meanings. You will also remember words longer if you pair them in your mind.

Show You Know

Answer the questions below to show you know the meaning of each
Word Bank word.

1. What are your best friend's best **attributes**?

____

____

2. If you **illustrate** an idea in a paragraph, what do you do?

____

____

3. What is the name of a **legendary** musician, singer, or actor whom you admire?

____

____

4. How might you show **selflessness** to your family?

____

____

A Suffix That Means "Connected with": *-ary*

- When you add the suffix *-ary* to a noun, you create an adjective.
  Noun: Do you know the **legend** of King Arthur?
  Adjective: His fame in battle is **legendary.**

**Add the *-ary* suffix to each word below. Then write a sentence using
the new adjective that you form.**

1. second + *-ary*: ______________________________________

Sentence: ______________________________________

2. honor + *-ary*: ______________________________________

Sentence: ______________________________________

3. custom + *-ary*: ______________________________________

Sentence: ______________________________________

  Our Hero!

Peacekeepers

Write About It!

You have read an article about the United Nations. Now you will write about the topic. Read the writing prompt. It gives your writing assignment.

Writing Prompt

What should young people know about the United Nations? Imagine that you are creating a Web site for kids about the U.N. Write a short description of the U.N. and its goals and challenges. Use ideas from the article and at least one word from the Word Bank.

conduct • honor • principles • responsibility • sacrifice

Prewrite It

Once you are sure you understand the prompt, plan what you want to say.

1. Review your notes from the class discussion. Use the organizer on the right to jot down your thoughts.

2. Reread the article. Look for facts and ideas about the U.N.'s goals and challenges, and add them to your organizer.

3. Take another look at your organizer. Read over the information you have included. Is there anything else young people should know about the U.N.? If so, add it.

WRITING RUBRIC

In your response, you should:

- Write a short description of the U.N., its goals, and its challenges.

- Include ideas from the article.

- Use at least one word from the Word Bank.

- Use correct grammar, usage, and mechanics.

U.N. Description

What is the U.N.?

What are its main goals?

What challenges does it face?

Draft It

Now use your organizer to draft, or write, your description of the U.N. The writing frame below will help you.

1. Complete the first sentence starter by writing a general description of the U.N. Include what it is, when it started, and how many members it has.

2. Then finish the second sentence starter by writing about the U.N.'s main goals. Follow up by briefly describing one of the U.N.'s challenges. Be sure to use facts and ideas from the article.

If you are not sure what information to include in your description, try asking and answering the five *W*'s and an *H* questions with a partner. Take notes on your answers, and use them to write.

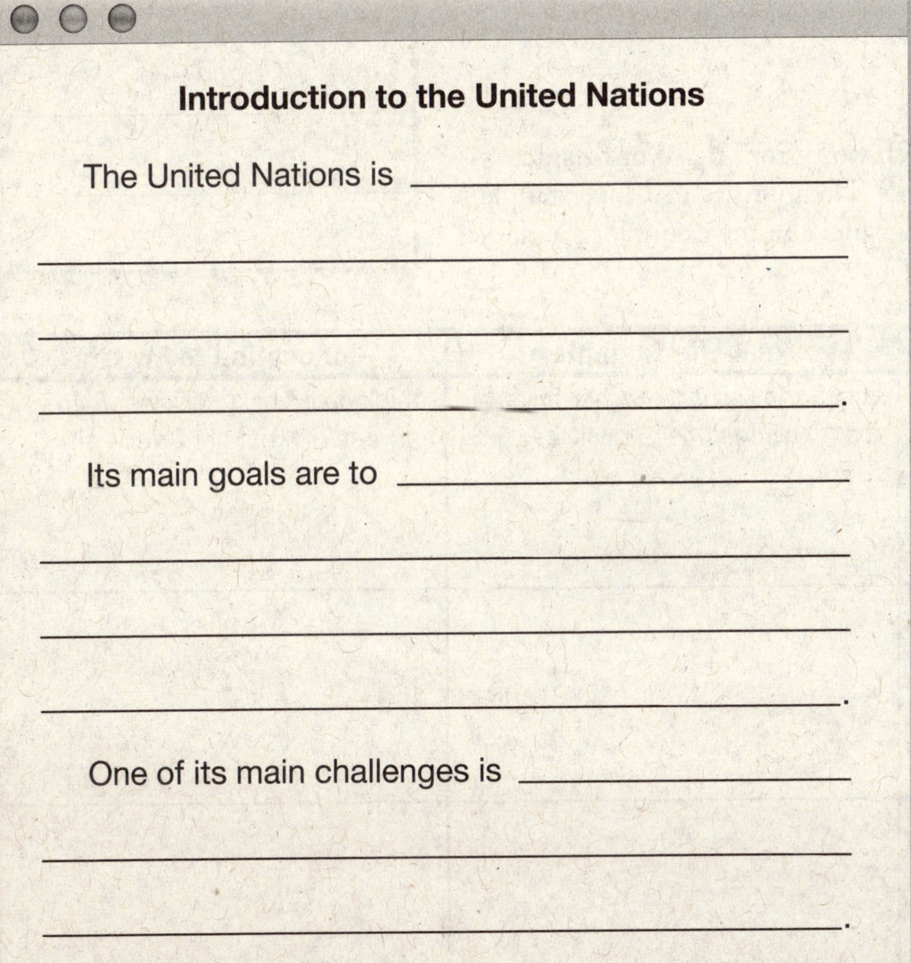

Introduction to the United Nations

The United Nations is __________________

____

____

_________________________________.

Its main goals are to __________________

____

____

_________________________________.

One of its main challenges is _____________

____

_________________________________.

Evaluate your writing.
A score of "5" is excellent.
A score of "1" means you need to do more work.
Then ask a partner to rate your writing.

1. Is the description of the U.N. clear and complete?

Me: 1 2 3 4 5
Partner: 1 2 3 4 5

2. Does it include the U.N.'s main goals and one of its challenges, based on the article?

Me: 1 2 3 4 5
Partner: 1 2 3 4 5

3. Is there at least one word from the Word Bank?

Me: 1 2 3 4 5
Partner: 1 2 3 4 5

4. Are grammar, usage, and mechanics correct?

Me: 1 2 3 4 5
Partner: 1 2 3 4 5

Check It and Fix It

After you have written your description, check your work. Try to read it as if you were a young person who knows nothing about the U.N.

1. Is everything written clearly and correctly? Use the checklist on the right to decide.

2. Trade descriptions with a classmate. Discuss whether your description is clear and complete. If not, note how you might improve your description, and use the ideas to revise your work.

3. For help with grammar, usage, and mechanics, go to the Handbook on pages 189–231.

Vocabulary Workshop

Add these words to your personal word bank by
practicing them.

**conduct • honor • principles •
responsibility • sacrifice**

Your Choice

What other new words in
the article would you like
to remember? List them.

____

____

____

Define It

Complete the chart below using each word from the Word Bank.
Give the meaning in your own words. Then write a real-life example
and an example that connects to your life. Use the example as a guide.

Word	Real-Life Example	Connection to My Life
principles: rules to live by	My Sunday school teacher talks about having strong principles.	I think about my principles when I have to make a hard decision.

Show You Know

In the space below, write a short, short story (just a paragraph!) using the Word Bank words. Be sure your sentences show that you understand the meanings of the words.

Once upon a time, ___________________________________

____

____

____

____

____

____

____

____

____

Ask a partner to read your story and check to see whether you used the Word Bank words correctly.
If not, discuss how to revise your story; then make the revisions.

Roots That Mean "To Lead": *duc, duct*

- The Word Bank word *conduct* means "to lead together" or "to guide or carry out." A *conductor* is someone who leads. *Conduction* is the act of leading. Other *duc* or *duct* words are *production*, *reduce*, and *introduction*.

Complete each sentence below by underlining the correct word in parentheses.

The repairman said he had to (conduct, conductor, conduction) an inspection of our house. He found that the electrical system was old and that the process of electricity (conduct, conductor, conduction) was not working properly. He suggested that we replace the wiring and the main supply (conduct, conductor, conduction).

The following words belong to the same word family. Underline the words that appear in the article.

Write About It!

You have read an article about smokejumpers. Now you will write about a hero you know. Read the writing prompt. It gives your writing assignment.

Writing Prompt

After reading "Leaping into the Fire," what other everyday heroes come to mind? Whom could you call a hero? Write a tribute to a heroic person you know, explaining the qualities and actions that make him or her a hero. Include relevant ideas from the article, if any, and at least one word from the Word Bank.

conduct • courage • determination • devise • inherent

WRITING RUBRIC

In your response, you should:

- Write a tribute to an everyday hero you know.

- Explain the qualities and actions that make the person a hero. Use ideas from the article to suggest heroic attributes.

- Use at least one word from the Word Bank.

- Use correct grammar, usage, and mechanics.

Prewrite It

Once you are sure you understand the prompt, plan what you want to say.

1. Review your notes from the class discussion. Jot down your thoughts on the organizer on the right. Write the name of the person in the center and heroic qualities in the points.

2. Reread the article. Look for qualities that might also apply to your hero. Add those to your organizer.

3. Take another look at your organizer. Read over the qualities you have included. Do they all describe your hero? If not, revise them.

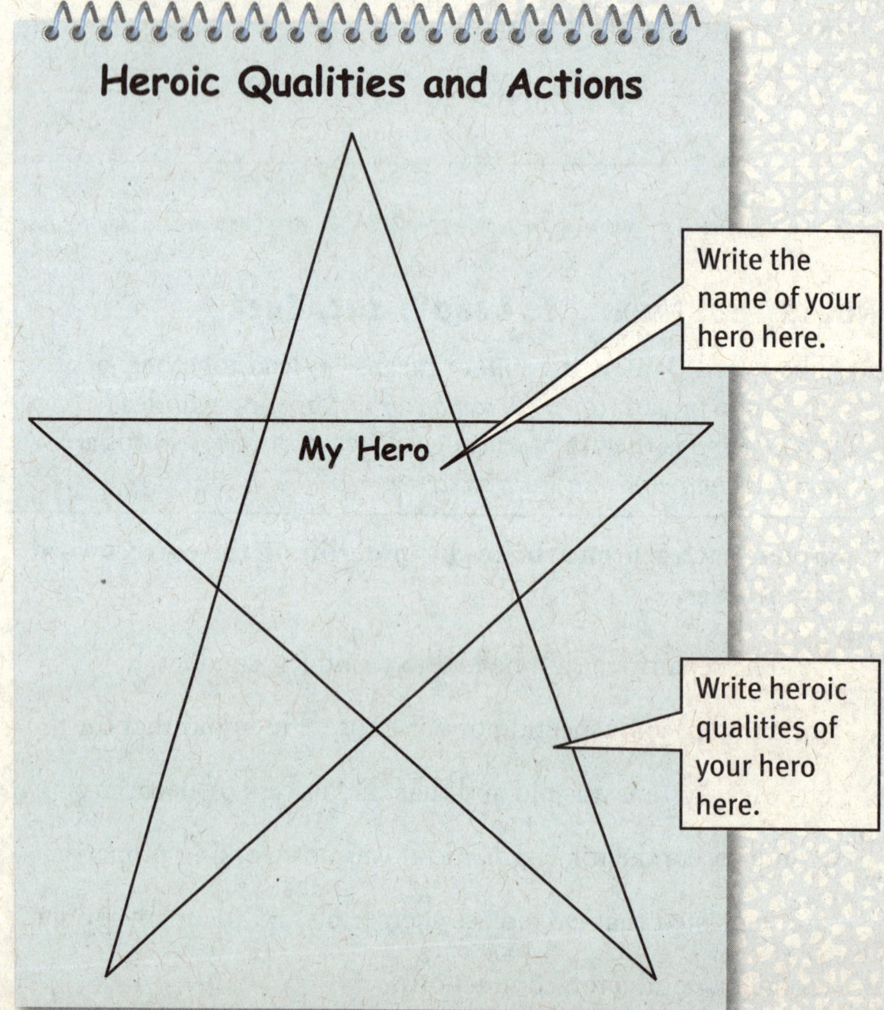

Draft It

Now use your organizer to draft, or write, your tribute to the hero you have selected. The writing frame below will help you.

1. Read the first sentence. Complete the sentence by writing the name of your hero.

2. Then finish the next sentence starter by explaining why you think this person is a hero. Be sure to include in your tribute any related ideas from the article.

The purpose of a tribute is to honor a person. Therefore, the language in a tribute is usually formal and positive. Read your tribute to a classmate. Does it sound formal? Is the language positive in tone? If not, discuss how you might reword your tribute to make it sound better.

My Hero

The hero I know is _____________. I think this person is heroic

because ____.

____

____

____

____

____

____

____

____.

✔ CHECKLIST

Evaluate your writing. A score of "5" is excellent. A score of "1" means you need to do more work. Then ask a partner to rate your writing.

1. **Does the tribute name an everyday hero?**

   Me: 1 2 3 4 5
   Partner: 1 2 3 4 5

2. **Does it clearly explain why this person is a hero?**

   Me: 1 2 3 4 5
   Partner: 1 2 3 4 5

3. **Is there at least one word from the Word Bank?**

   Me: 1 2 3 4 5
   Partner: 1 2 3 4 5

4. **Are grammar, usage, and mechanics correct?**

   Me: 1 2 3 4 5
   Partner: 1 2 3 4 5

Check It and Fix It

After you have written your tribute, check your work. Try to read it with a "fresh eye," as if you have never before seen it.

1. Is everything written clearly and correctly? Use the checklist on the right to decide.

2. Trade tributes with a classmate. Discuss ways to improve your tributes. Use the ideas to revise your work.

3. For help with grammar, usage, and mechanics, go to the Handbook on pages 189–231.

Vocabulary Workshop

Add these words to your personal word bank by
practicing them.

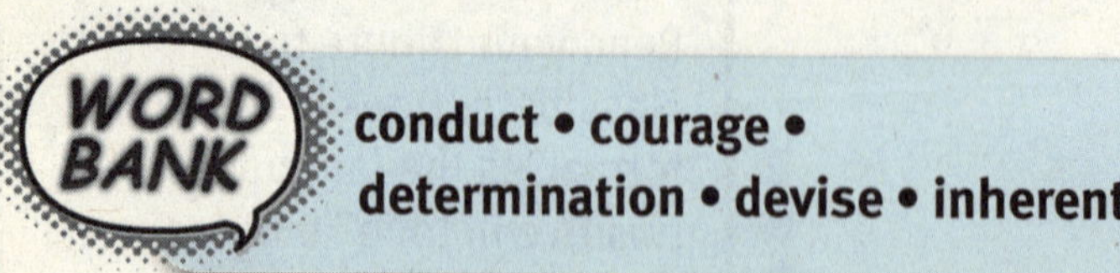

Define It

Complete the chart below using the Word Bank words. First, tell
what the word means. Then tell what the word does not mean.
Use the example as a guide.

Word	What It Is	What It Is Not
courage	the quality of being brave	being fearful or afraid

Show You Know

To show that you understand the Word Bank words, write a clue for
each word. Exchange clues with a partner. See whether your partner
can identify the correct word for each clue.

1. ____

2. ____

3. ____

4. ____

5. ____

Word Sort

Organize the Word Bank words into categories. Sort them by
prefixes and suffixes, and add them to the chart below. Then scan
the article for other words that have the same prefixes and suffixes
and add them to the correct columns. The first column is started
for you.

Prefix *con-*	Suffix *-tion*	Suffix *-age*
conduct control contain		

The Sport Entertainment Hero

Write About It!

You have read an article about sport entertainment heroes.
Now you will write about the topic. Read the writing prompt.
It gives your writing assignment.

In your response, you should:

- Give your opinion about whether a celebrity of your choice is a hero.

- Support your opinion with reasons from the article or real life.

- Use at least one word from the Word Bank.

- Use correct grammar, usage, and mechanics.

Writing Prompt

Do you think entertainers can also be real heroes?
Choose a celebrity whom teens look up to. The person
could be a professional wrestler or a different kind of
entertainer, such as a singer or actor. Write a paragraph
giving your opinion about whether or not this person is
a real hero. Support your opinion with reasons from the
article or real life, and use at least one word from the
Word Bank.

character • honor • legendary • persevere • principles

Prewrite It

Once you are sure you understand
the prompt, plan what you want
to say.

1. Review your notes from the
   class discussion. Jot down your
   thoughts on the organizer on
   the right.

2. Reread the article. Look for
   examples of entertainment
   heroes and reasons why they are
   or are not real heroes. Add the
   examples and reasons to your
   organizer.

3. Now take another look at your
   organizer. Reread your notes.
   Do you have ideas to write a
   paragraph? If not, brainstorm
   with a partner.

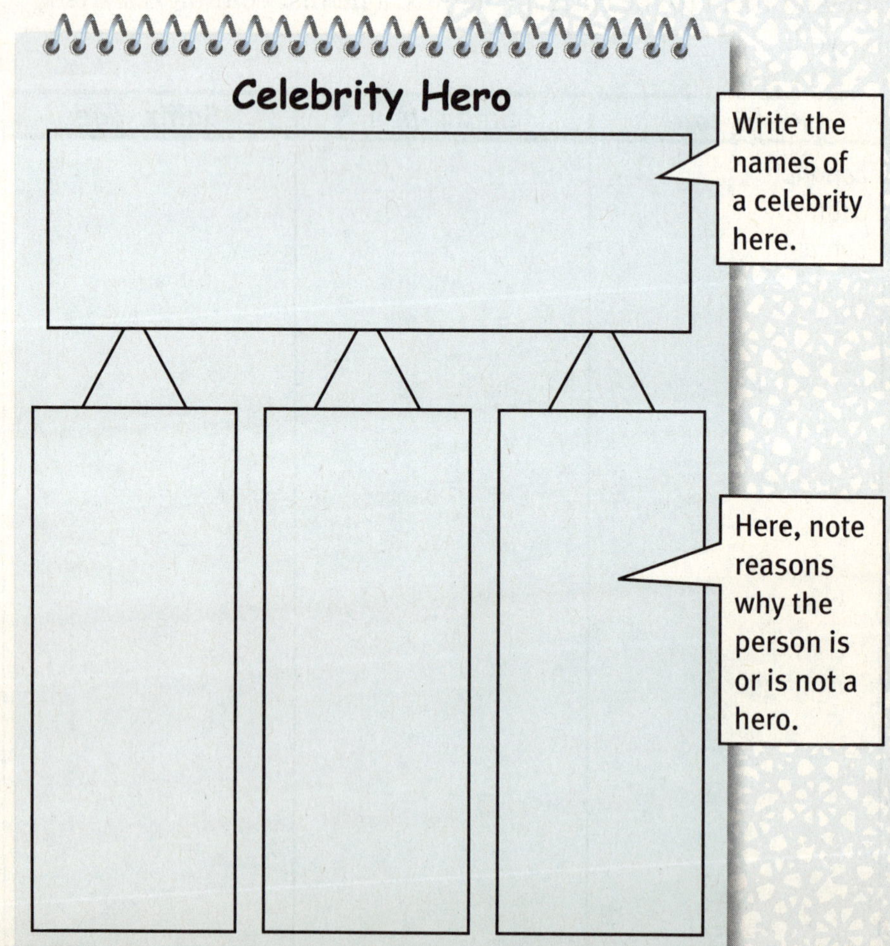

Draft It

Now use your organizer to draft, or write, your opinion paragraph.
The writing frame below will help you.

1. Start by completing the first sentence starter. Give the name of
   a celebrity hero.

2. Then complete the second sentence starter by underlining your
   opinion and supporting it with reasons and examples. Your
   supporting details may come from the article or from real life.

For an extra challenge,
end your paragraph with a
summary statement. Work
with a partner to write a last
sentence that sums up the
main idea.

Celebrity Heroes?

Some kids think that ______________ is a hero. I, for one, (agree,

disagree), because ____

____

____

____

____

____

____

____

____

____ .

✔ CHECKLIST

Evaluate your writing.
A score of "5" is excellent.
A score of "1" means you
need to do more work.
Then ask a partner to rate
your writing.

1. **Does the paragraph
   clearly state an opinion
   about whether a celebrity
   is a hero?**

   Me: 1 2 3 4 5
   Partner: 1 2 3 4 5

2. **Does the paragraph
   include related ideas
   from the article or from
   real life?**

   Me: 1 2 3 4 5
   Partner: 1 2 3 4 5

3. **Is there at least one word
   from the Word Bank?**

   Me: 1 2 3 4 5
   Partner: 1 2 3 4 5

4. **Are grammar, usage, and
   mechanics correct?**

   Me: 1 2 3 4 5
   Partner: 1 2 3 4 5

Check It and Fix It

After you have written your opinion paragraph, check your work.
Try to read your paragraph as if you have never before seen it.

1. Is everything written clearly and correctly? Use the checklist on the
   right to decide.

2. Trade paragraphs with a classmate. Talk over ways you might
   improve your paragraphs. Use the ideas to revise your work.

3. For help with grammar, usage, and mechanics, go to the Handbook
   on pages 189–231.

Vocabulary Workshop

Add these words to your personal word bank by
practicing them.

**character • honor • legendary •
persevere • principles**

Define It

Fill in the chart. In the center oval, write two or three subjects you
could write about using the Word Bank words.

Your Choice

What other new words in
the article would you like
to remember? List them.

____

____

____

What It Means	What It Means	What It Means
	Subjects:	
What It Means		**What It Means**

Show You Know

Write a comic strip in the space below. Use all the Word Bank words in a way that shows you understand their meanings.

Context Clues

Often you can figure out what unfamiliar words mean by using context clues. The *context* of a word is the way it is used in a sentence and in other nearby sentences. What clue or clues tell what the word *persevere* means in this sentence?

- I wanted to quit, but Mom convinced me to persevere and keep trying.

From the clues "wanted to quit, but" and "keep trying," you can guess that *persevere* means "to refuse to give up in spite of difficulties."

Underline the context clues in each sentence that tell what the boldface word means.

1. Amy dislikes the new kid's **character** because she thinks his personality is phony.

2. The civil servant agreed to **honor** her promise to the state by carrying out all her duties well.

3. Many climbers admire the **legendary** skills and feats of the first man who scaled Mt. Everest.

4. A code of behavior often includes **principles** to live by and believe in.

Writing Reflection

Can anyone be a hero?

Look through your writing from this unit and choose the best piece. Reflect on this piece of writing by completing each sentence below.

My best piece of writing from this unit is _______________________________

____

I chose this piece because ____

____

____

While I was writing, one goal I had was _____________________________________

____

I accomplished this goal by ____

____

____

This writing helped me think more about the Big Question because

____

____

One thing I learned while writing that can help me in the future is

____

____

GRAMMAR, USAGE, AND MECHANICS HANDBOOK

Nouns

A **noun** names a person, a place, or a thing.

Person: <u>Mona</u> is a <u>student</u>.
Place: My <u>school</u> is <u>Harrison High School</u>.
Thing: That <u>article</u> is about <u>baseball</u>.

Regular Plurals

A **singular noun** names a person, a place, or a thing.
A **plural noun** names more than one person, place, or thing.
To form the plural of most nouns, add –*s* to the end of the noun.

Singular	Plural
one teenager	two teenager<u>s</u>
this computer	these computer<u>s</u>
that government	those government<u>s</u>
a site	many site<u>s</u>

A noncount noun, which names something you cannot count, does not have a plural form. Some common noncount nouns are *clothing, equipment, furniture, information, knowledge,* and *water*.

Exercise: Regular Plurals

Highlight and fix the seven mistakes in noun plurals.

(1) There are many camp that kids can attend in the summer.

(2) A circus camp is fun. **(3)** Campers can learn several thing. **(4)** Riding the unicycle, clowning, and juggling are skill that campers can learn.

(5) Kid can also learn timing and balance. **(6)** Some camps meet five day a week. **(7)** Other camps meet every day. **(8)** These days, camps can be expensive. **(9)** Most parent do not complain about the cost. **(10)** They know that circus equipments is expensive, and they are happy to pay for their kids to gain knowledge.

Nouns continued

Special Noun Plurals

To make some nouns plural, you need to do more than add an *-s* ending.
Use the chart to figure out how to spell these plurals.

Singular Noun Ending	Singular	Plural
When a noun ends in *ch, s, sh, x,* or *z,* add *-es.*	a lun**ch** one dre**ss** that di**sh** this bo**x** each walt**z**	two lunch**es** many dress**es** those dish**es** these box**es** several waltz**es**
When a noun ends in a consonant + *y,* change the *y* to *i* and add *-es.*	a coun**try** one pen**ny** every **city**	many count**ries** several pen**nies** ten ci**ties**
When a noun ends in *f* or *fe,* change the *f* to *v* and add *-es.* Note exceptions to this rule.	this lea**f** one kni**fe** a chie**f** one roo**f**	these lea**ves** two kni**ves** several chief**s** many roof**s**
When a noun ends in a consonant + *o,* add *-es.* Note exceptions to this rule.	that he**ro** a pota**to** one pi**ano** an au**to**	those hero**es** a dozen potato**es** many piano**s** several auto**s**

Do not use an apostrophe to form the plural of a noun.
Wrong: many belief's   **Right:** many beliefs

Exercise: Special Noun Plurals

Highlight the misspelled noun plural in each sentence. Then fix the spelling
mistake. Use the chart or a dictionary for help.

(1) School lunchs have become more healthful. (2) Some school policys
require cafeterias to have salad bars. (3) Students can top their salads with
tomatos. (4) Sandwich's are made with grilled chicken rather than fried
chicken. (5) In fact, very few dishs are fried. (6) Cafeterias are now serving
loafs of high-fiber bread. (7) The goal is to help students live healthful lifes.
(8) Girls and boyes should eat three healthful meals a day.

Nouns continued

Irregular Plurals

Some plural nouns do not follow the rules. Memorize common **irregular plural nouns** like the ones below.

Singular	Plural
one <u>man</u>	two <u>men</u>
a <u>woman</u>	many <u>women</u>
this <u>person</u>	these <u>people</u>
that <u>child</u>	those <u>children</u>

Exercise: Irregular Plurals

Highlight and fix the misspelled irregular plural in each sentence.

(1) Many peoples try to climb Mount Everest. **(2)** Two womans set out on an expedition today. **(3)** Recently, some mens were rescued after a blizzard.

(4) No childs have climbed Everest; the youngest climber was sixteen.

Possessive Nouns

A **possessive noun** shows ownership or relationship.

Ownership: John's coat = a coat that belongs to John

To make the possessive of a singular noun, add an apostrophe and an -*s*.
To make a regular noun plural possessive, add an -*s* and an apostrophe.
Singular: that boy<u>'s</u> basketball **Plural:** the boys<u>'</u> basketball team

The plurals of irregular nouns do not end in -*s*. Add an apostrophe and an -*s* to make them possessive.
Wrong: childrens<u>'</u> shoes   **Right:** children<u>'s</u> shoes

Exercise: Possessive Nouns

Highlight and fix the mistake in possessive nouns in each sentence.

(1) Lynns parents were nervous about her trip to Everest. **(2)** A few friend's went with Lynn. **(3)** When a storm hit, they used Davids cell phone to call for help. **(4)** The mens' hands were frostbitten. **(5)** To the climbers relief, they were rescued.

Pronouns

A **pronoun** takes the place of a noun or another pronoun. The word that a pronoun refers to is its **antecedent** (an tuh SEE duhnt).

<u>Jamal</u> plays the guitar. <u>He</u> is also learning the drums.
Antecedent   Pronoun

Subject and Object Pronouns

Pronouns take different forms depending on how they are used in sentences. A **subject pronoun** tells who or what a sentence is about. An **object pronoun** receives the action in a sentence or comes after a preposition (a word like *for, from, in, on,* or *with*).

Subject Pronoun: <u>She</u> is a very fast swimmer.
Object Pronoun: The swim team gave <u>her</u> an award.
Object Pronoun: Swimming is fun for <u>her</u>.

	Singular Pronouns	Plural Pronouns
Used as Subjects	I you he, she, it	we you they
Used as Objects	me you him, her, it	us you them

Do not use self-ending pronouns as subject or object pronouns.
Wrong: She and <u>myself</u> are on the swim team.
Right: She and <u>I</u> are on the swim team.

Exercise: Subject and Object Pronouns

Underline the right pronoun form in each pair.

(1) Shark attacks are a concern; however, (they, them) are not as common as most people think. **(2)** Most people are terribly afraid of sharks, even though other animals pose a greater danger to (they, them). **(3)** When sharks are feeding, they may confuse (we, us) with prey. **(4)** The best thing for (we, us) to do is stay out of waters where sharks live.

Pronouns continued

Pronouns in Compounds

Pronouns can be joined together with the word *and*. These are called **compound pronouns**.

Compound: <u>Sam and I</u> went to a movie.
Compound: The movie was exciting to <u>Sam and me</u>.

If you are not sure whether a pronoun in a compound should be in the subject form or the object form, leave out the noun. You may "hear" which form is right.

Example: My dad cooked hamburgers for ~~my brother and~~ (I, <u>me</u>).

Exercise: Pronouns in Compounds

Highlight and fix the three pronoun mistakes.

(1) My best friend and me split the cost of a lottery ticket. **(2)** We agreed that the winnings would be shared equally between him and I. **(3)** He and I dreamed about what we would do with the money. **(4)** Imagining that we were rich was fun for him and me. **(5)** Everyone said that him and I could not win, but people were wrong about us. **(6)** He and I won!

Possessive Pronouns

Possessive pronouns show who owns something. They can be used to describe nouns or in place of possessive nouns.

	Singular	Plural
Describer	<u>my</u> book <u>your</u> book <u>his</u>, <u>her</u>, <u>its</u> book	<u>our</u> books <u>your</u> books <u>their</u> books
Noun Substitute	<u>Mine</u> has my name in it. Did you forget <u>yours</u>? <u>His</u> and <u>hers</u> are missing.	<u>Ours</u> are here. <u>Yours</u> are there. <u>Theirs</u> are missing.

Exercise: Possessive Pronouns

Highlight and fix the pronoun mistake in each sentence.

(1) Some of these trophies are mines. **(2)** Are those trophies your's?

(3) Some trophies are their. **(4)** Do you want to look at mine trophy?

(5) She should be proud of her's.

Pronouns continued

Demonstrative Pronouns

The words *this*, *that*, *these*, and *those* are **demonstrative pronouns.** They point to a specific person, place, or thing. *This* and *these* point to things near the speaker. *That* and *those* point to things farther away. *This* and *that* are singular. *These* and *those* are plural.

Never use *them* as a demonstrative pronoun.
Wrong: Bring me <u>them</u> books.
Right: Bring me <u>those</u> books.

Exercise: Demonstrative Pronouns

<u>Underline</u> the right pronoun to use in each pair.

(1) (This, That) movie theater is far away. **(2)** I would rather watch a movie at (this, that) theater, here. **(3)** Have you ever seen one of (them, those) 3-D movies? **(4)** (These, That) are the glasses that you wear to watch 3-D movies.

Indefinite Pronouns

Indefinite pronouns refer to people, places, or things that are not specifically identified. Some indefinite pronouns are always singular. Others are always plural.

Singular	anybody everybody no one	anyone everyone nothing	anything everything somebody	each neither someone	either nobody something
Plural	both	few	many	several	

Exercise: Indefinite Pronouns

Highlight the indefinite pronoun in each sentence. Write *S* above the pronoun if it is singular or *P* if it is plural.

(1) All were excited to skydive. **(2)** Nobody is volunteering to jump off the plane first. **(3)** Many are having second thoughts. **(4)** Anybody who wants to can stay on the plane. **(5)** Most are going to jump eventually.

(6) Each is aware of the risk. **(7)** Somebody is talking to the instructors.

(8) Both are very supportive.

Pronouns continued

Pronoun-Antecedent Agreement

A pronoun and its antecedent—the word the pronoun refers to—must **agree,** or match. To match in number, both must be singular or both must be plural.

Wrong: <u>Nobody</u> raised <u>their</u> hand.
    singular   plural

Right: <u>Nobody</u> raised <u>his or her</u> hand.
    singular   singular

	Singular	**Plural**
First person	<u>I</u> have <u>my</u> pen.	<u>We</u> have <u>our</u> pens.
Second person	<u>You</u> have <u>your</u> pen.	<u>You</u> have <u>your</u> pens.
Third person	<u>He</u> has <u>his</u> pen. <u>She</u> has <u>her</u> pen. <u>It</u> has <u>its</u> merits.	<u>They</u> have <u>their</u> pens. <u>They</u> have <u>their</u> pens. <u>They</u> have <u>their</u> merits.

To avoid using the phrase *his or her,* make the noun and the pronoun plural.

Singular: <u>Everybody</u> brought <u>his or her</u> ticket.

Plural: <u>All the students</u> brought <u>their</u> tickets.

Exercise: Pronoun-Antecedent Agreement

Highlight and fix the five pronoun mistakes in the paragraph.

(1) The class project is to make maple syrup; they will be fun. (2) Did everyone bring their coat to class today? (3) We will look for sugar maples. (4) Sugar maples can be identified by its bark, buds, and leaves. (5) Red maples also produce sap, but its sap is not as sweet. (6) Mrs. Donohoe will explain how to pick a tree, and then she will show how to drill a tap hole. (7) Did anybody forget their spout in the classroom? (8) Each student will collect sap daily from his or her pail.

Pronouns continued

Relative Pronouns

A **relative pronoun** is used to introduce a clause (a group of words containing a subject and its verb). The relative pronoun *relates* the clause to the rest of the sentence.

Relative Clause: Marisa is the student <u>who won the award</u>.

relative
pronoun

Relative Pronouns
who, whom, whose, whoever, whomever, which, what, that

Use relative pronouns to combine two or three short choppy sentences into one smooth sentence.

Choppy: The music is good. The music is on the radio.

Better: The music <u>that is on the radio</u> is good.

Exercise: Relative Pronouns

Use the relative pronoun in parentheses to combine each pair of sentences into one sentence.

1. (that) Folk tales are traditional stories. Folk tales change over time.

____.

2. (that) Urban myths are folk tales. Urban myths often reflect social problems.

____.

3. (who) Urban myths are created by imaginative people. Imaginative people make them up for many reasons.

____.

4. (who) Jan Harold Brunvand is an expert on urban myths. Jan Harold Brunvand has written several books about them.

____.

5. (which) Some urban myths are cautionary tales. Cautionary tales are stories that warn people about a potential danger.

____.

Verbs

A **verb** expresses action or links important parts of a sentence together. Every sentence has at least one verb. The verb is the main word or group of words in the **predicate** (PRE di kuht), which is the part of the sentence that tells about the subject.

Example: Bob <u>is</u> my brother.

The sentence is about Bob, so *Bob* is the subject. The verb *is* links *Bob* to *my brother*, which tells who Bob is. That makes *is* the verb in the predicate.

Example: Bob <u>writes</u> wonderful songs.

The sentence is about Bob, so *Bob* is the subject. The verb *writes* tells what Bob does, so *writes* is the predicate.

Action Verbs and Linking Verbs

Many **action verbs** name an action you can see—for example, *run, jump, smile.* Other action verbs name an action you cannot see—for example, *think, wonder, hope.* An action verb may stand alone with a subject to state a complete thought, or it may have an **object**—a person, place, or thing that receives the action.

Subject and Action Verb: <u>Darnella</u> <u>dances</u>.
                                  subject   verb

Subject, Action Verb, and Object: <u>Carmelita</u> <u>plays</u> piano.
                                  subject   verb object

Linking verbs do not show action. They connect subjects with complements. Complements help complete the thought that subjects and their linking verbs begin to express. The most common linking verbs are forms of *to be—am, is, are, was, were, being, been.*

Thought Seems Incomplete: <u>Terrell</u> <u>is</u>.

Thought Is Complete: <u>Terrell</u> <u>is</u> a <u>firefighter</u>.

Exercise: Action and Linking Verbs

Highlight each action verb. <u>Underline</u> each linking verb.

(1) Circus people depend on each other. (2) Trapeze artists hang from each other's ankles. (3) Clowns shoot each other out of cannons. (4) The performers fly through the air. (5) Mindy is a clown for a large circus.

(6) She teaches safety techniques to other clowns. (7) These techniques are important. (8) Performers cannot be too careful.

Verbs continued

Present Tense Verbs

The **tense** of a verb tells the time of an action or a state of being. It may tell when an action happened, happens, or will happen—in the past, the present, or the future. Use the **present tense** to express something that happens or exists in the present, happens regularly, or is always true.

Happens Regularly: I <u>enjoy</u> the sunset nearly every day.
Always True: The sun <u>sets</u> in the west.

Use the chart below to form the present tense of **regular verbs** (verbs that follow regular rules). Notice that the form of a present tense verb depends on the subject that goes with it. If the subject is *he, she,* or *it,* the verb ends in *-s.* If the subject is *I, you, we,* or *they,* the verb does not end in *-s.*

Singular	Plural
I <u>like</u> you <u>like</u> he, she, it <u>likes</u>	we <u>like</u> you <u>like</u> they <u>like</u>

If a subject is a noun and you are not sure which verb form to use, change the noun into the pronoun that could substitute for it. Then use the chart.

Noun Subject: <u>Victor</u> (like, likes) rap.
Pronoun Subject: *Victor = he.* <u>Victor</u> (like, <u>likes</u>) rap.

Exercise: Present Tense Verbs

Underline the right verb form in parentheses. Use the chart if you need to.

(1) Damian's grandfather (take, takes) him fishing every spring.

(2) Damian and his grandfather (prefer, prefers) to fish for salmon or trout.

(3) Damian (catch, catches) trout in streams and lakes near his home.

(4) He and his grandfather (travel, travels) several hours away to fish for salmon. **(5)** These fish (run, runs) up northern rivers in April. **(6)** They (return, returns) to the sea near the end of July. **(7)** In Oregon, trout season (begin, begins) at the end of April. **(8)** It (end, ends) at the end of October.

Verbs continued

Tricky Present Tense Verbs

Some verbs do not form the present tense in the regular way, by adding *-s*. The only way to learn tricky verbs like *have, do,* and *be* is to memorize them. Study the chart.

	To Have	**To Do**	**To Be**
Singular	I <u>have</u> (<u>haven't</u>) you <u>have</u> (<u>haven't</u>) he, she, it <u>has</u> (<u>hasn't</u>)	I <u>do</u> (<u>don't</u>) you <u>do</u> (<u>don't</u>) he, she, it <u>does</u> (<u>doesn't</u>)	I <u>am</u> (<u>I'm not</u>) you <u>are</u> (<u>aren't</u>) he, she, it <u>is</u> (<u>isn't</u>)
Plural	we <u>have</u> (<u>haven't</u>) you <u>have</u> (<u>haven't</u>) they <u>have</u> (<u>haven't</u>)	we <u>do</u> (<u>don't</u>) you <u>do</u> (<u>don't</u>) they <u>do</u> (<u>don't</u>)	We <u>are</u> (<u>aren't</u>) you <u>are</u> (<u>aren't</u>) they <u>are</u> (<u>aren't</u>)

These tricky verbs can stand alone as **main verbs**, or they can be helping verbs. A **helping verb** helps a main verb express when an action happened or a situation existed.

Main Verb: Sinclair <u>has</u> a cell phone.
Helping Verb + Main Verb: Sinclair <u>has</u> <u>called</u> me on her phone.

Avoid using *ain't.*
Wrong: I <u>ain't</u> tired.   **Right:** I <u>am</u> <u>not</u> tired. OR <u>I'm</u> <u>not</u> tired.

Exercise: Tricky Present Tense Verbs

Highlight and fix the six verb mistakes in the paragraph.

(1) My parents does not know much about computers. **(2)** Computer problems do not bother me. **(3)** I ain't afraid to work with computer programs. **(4)** Unless the problems is with the hard drive, I can figure out what to do. **(5)** Lately, our computer have been freezing up a lot. **(6)** Unfortunately, we has spyware on our computer. **(7)** My parents was upset to hear this. **(8)** They have warned me not to play games over the Internet.

Verbs continued

Agreement with Compound Subjects

A **compound subject** is two or more subjects joined by the word *and* or *or.*
When the subjects are joined by *and,* the compound subject is plural. To
match, or agree, the verb must be in the plural form. When the subjects
are joined by *or,* the verb must agree with the subject closer to it, whether
singular or plural.

Compound with *And:* <u>Benoit and I</u> (am, is, <u>are</u>) friends.
Compound with *Or:* Benoit or <u>I</u> (<u>am</u>, is, are) happy to help.
Compound with *Or:* I or <u>Benoit</u> (am, <u>is</u>, are) happy to help.

Exercise: Agreement with Compound Subjects

Highlight and fix the three verb mistakes.

(1) Derrick and Hillary are in the school musical. (2) Derrick or Favian

have been selected for the lead role. (3) The chorus director or the theater

teacher know which. (4) You and I have heard Derrick and Favian.

(5) Samantha and I am working on the stage crew.

Agreement in Questions

In most questions, all or part of the verb comes before the subject. Make
sure the verb at the beginning of a question agrees with the subject.

Statement: <u>Thomasina</u> <u>is</u> <u>going</u> to the party.
           subject   **verb**

Question: <u>Is</u> <u>Thomasina</u> <u>going</u> to the party?
       verb   **subject**   **verb**

Exercise: Agreement in Questions

For each sentence, underline the right verb form in parentheses.

1. (Are, Is) you still collecting Spiderman comic books?

2. How (do, does) Peter Parker turn into Spiderman?

3. (Do, Does) you know how he does it?

4. (Have, Has) Parker's superpowers caused problems for him?

5. Where (do, does) the Parkers live?

Verbs continued

Past and Perfect Tenses

Use the **past tense** of a verb to show that something has already happened. To form the past tense of a regular verb, add an *-ed* ending.

Past: Yesterday, Lucie <u>called</u> me on her new phone.

Use the **present perfect tense** to show that something began in the past and is still happening or happened at an indefinite time in the past. To form the present perfect, use the helping verb *has* or *have*.

Present Perfect: People <u>have</u> <u>used</u> cell phones since the 1970s.

Use the **past perfect tense** to show that something happened before another action in the past. To form the past perfect, use the helping verb *had*.

Past Perfect: I <u>had</u> already <u>walked</u> out the door when Lucie called.

	Present Perfect *Have* or *has* + verb + *-ed*	**Past Perfect** *had* + verb + *-ed*
Singular	I <u>have</u> <u>walked</u> you <u>have</u> <u>walked</u> he, she, or it <u>has</u> <u>walked</u>	I <u>had</u> <u>walked</u> you <u>had</u> <u>walked</u> he, she, or it <u>had</u> <u>walked</u>
Plural	we <u>have</u> <u>walked</u> you <u>have</u> <u>walked</u> they <u>have</u> <u>walked</u>	we <u>had</u> <u>walked</u> you <u>had</u> <u>walked</u> they <u>had</u> <u>walked</u>

Remember to make the helping verb agree in number with the subject.

Wrong: <u>Haven't</u> <u>he</u> listened to the news?

Right: <u>Hasn't</u> <u>he</u> listened to the news?

Exercise: Past and Perfect Tenses

Highlight and fix the verb mistake in each sentence.

(1) For many years, Jeremy has want to be a firefighter. **(2)** When his family had a kitchen fire, he watches the firefighters work. **(3)** One firefighter rescue Jeremy's dog. **(4)** By the time they have put out the fire, neighbors filled the street. **(5)** Everyone call the firefighters heroes.

(6) Jeremy and his parents visit the fire department to say thank you.

Verbs continued

Irregular Verbs: Past and Perfect of *To Be*

Irregular verbs do not take an *-ed* ending to form the past and perfect tenses. The most irregular verb in English is *to be*.

	Past Tense	Present Perfect Tense
Singular	I <u>was</u> (wasn't) you <u>were</u> (weren't) he, she it <u>was</u> (wasn't)	I <u>have</u> (haven't) <u>been</u> you <u>have</u> (haven't) <u>been</u> he, she, it <u>has</u> (hasn't) <u>been</u>
Plural	we <u>were</u> (weren't) you <u>were</u> (weren't) they <u>were</u> (weren't)	we <u>have</u> (haven't) <u>been</u> you <u>have</u> (haven't) <u>been</u> they <u>have</u> (haven't) <u>been</u>

	Past Perfect Tense
Singular	I <u>had</u> (hadn't) <u>been</u> you <u>had</u> (hadn't) <u>been</u> he, she, it <u>had</u> (hadn't) <u>been</u>
Plural	we <u>had</u> (hadn't) <u>been</u> you <u>had</u> (hadn't) <u>been</u> they <u>had</u> (hadn't) <u>been</u>

Exercise: Irregular Verbs: Past and Perfect of *To Be*

Highlight and fix the six verb mistakes.

(1) I were excited to see Minuella. **(2)** For weeks, we has been too busy to get together. **(3)** For the first hour, our visit were boring. **(4)** She was more interested in playing video games than talking. **(5)** If it have not been for her mother, I would have left. **(6)** She told Minuella that she weren't being polite. **(7)** At first, Minuella was angry. **(8)** Then she said, "If I has been rude, I am sorry."

Irregular Verbs 2: Past and Perfect That Stay the Same

Some irregular verbs keep the same form for every tense. The most common are *cost, cut, hit, let, put, read, set,* and *shut*.

Present: I <u>read</u> every day.
Past: Yesterday, I <u>read</u> the sports pages.
Present Perfect: I <u>have</u> <u>read</u> ten books this year.
Past Perfect: My mom gave me a book, but I <u>had</u> already <u>read</u> it.

Verbs continued

Irregular Verbs 3: Past and Perfect That Change Vowels

Some irregular verbs change only a vowel to go from present tense to past or perfect. Others add *-n* or *-en* to form the perfect tenses.

Present Tense	Past Tense	Perfect Tenses (has, have, had)
become	became	become
begin	began	begun
break	broke	broken
come	came	come
drink	drank	drunk
drive	drove	driven
forget	forgot	forgotten
give	gave	given
grow	grew	grown
know	knew	known
ride	rode	ridden
ring	rang	rung
rise	rose	risen
run	ran	run
see	saw	seen
sing	sang	sung
sit	sat	sat
speak	spoke	spoken
swim	swam	swum
write	wrote	written

Exercise: Irregular Verbs 3: Past and Perfect That Change Vowels

Highlight and fix the verb mistake in each sentence.

(1) I knowed that the wrestling match was today. **(2)** I had forgot to ask Mom if I could go. **(3)** Before I got on the bus, my cell phone ringed. **(4)** She had saw the wrestling schedule. **(5)** She know that I wanted to see my boyfriend's match. **(6)** As soon as I sitted down, I saw André. **(7)** He looked around to see if I had came. **(8)** André smiled when he seen me.

Verbs continued

Irregular Verbs 4: Past and Perfect That Change Completely

Some verbs change their form completely to form the past or perfect tenses.
Many of them (like *bring* and *buy*) have the same form for both past and
perfect tenses. A few (like *do* and *fly*) change to different forms for past and
perfect tenses.

Present Tense	Past Tense	Perfect Tenses (has, have, had)
bring	brought	brought
buy	bought	bought
catch	caught	caught
do	did	done
fight	fought	fought
find	found	found
fly	flew	flown
go	went	gone
sell	sold	sold
take	took	taken
teach	taught	taught
think	thought	thought

Exercise: Irregular Verbs 4: Past and Perfect That Change Completely

Highlight and fix the verb mistake in each sentence.

(1) Have you ever buyed anything on eBay? (2) My mom teached me
how to place a bid. (3) I was a little nervous the first time I done it.

(4) Since then, I have bought items on eBay, and I have selled a few things.

(5) Many times, I have finded gifts to buy for my friends. (6) My parents
thunk I paid a good price. (7) I catched my cousin looking at a set of DVDs
of his favorite TV show. (8) I telled my aunt and uncle about it. (9) They
boughten the DVDs for David's birthday. (10) David was so excited, he
brang them over to show me.

Verbs continued

Verbs as Describers

Certain verb forms can act as describers. These **verbals** describe nouns or pronouns. Verbals can end in *-ing, -ed*, or, when the verb is irregular, the perfect form. Be sure to use the right ending or form.

Verbal with *-ing* ending: A freezing rain fell.

Verbal with *-ed* ending: Chantel wore faded jeans.

Verbal in Perfect Form: Her jacket has a broken zipper.

Exercise: Verbs as Describers

Highlight and fix the four mistakes in verbals.

(1) Yesterday, we had an old-fashion barbecue. (2) Alesha made grill chicken. (3) Roberto made bake potatoes. (4) I accidentally made flaming marshmallows! (5) For dessert, we had freshly pick strawberries.

Future Tense

The **future tense** shows that an action will happen some time in the future. To form the future tense, use the helping verb *will* and a main verb.

Present: I walk to school every day.

Future: I will walk to soccer practice after school today.

Exercise: Future Tense

Change each underlined verb to future tense.

1. We _____________ take the SATs next fall.

2. The school _____________ give us practice tests.

3. We _____________ register for the SAT in the guidance office.

4. We _____________ get our results a month later.

5. When we apply to colleges, they _____________ consider our SAT results.

6. I _____________ do my best on the SAT.

7. I _____________ try to answer all the questions.

8. I _____________ go to bed early the night before the test.

Verbs continued

Progressive Tenses

The **progressive tense** shows that something is in progress, or still happening. To form present and past progressive, use a form of *to be* and a main verb with an *-ing* ending. To form the future progressive, add the future-tense helping verb *will*.

Present Progressive: I <u>am</u> <u>biking</u>.
Past Progressive: I <u>was</u> <u>biking</u>.
Future Progressive: I <u>will be</u> <u>biking</u>.

Exercise: Progressive Tenses

Write a sentence to answer each question below. Make sure your answers are in the correct tenses.

1. What are you reading for your book report in English class?

____

2. What movie were you watching when I called last evening?

____

3. When will you be eating dinner tonight?

____

Modals

Modals are a kind of helping verb. They include *can, could, will, would, must, should, may, might,* and *ought to*. A main verb paired with a modal never takes an *-ed* or *-s* ending. It does not change form.

Wrong: I <u>should</u> **called** him.   **Right:** I <u>should</u> **call** him.
Wrong: She <u>can</u> **sings**.   **Right:** She <u>can</u> **sing**.

Exercise: Modals

Highlight and fix the five mistakes in verbs.

(1) You should spends the night at my house on Friday. **(2)** You could

rided the bus home with me. **(3)** We ought to see a movie. **(4)** My mom

can drops us off at the theater. **(5)** She must take my brother to work first.

(6) Serena might meets us at the movies. **(7)** I will calls her to find out if she

is coming.

Adjectives

Adjectives describe nouns and pronouns. Adjectives answer these questions: *Which one? What kind? How many? How much?*

Which One: The <u>blue</u> coat is mine.

What Kind: It is a <u>wool</u> coat.

How Many: I own <u>two</u> coats.

How Much: That is <u>enough</u> coats for anyone.

Articles

The most often used adjectives are *a, an,* and *the. The* is called a **definite article** because it is used to refer to a particular person, place, or thing. *A* and *an* are called **indefinite articles** because they do not refer to a particular person, place, or thing.

Definite Article: Buy your ticket from <u>the</u> man in the booth.

Indefinite Article: <u>A</u> ticket costs $10.

Use *a* with words that begin with a consonant sound. Use *an* with words that begin with a vowel sound. (It is the *sound* that matters, not the spelling.)

A: <u>a</u> car, <u>a</u> song, <u>a</u> unit (*u* with the consonant *y* sound)

An: <u>an</u> ant, <u>an</u> olive, <u>an</u> umbrella (*u* with the vowel *u* sound)

Use *a* or *an* if the noun can be counted. Use *the* if the noun cannot be counted. **Example:** I spilled <u>a</u> cup of coffee. (You can count a cup.) I spilled <u>the</u> coffee. (You cannot count coffee that is not in a cup.)

Exercise: Articles

Highlight and fix the mistake in articles in each sentence.

1. My brother has a aquarium in his room.

2. He has an neon tetra or two.

3. A colors of those fish are so bright.

4. It's an kick to watch them swim around.

5. He also has a angelfish.

6. It has to be kept separate from a tetras, or it will fight them.

7. His old aquarium broke, and a water went everywhere.

Adjectives continued

Adjectives That Compare

Adjectives can be used to make comparisons. Use the **comparative** (kuhm PER uh tiv) **adjective** form to compare two people, places, or things. To form the comparative of one-syllable adjectives and many two-syllable adjectives, add -*er*. To form the comparative of adjectives of three or more syllables, add the word *more* or *less* in front of the adjective.

One-Syllable Adjective: Sara is <u>younger</u> than I am.
Three-Syllable Adjective: I am <u>more</u> <u>athletic</u> than she is.

Use the **superlative** (soo PUHR luh tiv) **adjective** form to compare three or more people, places, or things. To form the superlative of one-syllable adjectives and many two-syllable adjectives, add -*est*. To form the superlative of adjectives of three or more syllables, add the word *most* or *least* in front of the adjective.

One-Syllable Adjective: Caryn is the <u>oldest</u> girl in our family.
Three-Syllable Adjective: She is our <u>most</u> <u>talented</u> musician.

Exercise: Adjectives That Compare

Fill in each blank with the right form of the adjective in parentheses.

1. Mt. Everest is the _______________ mountain in the world. **(tall)**

2. No American _______________ than Samantha Larson has reached the top. **(young)**

3. Samantha is _______________ than a girl from Nepal who reached the summit. **(old)**

4. A 71-year-old Japanese man is said to be the _______________ person to climb Mt. Everest. **(old)**

5. Sir Edmund Hillary is the _______________ person to climb the mountain. **(famous)**

6. Mountain climbing is _______________ than skiing. **(dangerous)**

7. My friend Mudar is _______________ than I am. **(brave)**

8. I am _______________ than my best friend. **(adventurous)**

Adjectives continued

Irregular Adjectives

Not all adjectives form comparisons in regular ways. The chart shows how
to form common irregular adjectives.

Adjective	Comparative	Superlative
good, well	better	best
bad	worse	worst
many, much	more	most
little	less	least

Exercise: Irregular Adjectives

Fill in each blank with the right form of the adjective in parentheses.

1. I feel _________________ today than I did yesterday. **(bad)**

2. This is the _________________ cold I have ever had. **(bad)**

3. I have missed _________________ days of school than my sisters. **(many)**

4. I am usually the _________________ student. **(good)**

5. I usually miss the _________________ amount of school. **(little)**

Double Comparisons

Never use *more* or *most* with an adjective that ends with *-er* or *-est*.
This mistake in grammar is called a **double comparison.**

Wrong: My hometown is the <u>most</u> <u>bestest</u> place on earth.
Right: My hometown is the <u>best</u> place on earth.

Wrong: It is <u>more</u> <u>warmer</u> here than in Miami.
Right: It is <u>warmer</u> here than in Miami.

Exercise: Double Comparisons

Highlight and fix the three adjective mistakes.

(1) I like math more better than English. **(2)** To me, balancing equations
is more interesting than reading poems. **(3)** The most worstest problems
in math class are story problems. **(4)** They are more harder than any other
kind. **(5)** When I get an answer right, I am the proudest student in class.

Adverbs

Adverbs describe verbs, adjectives, and other adverbs. Adverbs answer these questions: *How? When? Where? How much? How often?*

How: Jim spoke <u>quietly</u>.

When: He is <u>never</u> loud.

Where: He arrived <u>here</u> at five o'clock.

How Much: He was <u>too</u> late.

How Often: He <u>usually</u> arrives at four o'clock.

The *-ly* Adverb Ending

Many adverbs are formed by adding *-ly* to the end of an adjective.

Example: quiet + ly = quietly

Not all adverbs end in *-ly,* however, and not every word that ends in *-ly* is an adverb. For example, the word *friendly* ends in *-ly*, but it is an adjective, not an adverb.

The word *real* is an adjective. The word *really* is an adverb. Use *really* when you are describing an adjective.

Wrong: Sherelle is <u>real</u> happy.

Right: Sherelle is <u>really</u> happy.

Exercise: The *-ly* Adverb Ending

Add *-ly* to each adjective in parentheses to form an adverb.

1. The receiver ran _________________ down the field. **(graceful)**

2. The fans cheered _________________. **(wild)**

3. He _________________ neared the end zone. **(quick)**

4. He _________________ placed the football in the end zone. **(happy)**

5. Then he _________________ called out to the fans. **(joyous)**

6. They _________________ chanted his name. **(repeated)**

7. I _________________ do not enjoy football games. **(usual)**

8. However, I _________________ enjoyed this game. **(real)**

Adverbs continued

Good and Well

Use the adjective *good* to describe people, places, and things.

Example: That is a good song.

Use *well* as an adverb to describe action verbs and adjectives. Use *well* as an adjective to describe someone's health.

Example: The band played well.

Example: Jen felt well after a good night's rest.

Exercise: *Good* and *Well*

Highlight and fix the two mistakes in the use of *good* and *well*.

(1) Janelle did not feel good. **(2)** Therefore, she did not sing good.

(3) She did write one good song, however.

Double Negatives

Do not form a **double negative** by using two negative words in one clause. The adverb *not* is negative. Also negative are contractions that contain the word *not* (*can't, don't, haven't, isn't, wasn't, wouldn't,* and so on).

To fix a double negative, change one of the negatives into a positive, or drop one of the negative words.

Wrong: I don't have no money.
Right: I don't have any money. OR I have no money.

Negatives	Positives
never	ever
nobody, no one	somebody, someone
none	some
nothing	something, anything
nowhere	somewhere
hardly, barely	

Exercise: Double Negatives

Highlight and fix the double negative in each sentence.

(1) Ben didn't have hardly any time. **(2)** He couldn't stop for nothing.

(3) I didn't have no spare time either.

Prepositions

A **preposition** (pre puh ZI shuhn) shows the relationship between a noun
or pronoun and another word in a sentence.
The stars shone <u>above</u> us.
We sat <u>on</u> a bench <u>beside</u> the lake.

Prepositions					
about	among	beneath	for	on	under
above	around	beside	from	onto	underneath
across	at	between	in	over	until
after	before	beyond	into	through	with
against	behind	by	near	to	within
along	below	during	of	toward	without

Prepositional Phrases

A **prepositional phrase** is a group of words that go together and that begin
with a preposition and end with a noun or pronoun. The noun or pronoun
at the end of the phrase is called the **object of the preposition.**

Prepositional Phrase: The moon rose <u>over the calm lake</u>.
preposition   object

Exercise: Prepositional Phrases

<u>Underline</u> the prepositional phrase in each sentence below.

1. Last year, I ran for class president.

2. I got help from my friends.

3. They hung campaign posters in the school hallways.

4. After school, they distributed campaign flyers.

5. They helped me write speeches about my plans.

6. I would have lost the election without their help.

7. I will always be grateful to them.

8. One of my friends is the new class president.

Conjunctions

Conjunctions (kuhn JUHNG shuhns) connect, or join, words or groups of words. There are three kinds of conjunctions:

1. coordinating

2. correlative

3. subordinating

Coordinating Conjunctions

Coordinating (koh AWR duh nay ting) **conjunctions** connect similar words or groups of words. They can link parts of sentences or whole sentences. The coordinating conjunctions are as follows:

Coordinating Conjunctions
and, but, for, nor, or, so, yet

Coordinating Conjunctions: and, but, for, nor, or, so, yet
Sentence Parts: Kim and her mom went on a trip.
Sentences: They went to Ohio, and they saw the Columbus Zoo.

Exercise: Coordinating Conjunctions

Highlight the coordinating conjunction in each sentence.

1. I like all holidays, but Independence Day is my favorite.

2. My cousins come to my house, or we go to theirs.

3. We always eat hamburgers, potato salad, and watermelon.

4. I do not mean to overeat, yet I always do.

5. I cannot cook, nor do I want to learn how.

6. I am spoiled, for everyone else in my family can cook.

7. Our parents are against fireworks, so we never have any.

8. We go to the park, and we watch the fireworks show.

Conjunctions continued

Subordinating Conjunctions

A **subordinating** (suh BOR duh nay ting) **conjunction** introduces and connects a subordinate clause to a main clause.

Subordinating Conjunctions			
after	because	since	until
although	before	so that	when
as	even though	than	where
as if	if	though	whereas
as though	in order that	unless	while

Example: While we were in Chicago, we visited museums.
        subordinate clause   main clause

Exercise: Subordinating Conjunctions

Highlight the subordinating conjunction in each sentence and underline the subordinate clause.

(1) Though Leticia is my twin, we are very different. **(2)** I like sports, whereas she likes music. **(3)** When she sings, I cover my ears. **(4)** I act as if she is the worst singer on earth. **(5)** I tease her just because she is my sister.

Correlative Conjunctions

Correlative (kuh RE luh tiv) **conjunctions** work in pairs.

Correlative Conjunctions	
both . . . and	either . . . or
not only . . . but also	neither . . . nor

Example: Both Lia and Raj are in the chess club.
Example: Neither Lia nor Raj likes to lose.

Exercise: Correlative Conjunctions

Highlight the pair of correlative conjunctions in each sentence.

(1) Both my sister and I want to be artists. **(2)** My sister not only draws but also paints. **(3)** Neither my mom nor my dad is artistic!

Sentences

A **complete sentence** is a group of words that has a subject and a predicate and that expresses a complete thought. The **subject** tells who or what the sentence is about. The **predicate** tells what the subject is or does. The verb is the main word or words in the predicate.

Complete Sentence: <u>Josephina</u> <u>overslept this morning</u>.
               subject   predicate

1. A **declarative** (di KLER uh tiv) sentence makes a statement.

- <u>Josephina</u> <u>missed</u> her bus.

2. An **imperative** (im PER uh tiv) sentence gives an order.

- <u>Set</u> the alarm. (The "understood" subject is <u>you</u>.)

3. An **exclamatory** (iks KLA muh tawr ee) sentence shows emotion.

- What a nightmare <u>she</u> <u>had</u>!

4. An **interrogative** (in tuh RAH guh tiv) sentence asks a question.

- What time <u>did</u> <u>she</u> <u>go</u> to bed last night?

Clauses and Types of Sentences

All sentences are made up of clauses. A **clause** is a group of words that contains a verb and its subject. A **main clause** can stand alone as a complete sentence. A **subordinate clause** cannot stand alone as a complete sentence. It does not express a complete thought because it begins with a subordinating conjunction.

Main clause: <u>Lenny</u> <u>is</u> afraid to speak in public.
Subordinate clause: because <u>he</u> <u>is</u> very shy

The three major types of sentences are made up of main clauses or main and subordinate clauses.

1. Simple Sentence = 1 Main Clause

- <u>Lenny</u> <u>is</u> afraid to speak in public.

2. Compound Sentence = 1 Main Clause + 1 Main Clause

- <u>Lenny</u> <u>is</u> afraid to speak in public, so <u>he</u> <u>dislikes</u> making speeches.
        main clause   main clause

3. Complex Sentence = 1 Main Clause + 1 or more Subordinate Clauses
OR 1 or more Subordinate Clauses + 1 Main Clause

- <u>Lenny</u> <u>is</u> afraid to speak in public because <u>he</u> <u>is</u> very shy.
        main clause   subordinate clause

- Because <u>he</u> <u>is</u> very shy, <u>Lenny</u> <u>is</u> afraid to speak in public.
    subordinate clause   main clause

Sentences continued

Run-on Sentences

Do not write a **run-on sentence**—two or more sentences run together as one sentence. There are three kinds of run-on sentences.

1. Main clauses are separated only by a comma.

- Roy walked home, it was autumn.

2. Main clauses are not separated by any punctuation.

- The sky was blue the leaves were red and gold.

3. Main clauses are separated by a coordinating conjunction, but the comma before the conjunction is missing.

- He felt like running but he did not want to make noise.

There are five ways to fix a run-on sentence.

Fix 1: Separate the main clauses with a period.

- Roy walked home. It was autumn.

Fix 2: Create a compound sentence by separating the main clauses with a comma and a coordinating conjunction.

- The sky was blue, and the leaves were red and gold.

Fix 3: Create a compound sentence by separating the main clauses with a semicolon, a conjunctive adverb like _however_ or _therefore_, and a comma.

- Roy walked home; however, he felt like running.

Fix 4: Create a compound sentence by separating the clauses with a semicolon (if the clauses are short and closely related).

- The sky was blue; the leaves were red and gold.

Fix 5: Create a complex sentence by making one of the main clauses into a subordinate clause.

- Although he felt like running, he did not want to make noise.

Exercise: Run-on Sentences

Fix the three run-on sentences below. There is more than one right way to fix each run-on.

(1) Charlie Nagreen sold meatballs at a fair but they did not sell well.

(2) They rolled off the bread, it was too hard to eat them. **(3)** Charlie

flattened the meat he created the first hamburgers!

Sentences continued

Subordinate Clause Sentence Fragments

A **sentence fragment** is an incomplete sentence capitalized and punctuated as if it were complete. A **subordinate clause fragment** is a subordinate clause that is not joined to a main clause. To fix a subordinate clause fragment, add it to the main clause it describes, or goes with.

Paragraph with Fragment: We should drop the curfew law. It has not reduced crime, and it is unfair to some teen workers who work late on weeknights. They cannot get home by 10 P.M. <u>Because they work late</u>.

fragment

Revised Paragraph: We should drop the curfew law. It has not reduced crime, and it is unfair to some teen workers who work late on weeknights. <u>They cannot get home by 10 P.M.</u> <u>because they work late</u>.

main clause   subordinate clause

When you join a subordinate clause and a main clause, punctuate correctly. If the subordinate clause is first, follow the clause with a comma. If the subordinate clause is second, do not use a comma.

Subordinate First: <u>If you agree</u>, you should attend the hearing.

Subordinate Second: You should attend the hearing <u>if you agree</u>.

Exercise: Subordinate Clause Sentence Fragments

<u>Underline</u> and fix the four subordinate clause fragments.

(1) Though we think of heroes as fearless. **(2)** Heroes often feel fear.

(3) The bravest people may not behave heroically. **(4)** When the opportunity arises. **(5)** They may be unwilling to help others. **(6)** In contrast, timid people may act selflessly. **(7)** Even though they are afraid. **(8)** They may react quickly to rescue another person. **(9)** In fact, their acts may seem even more heroic. **(10)** Because they are willing to put their fear aside.

Sentences continued

Fragments Missing Sentence Parts

A fragment occurs when an incomplete sentence is capitalized and punctuated as if it were complete. Avoid these common types of fragments.

1. A sentence missing a subject

Fragment: <u>Went</u> to a storytelling festival.
Complete: <u>Al and Beatrice</u> <u>went</u> to a storytelling festival.

2. A sentence missing a verb

Fragment: <u>Al and Beatrice</u> to a storytelling festival.
Complete: <u>Al and Beatrice</u> <u>went</u> to a storytelling festival.

3. A sentence missing a subject and a verb

Fragment: Among the storytellers.
Complete: <u>Paula and Danny</u> <u>were</u> among the storytellers.

Incomplete verbs can cause sentence fragments. To be complete, a verb that ends in *-ing* or that is in the perfect form must have a helping verb.

Fragment: The children <u>sitting</u> on the ground.
Complete: The children <u>were sitting</u> on the ground.

Fragment: Their favorite storyteller <u>given</u> first prize.
Complete: Their favorite storyteller <u>was given</u> first prize.

Exercise: Fragments Missing Sentence Parts

Follow the directions in parentheses to fix each fragment. Write the complete sentence on the line provided.

1. (Add a subject.) Always enjoy dancing.

____

2. (Add a verb.) It fun to perform.

____

3. (Add a subject and a verb.) Dancing in front of an audience.

____

4. (Add a helping verb.) The audience members clapping for me.

____

Paragraphs continued

Paragraph Organization

Organization is the sequence, or order, in which sentences are arranged.

1. In **chronological** (krah nuh LAH ji kuhl) **order,** actions are arranged in the order in which they happened. Chronological order is most often used in **narratives**—real-life or fictional stories—and "how to" paragraphs.

2. In **order of importance,** ideas are presented in the order of their strength as supporting details. Often, the least important idea is presented first and the most important idea is presented last. Order of importance is often used to organize opinion paragraphs and persuasive writing, such as editorials.

3. In the **cause and effect** pattern of organization, the causes and/or effects of an action are presented. **Causes** are reasons why something happens. **Effects** are results, or outcomes. Cause and effect is used to analyze why something happened and/or the outcomes of an event.

4. In the **comparison and contrast** pattern of organization, similarities and/or differences between two or more people, places, or things are presented. Comparison and contrast is often used to show that one person, place, or thing is superior to another.

Paragraph Coherence and Transitions

Coherence (ko HIR hunts) refers to the smooth and logical flow of sentences in paragraphs. One way to achieve coherence is through transitional words and phrases.

Pattern of Organization	Examples of Transitions
Chronological order Order of importance	first, before, after, then, next, later, finally
Cause and effect	because, since, so, therefore, thus, as a result, if . . . then
Comparison and contrast	also, like, similarly in contrast, but, however

Exercise: Paragraph Coherence and Transitions

Add a logical transition to each blank.

(1) I decided to find out where my classmates get their news.

(2) _______________ I created a survey listing local and national papers and news magazines. **(3)** _______________ I passed it out in homeroom.

(4) _______________ I counted the results.

Capitalization

Capitalize proper nouns and proper adjectives. A **proper noun** names
a specific person, place, or thing. A **common noun** names a general one.
A **proper adjective** is formed from a proper noun.

Common	Proper
man	Damion
street	Sloan Street
state	Texas

Capitalization Rules

1. Capitalize the proper name or title of a person.

   • Sue, Dad, Ms. Smith, Detective Jones, President Adams

2. Capitalize the proper name of a place.

   • Chicago, Utah, France, Main Street, the Sears Tower

3. Capitalize a proper adjective.

   • American, Mexican, Chinese

4. Capitalize the first word of a sentence.

   • The night was dark.

5. Capitalize the first word and name or title in the greeting of a letter, and
   the first word of the closing.

   • Dear Sir: • Sincerely yours,

6. Capitalize the first word and main words in a title.

   • *The Sound of Music*

Exercise: Capitalization

Highlight and fix the capitalization mistake or mistakes in each
numbered line.

   (1) Dear uncle Bob,

   (2) We had the best time today in chicago! (3) We went to see the Sears

tower. (4) then we went to see a play. (5) It was called *Tomorrow is only a*

Day Away. (6) Afterward, we ate at a korean restaurant.

Punctuation

Punctuation helps readers understand how sentences should be read.
Punctuation marks include commas, apostrophes, quotation marks, semicolons, and end marks (periods, question marks, and exclamation points).

A **comma** signals a pause or separates parts of a sentence:
• Berkeley, California, is her home.

An **apostrophe** can show possession, show where letters are missing in a contraction, or show that a letter or number is plural.
• Sara's ears almost froze when she didn't wear her hat.

A **semicolon** separates main clauses. It can go between two main clauses or before a conjunctive adverb that separates main clauses.
• I'm going to the library tonight; there's an art class for teens.
• I like to draw; however, I'm not a very good painter.

Quotation marks set off someone's exact words. Quotation marks are also used to set off titles of articles, short stories, and TV shows.
• "What did you say?" Homer asked.
• My favorite show is "My Best Friends."

End Marks

An **end mark** signals the end of a sentence.
A **period** ends a complete sentence that makes a statement.
• Roz went to school early today.

A **question mark** ends a direct question.
• Why did she go early?

An **exclamation point** ends a sentence that shows strong emotion.
• Be careful not to fall!

Put periods and commas inside closing quotation marks.
Example: "I am glad," Marcia said, "to meet you at last."

Exercise: End Marks

Add the correct end mark to each sentence.

1. Have you ever baked a pie

2. We baked one today in cooking class

3. The juice spilled in the oven

4. Smoke was everywhere

5. My teacher said, "Accidents will happen"

Punctuation continued

Commas

Commas make writing easier to understand by signaling pauses or separating parts of a sentence. Use commas in these situations:

1. To separate three or more items in a series.

- They walked past shops, houses, and parks.

2. To set off names and titles used in direct address.

- Have you seen my CD, Tim?   • No, Terrell, I haven't.

3. To set off dates and addresses.

- On July 25, 1999, my sister was born in St. George, Utah.

4. After an introductory word, phrase, or clause.

- Finally, the day ended.   • At last, we relaxed.   • If you want, sleep.

5. To set off groups of words that explain or rename.

- Felicia, our class president, does a good job.
- Soccer, my favorite sport, involves a lot of running.

6. To separate main clauses joined by a coordinating conjunction.

- Ron did his homework, but Ken did not do his.

Do not use a comma to separate the parts of a compound predicate.
Wrong: Ron sings well, and plays the guitar even better.
Right: Ron sings well and plays the guitar even better.
Right: Ron sings well, and _he_ plays the guitar even better.

Exercise: Commas

Add the missing comma or commas to each sentence.

(1) Have you ever played handball Matthew? (2) Handball can be played by two three or four players. (3) Really it is an easy game to learn. (4) One player serves the ball using a hand or a fist and the opponent tries to return the serve. (5) I went to my first handball tournament on June 10 2008 in Hightown California. (6) Carey my handball partner went with me. (7) We have traveled as far as Detroit Michigan to attend handball tournaments. (8) When the audience cheers it feels really great.

Punctuation continued

Apostrophes

Use an apostrophe to show where letters are missing in a contraction.
• aren't (are not), can't (cannot), haven't (have not).

Don't confuse contractions with possessives that sound like them. A possessive pronoun never takes an apostrophe.
• The cat licked <u>its</u> fur (fur belong to it), and now <u>it's</u> (it is) clean.

Also use an apostrophe to show possession.
• Cal's dad drove him to school. Some kids' parents drive to school.

Exercise: Apostrophes

Fix the apostrophe mistake in each sentence.

(1) Bills favorite sport is basketball. **(2)** Its almost an obsession with him.

(3) When he isn't playing basketball, hes watching it on TV. **(4)** He wants

to be a professional basketball player some day, but my parents plans for

him are different.

Semicolons

A **semicolon** separates main clauses. It can separate main clauses by itself or can precede a conjunctive adverb that is used to separate main clauses. When a conjunctive adverb separates main clauses, a semicolon goes before the adverb and a comma goes after it.
• I'm friends with the collie next door; I visit her almost every day.
• My father has allergies; therefore, we do not have a dog.

Exercise: Semicolons

Add a semicolon to each sentence to punctuate correctly.

(1) Skateboarding is not a new sport it started in the 1950s. **(2)** The

first skateboards were homemade therefore, they were not fancy. **(3)** They

were very simple in fact, they were just boards attached to rollerskates.

(4) Californians thought skateboarding was similar to surfing therefore,

they called it sidewalk surfing. **(5)** Skateboarding has come a long way it's

popular all over the world.

Punctuation continued

Quotation Marks

Use quotation marks before and after someone's exact words. Do not use them to set off an indirect quotation.

Direct quotation: "I'm ready," Shari said, "to work."
Indirect quotation: Shari said she was ready to work.

Set off titles of articles, short stories, poems, songs, and TV episodes with quotation marks.

Title of Article: Did you read the article "Sports Shorts"?
Title of Story: My favorite story is "Amigo Brothers."
Title of Song: My mom's favorite song is "You Are My Sunshine."

Exercise: Quotation Marks

Add quotation marks where needed in the sentences below. Some sentences may not need quotation marks.

1. Did you practice playing your guitar? Mickey asked.

2. I started to, Mauricio replied, but then I decided to watch TV.

3. Mickey said that he practiced playing the drums.

4. Mauricio needs to learn the chords to the song Wishful Thinking.

5. He should read the article Play Guitar Like a Pro.

Italics and Underlining

Use italics to set off the titles of books, plays, movies, TV series, magazines, newspapers, and works of art. When you are writing by hand instead of on a computer, underline such titles instead of italicizing them.

Title of Book: Did you read *The Hobbit*?
Title of Movie: I saw *Spiderman 3*.
Title of Magazine: Julio wrote a story for *Stone Soup*.
Title of Newspaper: I read a good article in *The New York Times*.

Exercise: Italics and Underlining

<u>Underline</u> the words that should be italicized in the sentences below.

1. My mom is reading the book Gone with the Wind.

2. I prefer short stories, likes the ones in Teen Magazine.

3. Have you ever seen the movie The Wizard of Oz?

4. We are going to go see the play Wicked, which is about the witches in Oz.

Spelling

Though some words are spelled exactly the way they sound, many are not. Use these rules to help guide your spelling. When in doubt, turn to a dictionary for help.

1. Put *i* before *e* except after *c* or the sound "*ay*."

Examples: bel*ie*ve, fr*ie*nd, p*ie*ce, rel*ie*f, sh*ie*ld
Examples: *ce*iling, re*ce*ipt, re*ce*ive, n*ei*ghbor, w*ei*ght

2. When adding an ending that starts with a vowel (like *-ed*, *-er*, or *-ing*), double these final consonants: *b*, *d*, *g*, *l*, *m*, *n*, *p*, *r*, and *t*.

Examples: sob*bed*, nag*ged*, begin*ner*, win*ner*, tap*ping*, bat*ting*

3. When adding *-ed*, *-es*, *-ing*, or *-y* to a word that ends with a silent *e*, drop the *e*.

Examples: bake + *-ed* = bak*ed*, tape + *-ing* = tap*ing*, rose + *y* = ros*y*

4. When a word ends in a consonant plus *y*, change the *y* to *i* before adding an ending like *-ed*, *-es*, *-est*, or *-ly*.

Examples: supply + *-ed* = suppl*ied*, fly + *-es* = fl*ies*,
easy + *-est* = eas*iest*, happy + *ly* = happ*ily*

5. When a word ends in a vowel plus *y*, do not change the *y* to *i* when adding *-ed*, *-er*, or *-s*.

Examples: del*ayed*, pl*ayer*, s*ays*, k*eys*, t*oys*, g*uys*

Exercise: Spelling

Highlight and fix the spelling mistake in each sentence.

(1) Coach, did you recicve the shipment of shoes for the soccer team?

(2) How about the other supplys we need? **(3)** My nieghbor Lonny wants to play this year. **(4)** Last year, he played sloppyly. **(5)** This year he amazeed me with his speed. **(6)** Also, Sal's footwork is dazzleing. **(7)** All the plaiers are ready for the season. **(8)** Some of the guyes have been training for months.

(9) This will be the crazyest season ever for our team. **(10)** I predict that we'll be winers by December.

Commonly Confused Words

The words on this list give many writers trouble. Use the list to figure out the right word to use.

accept, except
Accept means "to agree to" or "to welcome." *Except* means "but."

- I hope everyone will <u>accept</u> the new student to our class.
- We go to school every day <u>except</u> Saturday and Sunday.

affect, effect
Affect means "to influence" or "to have an impact." An *effect* is a result or outcome.

- I hope the canceled flight will not <u>affect</u> your travel plans.
- A high fever was one <u>effect</u> of the disease.

a lot
The expression *a lot* means "a large number" or "a large amount." It must be written as two words.

- <u>A</u> <u>lot</u> of people came to the championship game.

all ready, already
The expression *all ready* means "completely prepared." It is written as two words. *Already* means "before now." It is one word.

- Dinner was <u>all</u> <u>ready</u> by the time the guests arrived.
- I came to the stadium so late the game was <u>already</u> over.

amount, number
The word *amount* describes a quantity that cannot be counted. Use *number* to describe things that can be counted.

- The cake contained a large <u>amount</u> of sugar.
- She was impressed by the <u>number</u> of tickets that were sold.

beside, besides
Beside means someone or something is next to something else. *Besides* means "as well as" or "other than."

- She stood <u>beside</u> the lamppost, waiting for the bus.
- <u>Besides</u> math, I also like to study science and English.

Commonly Confused Words continued

can, may

The verb *can* means that someone is able to do something. *May* means that someone is allowed to do it.

- She <u>can</u> repair the car because she has the right tools.
- He <u>may</u> watch the concert because he has a ticket.

fewer, less

Fewer compares numbers of people or things that can be counted.
Less compares amounts or quantities that cannot be counted.

- The class had <u>fewer</u> boys than girls.
- My new car uses <u>less</u> gas than my old one.

like, as

Like is a preposition. *As* is a subordinating conjunction. It should be followed by a clause that contains both a subject and a verb.

- She sings <u>like</u> a bird.
- She sings <u>as</u> a <u>bird</u> <u>would sing</u>.

loose, lose

Loose is an adjective meaning "not strongly connected." *Lose* is a verb that is the opposite of "to win" or "to find."

- The stones in the wall were <u>loose</u> and fell to the street.
- The team that does not practice is sure to <u>lose</u> the game.

rise, raise

Rise means "to go up." *Raise* is used with an object and means to "move something else upward."

- Please <u>raise</u> your hand if you have a question.
- The sun will <u>rise</u> at 7 o'clock tomorrow morning.

sit, set

Sit means "to seat yourself." Use *set* when you are putting something in a certain place.

- I will <u>sit</u> at the table during dinner.
- I will <u>set</u> the dishes on the table.

Commonly Confused Words continued

than, then
Than is used to compare one person or thing to another. *Then* is used to show that something will happen next.

- An elephant is larger <u>than</u> a mouse.
- First beat the eggs, and <u>then</u> add the milk.

their, there, they're
Their is a possessive pronoun that is used to show that something belongs to someone. The adverb *there* is used to show where something is located. *They're* is the contraction for *they are*.

- <u>They're</u> going to swim during <u>their</u> visit to Florida.
- The weather is sunny and warm <u>there.</u>

to, too, two
To shows a direction or location. *Too* means "as well" or "in addition." *Two* is the number between one and three.

- I bought <u>two</u> tickets for the concert, so you can come, <u>too.</u>
- We should take a bus <u>to</u> the theater.

who, whom
Who refers to the subject of a sentence. *Whom* is an object and receives the action expressed by the predicate or ends a prepositional phrase.

- <u>Who</u> wrote the letter?
- I did not know <u>whom</u> to call.
- For <u>whom</u> did you ask?

who's, whose
Who's is a contraction meaning "who is." *Whose* is a possessive pronoun that refers to an owner.

- <u>Who's</u> going to be our teacher next year?
- Do you know <u>whose</u> bicycle this is?

Editing Checklist

Use this checklist to edit your writing.

1. I found misspelled words and spelled them correctly.

2. I checked to be sure that I used the correct homophone, such as *your/you're, to/too/two,* or *they're/their/there.*

3. I fixed run-on sentences and sentence fragments.

4. I looked to be sure that each new idea started a new paragraph.

5. I correctly placed punctuation marks where they belong.

6. I used uppercase letters for proper nouns.

7. I made sure that subjects and verbs agree.

Proofreaders' Marks

Use these marks as you review your writing.

Delete	Insert here
Close up; delete space	Insert comma
Let it stand	Insert apostrophe
Insert space	Insert quotation marks
Begin new paragraph	Insert period
Spell out	Insert question mark
Set in lowercase	Insert colon
Set in capital letters	Insert hyphen

Personal Word Bank

Use the Word Bank to keep track
of the "Your Choice" words from the articles.

For each word you add, do the following:

- Write the word in the box.

- Rate how well you understand it.

  1 = I do not know this word.

  2 = I have seen or heard this word.

  3 = I could use this word in a sentence.

  4 = I could teach this word to someone else.

- Write the definition in your own words.

- Write an example of the word or a connection you have with it.

- Use the word! Write with it, speak with it, and pay attention if
  you find it in your reading. Then go back to your rating and see
  if you can improve it.

<table>
<tr><td>

Word: ___________

Definition: ___________

Example or Connection: ___________
____
____

</td><td>

My Understanding
1 2 3 4

</td><td>

Word: ___________

Definition: ___________

Example or Connection: ___________
____
____

</td><td>

My Understanding
1 2 3 4

</td></tr>
</table>

wwWord: ___________ **My Understanding** 1 2 3 4
Definition: ___________
Example or Connection: ___________

Word: ___________ **My Understanding** 1 2 3 4
Definition: ___________
Example or Connection: ___________

Word: ___________ **My Understanding** 1 2 3 4
Definition: ___________
Example or Connection: ___________

Word: ___________ **My Understanding** 1 2 3 4
Definition: ___________
Example or Connection: ___________

Personal Word Bank

Word: _______________	My Understanding 1 2 3 4
Definition: _______________
Example or Connection: _______________

Word: _______________	My Understanding 1 2 3 4
Definition: _______________
Example or Connection: _______________

Word: _______________	My Understanding 1 2 3 4
Definition: _______________
Example or Connection: _______________

Word: _______________	My Understanding 1 2 3 4
Definition: _______________
Example or Connection: _______________

Word: _______________	My Understanding 1 2 3 4
Definition: _______________
Example or Connection: _______________

Word: _______________	My Understanding 1 2 3 4
Definition: _______________
Example or Connection: _______________

Word: _______________	My Understanding 1 2 3 4
Definition: _______________
Example or Connection: _______________

Word: _______________	My Understanding 1 2 3 4
Definition: _______________
Example or Connection: _______________

Word: _______________	My Understanding 1 2 3 4
Definition: _______________
Example or Connection: _______________

Word: _______________	My Understanding 1 2 3 4
Definition: _______________
Example or Connection: _______________